Endorsemen

Scott Shaum knows his topic. He doesn't just know abou...
living sufferer. As such, to read *The Uninvited Companion* is not just to be introduced to the abstract notion of suffering; it is to be submerged in it, and hence—if you are willing—to be submerged in your own version of the same. But our guide does not just know suffering. He knows the God of all suffering. He knows the Jesus who not only suffered supremely, but who is in the business of transforming our suffering into peace, wisdom and beauty. For you who suffer, for you who long and look for your suffering to be changed, I can think of no better place to start than here.

CURT THOMPSON, MD
Author of *The Soul of Shame* and *Anatomy of the Soul*

Like it or not, each of our lives are marked by challenges, adversity, and suffering. Scott's approach to suffering is authentic, deep, theologically sound, and, surprise! – incredibly hope-filled. Because while Scott's own life has been deeply marked by suffering and pain, he has personally experienced a re-orienting and transformation in his relationship with God. His easy writing style draws the reader in while taking us deeper; his use of biblical examples demonstrates a lifetime of wrestling with Scripture and with God that has led him to embrace suffering and its transformation. Scott invites us to engage with God through our pain; to ask the questions that will allow us to embrace this uninvited companion. His chapter on walking with others through their suffering is pure gold. This is a must-read for anyone struggling now with the "why" questions of suffering and for the rest of us who eventually will.

SUE PLUMB TAKAMOTO, PHD
Founder and Director of the Nozomi Project, Japan

Scott's book is a genuine and valuable Christian reflection on enduring in the face of adversity. It is written by an experienced global leader who personally suffers, draws alongside those who suffer, and witnesses suffering firsthand in many overseas contexts. Scott authentically lets us know that he is still learning to dig deep into his soul with irresistible hope that our loving, faithful, and compassionate God longs to comfort and companion us in our suffering. Scott meekly handles Scripture and normalizes the mysterious tension that coexists between God's comforting presence and a person's unremitting pain. Jesus was willing to endure because he knew he was loved. Scott is willing to endure because he experiences Trinitarian love in ever-deepening ways. As you read his book, you may discover that you are not alone.

DR. DUNCAN WESTWOOD
Clinical Director of Expat Care and Development, Missionary Health Institute

We all need good company and wise perspective when we face adversity. *The Uninvited Companion* generously provides both. By opening both the Scriptures and his life to us, Scott invites us to reconsider what we think about suffering and to be alert and receptive to God's compassionate presence and shaping purposes in our lives. Throughout these pages, he is both a teacher and a friend, encouraging thoughtfulness, honesty, and hope—in so doing, he is challenging us to be open to encountering the God and Father of our Lord Jesus Christ amidst everything life can throw at us.

ROBERT LOANE, President Vantage Point 3 Ministries
Coauthor of *Deep Mentoring: Guiding Others on Their Leadership Journey*

I've worked closely with Scott for the past 9 years in a shared leadership model in Barnabas International. My wife and I have witnessed Scott and Beth's journey up close and personal. We have seen them walk closely with their Chief Shepherd as He has shaped them through adversity. Scott's "Uninvited Companion" has moved him to a significantly deeper place with His Father and has also prepared him to shepherd thousands of global servants around the world. Suffering, pain, trials and hardship are never welcomed in our lives, often times they come "uninvited". It's during days of adversity that our Father draws us to a deeper intimacy with Him. Come and join Scott as he walks you through his own experience of suffering while leading you to the character and nature of The Father.

PERRY BRADFORD
Executive Director, Barnabas International

Diamonds, when they emerge out of the ground, are not that beautiful. Only after a long process of carving, grinding, and cutting do they reveal their true beauty. Scott Shaum, in "The Uninvited Companion," reveals the ways our good Father beautifully carves our souls into his likeness using a most unlikely tool: the pain of suffering. Drawing from personal experience, solid biblical exposition, and rich theology, Scott leads us to not only tolerate suffering, but to learn to welcome it as a means of our transformation. Contrary to our instincts, we do not grow by trying to get around suffering, but by trusting God through it. Both Scott's life, and his book, bear witness to that beautiful paradox.

REV. KENNETH ROBERTSON
Vicar, International Anglican Church, Colorado Springs, CO

I started reading this book and could not put it down. Scott shows us through his own personal journey supported by scripture how God was moving him from demanding an answer to the question '*why*' to asking the question '*how*'. A timely book much needed in the (mission) world today in dealing with pain and its accompanied questions.

SINY WIDMER
Executive Committee, Member Care Europe

As I've ministered in many far flung areas of the world, it is clear God is calling His Body to a deeper intimacy with Him. At the same time, so many in the global Church are dissatisfied with Sunday morning service. I venture to say that one of the challenges we face as leaders and elders needing to disciple the younger generation is the need to answer the questions being asked, instead of the usual "pat" answers. They don't want to hear "How to be happy;" they don't want the usual conceptual answers that "heal the wounds of my people lightly" (Jer 6:14). Instead, Scott answers the urgent question of "How do I deal with all the injustice and suffering I see and experience, and where is God in all of that?" Scott leads the reader through understanding this and applying the healing balm of Rev 22.2. Those in leadership will find this helpful in framing questions and perspective on the uninvited companions in our lives, and those in deep pain and trying to make sense of it will find answers they've been searching for. As Scott states, "The church dearly needs more loving, wise, listening elders in the faith to companion others during life's challenges. Suffering is a primary means of God to shape spiritual fathers and mothers of the faith." I highly recommend this book.

Dr. Anna Hampton
Author, *Facing Danger: A Guide Through Risk*

Hopeful and compelling, Uninvited Companion is an important read for anyone who suffers, or walks with those who do. Scott presents foundational truths that challenge the natural, worldly response to suffering. With humility, he speaks from the context of his own journey of suffering, inviting us to consider a broader, hope-filled reality...one in which God is very present and engaged.

Ruth Harrison
Member Care Director, Mission Aviation Fellowship

Although most of us would rather read a book on self-improvement than on suffering, our perspective on suffering undergirds much of our understanding of why we are here and what life is truly about. Scott Shaum's book handily addresses this often overlooked topic with painful honesty, scholarly insights, and practical wisdom. No matter what level of suffering you have encountered in your life, if you are brave enough to go on this journey with Scott and seriously ponder the questions at the end of each chapter, you will find your life deepened and enriched beyond what any self-help book could offer you.

Dr. Alex Galloway
Sent Well, Malaga, Spain

THE UNINVITED COMPANION

THE UNINVITED COMPANION

GOD'S SHAPING US IN HIS LOVE *through* LIFE'S ADVERSITIES

SCOTT E. SHAUM

ISBN 978-0-9994792-0-9

Editor: Ryan Adair | missiowriting.com

Cover & Interior: Sarah O'Neal | Eve Custom Artwork

Cover Photo Courtesy of Tyler L. Shaum | tylershaumphotography.com

to Beth

Your love and companionship has ever abided,

you constantly display immense trust and courage in the face of your own pain-filled uninvited companions,

and you do all this with a dazzling display of grace and beauty.

Contents

Acknowledgements

Anyone who has made some sort of contribution in life knows well it is never offered on one's own. There is a legion of loving presences in my life.

This project began many years ago. I was speaking on this subject at the annual Central Asian Consultation in Turkey. Siny Widmer, of Trans World Radio, approached me and asked if I would be willing to write a theology of suffering in the form of fifty-two sessions that could be translated into various languages and broadcast globally via radio. I was excited at the thought, so eagerly—and a bit naively—said yes. I had no idea what I had signed up for.

Due to normal life and leadership responsibilities, it took me four years to plow through those fifty-two sessions. Siny, Jonathan, and Karin have been so profoundly patient with me and offered many words of encouragement to stick with it. They knew far more than I what could come of this effort. I must especially thank Karin. Though we had never met, you provided a constant stream of encouragement and became the editor of the transcripts. I could not have gotten that project done without you. Thank you. Those transcripts are being translated into numerous languages in environments around the world that are harsh to the Christian faith.

The family at McCoy Baptist Church in Elkhart, Indiana, first launched me into the life of God, and they continue to encourage me decades later. Thank you for your constant support.

Our dear friends in the Dallas area have nurtured, encouraged, and supported us for thirty years. Walter and Sylvia, Charles and Pat, Cecil and Patty, Ondat and Eva, and Darcy and Stephanie, so many others: it is an amazing privilege to have known you from our youth to this day.

The community at Grace Community Church in Detroit, Michigan, graced me with the opportunity to grow in community and discover a teaching voice and shepherd's heart. It was there where I first received encouragement to write. Doug, Mike, and Dan: you guys are true friends, lifelong companions for whom I am forever grateful. Penny: you never cease to encourage and guide. How can I name each of the ones who make up this spiritual community? Doug and Meg, Mike and Sue, Dan and Peggy, John and Ginnie, Denny and Maureen, Bob and Victoria, Dawn, Steve and Janis, Bryce and Melissa, Chris and Stacey, Chris and Linnaea, Mark and Dawn, Bill and Ally, Kristine, Dave and Joya, Martin and Stacey, Jerry and Esther, Phil and Trina, Gary and Stacy, and DJ and MarySue—the list goes on and on. Thank you, for you are a constant spiritual home to us.

Of more recent years, International Anglican Church in Colorado Springs, Colorado, has allowed us to experience afresh the gospel of Jesus Christ every week. We are so glad to belong there. Pastor Ken: thank you for so ably shepherding the flock as you persistently present the gospel in Word and in sacrament.

Barnabas International is the most unique group of people I have ever been honored to work with. Perry, Sandi, Paul, Maribeth, John, and Kathryn: you have all shown me what it is to lead and serve with great faithfulness and quietude. I truly am humbled. Bob and Rachel: thank you for encouragement, modeling, and advice in this project. Tim and Renee: what a kick to be working together after all these years. Thanks to James and Jen for helpful and encouraging words on select chapters of an early manuscript. What a joy it is to be a fellow itinerant global shepherd with every one of BI's staff. You live the truths of this book so richly. My life is immeasurably blessed by each of you.

Randy R., I miss you. I wrote this book with your words daily ringing in my ears: "You must write." I have written. Thank you for all the "double-dog dare you's." I cannot tell you how it grieves me that I have lost your companionship in this journey and that I could not rely upon your voice and wisdom as I wrote. To the other Vantage Point 3 comrades—Rob, Pam, Kay, and Emily—you have beautiful hearts and are doing a grand work. Keep on. Thank you for the opportunities to teach some of this material at VP3 Gatherings, allowing me to hone my thinking and receive your encouraging words.

Duncan W.: thank you for your gentle, wise, orienting presence. Your words and counsel have both guided and cultivated confidence and faith to plow into this and many other ministry efforts, as well as the pilgrimage in general. Thank you for reminding me to invite Jesus into everything and to be responsive to the invitations of the Trinity.

Dave N.: yours has been a steady, caring, fun-loving friendship. Thank you for believing in me and pursuing my heart and for the ways you have walked your own many-layered life-challenges in these recent years. Let's go fly-fishing soon.

George and Connie, what a gift to have our paths cross at this stage of life. You have been with Beth and me in and through our uninvited companions' impact, and you have welcomed us into yours. Thank you for seeing me. But let's not meet in the ER anymore, okay?

To the Coconuts: Doug and Ruth, Bob and Rachel—Beth and I love having your laughter-filled and carrying presence in our lives during these years. Well done in your endurance with joy, pizza ovens, and great courage from Kabul to Ankara to where you are this day.

Beth and I have endured many adversities in the earlier years of our life. Front-row witnesses are our three sons—Andrew, Ty, and Ben. Each of you display hearts of good men—an amazing reflection of your God. You have already handled your own challenges well. I deeply long for you to know your Father's love and your parents' love, no matter what storms rage your way. Anna, love you, my first daughter. I am so grateful that our family is graced with your beautiful presence. Let it be known that I will show no mercy to any of you in Settlers of Catan!

Dad and Mom: thank you for your constant support, even if you do not always get what I am up to as I tromp the globe and scare the lights out of you along the way. Steve: it could be said that I have been an uninvited companion in your life in our boyhood days. Thanks for mercy toward your older brother from those childhood knockdowns. Jim, Bill, Esther, Mike, and Lynn, and all the "cousins:" thank you for your love and support all these years.

Beth: thank you. What more can I say? You are my *invited* companion in this journey, and you have so wondrously walked every straight and crooked path with me. Isn't the Father so good? What bounty he has lavished upon us. I am giddy that I get to experience it all—for better and for worse—with you. Here's to more chapters together as we give our lives away for Jesus.

Father, Son, and Holy Spirit, one God forever and ever: I am alive because you will it. I am loved because you *are* Love. All I am is yours. I do not always understand your ways, but I trust you. You are my good, good Father. This book is a simple offering to you. *Amen.*

Introduction

Settlers of Catan is a wonderfully awful game. Those who know this game are either knowingly smiling or ready to chuck this book across the room after the first sentence. Board games are a way to bring families together, but this game ought to come with a warning label: "Warning: this game has been known to splinter families, alienate friends, and instigate civil war in small nations."

For those who have not played it, it is kind of like Monopoly and Risk rolled into one. The objective is to obtain as many resources and as much territory as possible, and, in the process, humiliate the other players until they are on the family room floor in the fetal position.

Fun game.

Except for the Robber. The Robber is a bulbous piece of wood that is kind of snowman shaped. The Robber begins the game in the area of the board called the desert. That is where it belongs, forever and ever, amen. Except that at the roll of a seven on the dice, the Robber comes into play and wreaks all sorts of havoc on your possessions and relationships. I've fantasized about encasing the Robber in raw hamburger and throwing it over the neighbor's fence so one of their German shepherds could eat it.

You know what? Forget it. It's a stupid game anyhow.

A Robber in This World

The truth is that I have been graced with a beautiful life. God has adorned my life with the beautiful presence of Beth, my wife. I have three sons who are maturing as amazing young men. We now even have a daughter-in-law who has adorned the family with more beauty (but don't play her in Settlers!). I have traveled to dozens of nations working with some of the most amazing people. The world is bursting with the magnificent, lavish expressions of our Father's love. At times, it is a challenge to take in the abounding wonders of beauty all around us.

But there is a robber who is present, coming into play and wreaking all sorts of havoc on our lives. In this beautiful world, suffering is everywhere present. Despite all the "Life is Good" T-shirts, sometimes life is utterly crushing. Fifteen years ago, my mother-in-law was instantly killed in a car accident. She was ripped from our lives in a second. There was no goodbye. With one phone call, a void is torn in a person's life, which can never be filled again. Many of us have received that sort of impacting news:

- Cancer.
- An affair.
- Laid off from a job.
- Chronic depression.

The society I have been raised in—the United States—is radically committed to avoiding, fixing, and otherwise numbing itself of pain. Ironically, however, those efforts usually only magnify it. Unfortunately, the church often subtly facilitates this mind-set as well. But the Word of God never minimizes the human experience, whether it be beautiful or horrifying. And God invites us to do the same.

Where We Are Headed

We are striking out on a journey to lean into the truth of being invited by God to be drawn deeper into communion with him *as* we endure many hardships. These waters are deep, requiring much reflection.

The first section will guide us through reflections upon God's loving, mysterious wisdom, the place of suffering in our lives, and what God is up to in the hard stuff. Knowing what God is actively doing in us through suffering grants us perspective and enables us to more quickly join him in his redemptive efforts.

The second section will provide ways for how we can respond well to God and others amidst sufferings. As we learn that life's adversities, as painful as they can be, are gifts to draw us deeper into God's love and shape us for his purposes, we will reflect on how we can respond in trusting, wise, and loving ways. The church dearly needs more loving, wise, listening elders in the faith to companion others during life's challenges. Suffering is a primary means of God to shape spiritual fathers and mothers of the faith.

Within each chapter, there will be a story of how others have suffered, how they responded to their pain, and what God was doing in them through their adversities. These stories are tremendous gifts to us, for they offer us perspective and guidance.

Heart Reflection Invited

The primary objective of this book is to begin to shape a biblical theology of suffering immersed in the reality of our God of love. But we are after more than concepts we hold at arm's length; rather, we are seeking an applied theology that informs our responses to all of life. In other words, what does it look like to walk well with God amidst the adversities we find ourselves in? Could it be that pain, although painful, is a grace and therefore not necessarily "bad"? Can what others mean for evil be used by God for good?

As you venture into this book, I encourage you to not merely engage it cerebrally. For such a weighty subject, deep heart reflection is in order. What goes on inside you as you read? What is God stirring in you? What is he inviting you into? What emotions do you feel? When do you feel resistance? What are the evidences of a wise, loving Father's pursuit of you in the midst of all these dynamics?

A Prayer

Father, as we venture deeper into a fresh perspective of our journey, may you keep us in your love. Grace us with a growing ability to know your love, receive your love, and walk in your love—which is to say, to know, receive, and walk with you. You know how confounding life can be at times. Jesus, you have suffered the worst suffering of all humanity. You know us, you see us, you are with us. Please grow in us eyes to see and ears to hear that we may follow you and trust you wherever you lead. Our desire is to grow in your love and to become men and women of wisdom and faith so as to companion others in the beauty and sufferings of this life.

Amen.

THE UNINVITED COMPANION

section one

God's Loving Purposes Toward Us through Suffering

God is doing a deep, beautiful transformation through personal suffering. Knowing what he is up to provides perspective and the possibility of a trusting response as he shapes us in his love.

chapter 1

The Uninvited Companion Called Suffering

No one is exempt. It cannot be avoided. If you have a pulse, you will suffer. Adversity is all around us.

Several years into my personal version of long-term adversity, I dubbed it my "uninvited companion." I had not sought this out; it found me. I had not wanted this level of uncertainty, but nonetheless here I was. Every day that I awake, my "companion" is there to join me through the day. Many a dark night it has disrupted my sleep and sense of well-being.

There are no pills to cure it. No supplements make it scurry out of my life. No diets make it suddenly disappear. It's my uninvited companion, apparently for life. For the past 3,650 days in a row, I have experienced some version of crummy. Usually, it is not debilitating, but some days it is. Nearly every day it has an emotionally wearing effect and requires an act of faith in some way.

Depression. Cancer. Abuse. Rejection. ALS. Unemployment. Divorce. Singleness. Childlessness. Loneliness. Anxiety. Poverty. Doubt. Persecution. Fibromyalgia. MS. Neglect. What is the name of your uninvited companion?

Some uninvited companions come and go, some linger in the shadows for all our days, while others hover over us, eclipsing any sense of light. Does yours have a name? Are there more than one?

There seems to be as many hardships as there are people. No two people experience any of these realities in the same way. The truth is that our adversities impact each of us differently. These are our uninvited companions.

A Working Definition of Suffering

In Western societies, suffering is not an acceptable life experience. Pain is not to be endured well; it is to be remedied or otherwise numbed. We lack an adequate theology of suffering. Indeed, we are not sure how to bring hardship into our conversations with friends and family. We feel as if we are to apologize and cover up our struggles. Yet adversities are as normal as the sunrise. Because of this, we need a helpful reorientation on this subject. God's Word provides clarity and gives us a vocabulary for the adversities we experience.

In God's Word, there are many words that are translated as trials, tribulations, afflictions, temptations, persecutions, and other similar terms. Two Greek words are used in many of the central passages to which we will refer. *Parasmos* is used in key passages such as James 1 and 1 Peter 1. It has a dual meaning, referring to outward trials and inward temptations. *Flipsis* is another New Testament word that is used forty-five times. This word means pressure that squeezes painfully. Both these words are extremely generic—they can encompass the breadth of the human experience. Of course, they include our sufferings with Christ as well—the many adversities believers experience due to life lived in the reality of the gospel.

A tendency in the church is to dismiss and minimize suffering. But the Word of God never does that; it always honors the human experience. In this book, I will be using words like *trials*, *adversities*, and *sufferings* to be inclusive of any human hardship. If it is hard for you, then it is a form of suffering. This includes pains caused by another or those that are self-inflicted, and, of course, those pains that are a result of living in a fallen world, such as natural disasters, illnesses, and even death itself. In this book, the word *suffering* (and all synonyms such as *trials*, *adversities*, etc.) will refer to *any* human experience that causes pain—emotionally, mentally, spiritually, physically, relationally, or in any other area of one's life. There is danger in oversimplifying here. One of my objectives is to give vocabulary and permission to speak of life's hardships in a culture that constantly seeks to numb and minimize them.

With this understanding of suffering, we must lean into some jolting realities.

Hard Life Lessons

There are crucial lessons that God has taught me along the way regarding the experience of personal suffering. I cannot recall where I learned these lessons, but they have transformed my response to the reality of suffering. These two lessons can be startling, so we will take them on one at a time.

The Necessity of Suffering for Maturity

The first lesson is that God has designed the human soul to require suffering to reach maturity. We require many elements to mature throughout our lives. For example, we need love, grace, truth, forgiveness, community, time, and all sorts of daily provisions—all of which are graciously provided by God. But we also require suffering. For without suffering, we do not fully mature.

Both James and Paul, for example, argued that suffering is a means to maturity in various passages (e.g., James 1; Romans 5). Peter plainly states "though now for a little while, if *necessary,* you have been grieved by various trials" (1 Peter 1:7). Suffering is a necessary ingredient of maturation. God's Word does not give us stories of people who floated through life unscathed.

The central characters of faith in the Old Testament, for example, were all transformed by God through trials such as betrayal, barrenness, exile, failure, rejection, and isolation. We will press into many of these central passages and stories as we move through this book.

Some years ago, I sat with a man who was providing me with spiritual direction. I spoke candidly of my deep desolation over my chronic illness. The first comment he made after I had spoken for several minutes was, "I have never seen a conversion apart from suffering." His comment jolted me. We sat there together for a moment in silence, allowing the words to sink in. Then he repeated it, emphasizing the word *never*: "I have *never* seen a conversion apart from suffering."

By conversion, he did not mean coming to Christ as a new believer. Rather, he meant a significant inner transformation; a profound inner shift to a deeper level of spiritual depth and insight. One could call it a paradigm shift or a new insight into reality or a new openness to God's work in one's life. His observation was a deep affirmation of a truth God had been teaching me.

I had already experienced substantial growth through Jesus working *through pain* in my life. God had been showing me that I would not become the man he had created and redeemed me to be apart from sufferings.

Redemption Involves Suffering

The second lesson I learned was that God has designed the redemptive process to require suffering. This also was a striking reality for me to absorb. If you balk at this thought, then I point to exhibit A: Jesus Christ hanging on the cross.

Our redemption, or we could say, our maturation as a human being (i.e., all God has created and redeemed us to be), begins with the suffering of God. The Father purposely did not rescue his Son from the shame and torture of the cross. Jesus took upon himself our sin and his Father's loving wrath for that sin. He died a torturous death. Now we can have life, and have life to the full (we are reminded that life is a deepening relationship with he who is Life). Without this act of love expressed through suffering, we would have no hope of moving beyond being self-absorbed, God-rebellious, hurtful people.

Our justification is made possible by the just work of Jesus's suffering on the cross. Furthermore, our sanctification (that lifelong process of being drawn deeper into communion with the Triune God and, as a result, increasingly resembling Jesus and living for his purposes) also requires suffering. It must be emphasized that God's sufferings made way for us to have communion with the Father and Son by the Spirit. As we will see, God uses our sufferings to have the same impact—to draw us deeper into himself. This is about relationship first.

Knowing God's Purposes

These two lessons are like the two sides of a coin. Redemption is God's work of saving us from sin and death so we can become the women and men he created us to be in his love; suffering is an instrument in God's loving, wise hands that he uses to draw us deeper into communion with himself and to shape us.

The psalmist acknowledged this truth in his own life: "Before I was afflicted I went astray, but now I keep your word. You are good and do good; teach me your statutes. ... It is good for me that I was afflicted, that I might learn your statutes" (Psalm 119:67–68, 71). It was through some level of personal affliction that the psalmist learned to keep God's Word, which is a wise way to live one's life. Thus, the psalmist can call the affliction "good for me."

Not only that, but Paul calls us to "rejoice in our sufferings" (Romans 5:3), and James wrote that we are to "consider it pure joy, my brothers and sisters, whenever you face trials of many kinds ..." (James 1:2 NIV). These men were not masochists. Rather, they knew something about the work of God through life's hardships. They did not rejoice *in* the pain; they rejoiced in what God was doing in the midst of the pain. Knowing this reality caused them to have a profoundly different response to suffering. They knew suffering as a needed gift in this life.

Whether we fully understand these realities or not, they remain true. God created the human soul to require suffering in order to mature. He has also designed the redemptive process to necessitate suffering.

"I Do Not Like This"

I admit that I don't like any of this. The truth is that I would not have designed any of it this way. But then again, I am not a loving and wise God. When I have found myself baffled by what God is up to, I am reminded that God's ways are not my ways. He has a wisdom I will never fully grasp. In his wisdom, God has designed the redemptive process and created the human soul to require suffering. As we are taught by God how to walk with him in the pains of life, he is shaping us in beautiful and profound ways. Our pain in the hands of a loving Father brings forth amazing transformation that otherwise would not happen.

At the beginning of this chapter, I referred to my physical challenges as my uninvited companion. This uninvited companion has steered me to the crossroads of these realities. And in the same way, your uninvited companion, in the hands of a loving, wise Father, can be a means of him drawing you deeper into his love. On the surface, this seems ironic, even contradictory. Yet, as we will reflect upon in this book through biblical teaching and personal stories, we see that our loving, wise Father is redemptively drawing us deeper into communion with himself.

Pain stinks. It hurts. Suffering can be staggering. Often it seems mindless, ruthless, and horrifying. Our God is wiser and greater still. He alone is able to hold us, care for us, sustain us, and even take us to himself for eternity. Suffering never has the final say. Our God does.

A Trusting Response toward Our Father

Since suffering is normative in this fallen world, since each of us suffer in some way, since we are informed by God's Word that our loving Father in his wisdom uses suffering to draw us deeper into relationship with him and further shape us into wise and loving people, then *a trusting response toward our Father is possible.* As we trust God to walk with us through life's adversities, we are transformed by the one with whom we journey through these experiences. Hard experiences impact us, *and* far more reaching is the transformative presence of our redemptive God amidst these experiences.

Over the past decade, I have been prayed for by more people than I can count, yet God has not physically healed me. I know God does heal at times. My wife, Beth, has a wonderful story of a time God healed her instantly of a chronic physical ailment in her twenties. Yet I do not sense he will heal me physically.

As I share my story, I often say that God is using this physical malady to heal my soul—that is to say, mature me as a Christ-follower through a deeper communion with the Triune God. This physical malady I live with is the context in which he wants me to walk with him in my journey. Furthermore, it is the context in which he wants me to provide shepherding care to others. He has helped me see that I have been invited to steward this chronic illness. A very paradoxical way of saying it is that he has graced my life with this malady; it stinks, *and* it has worked beauty in me. This is my uninvited companion. A gratefulness is growing in me.

Story: When God Says No

Paul's Uninvited Companion

Paul also had an uninvited companion, his own version of a physical affliction. We really do not know what Paul's pain was—there are all sorts of theories about his ailment. And it is interesting that Paul does not tell us. However, I am not sure the circumstance is the key element to note. What is important is how it impacted Paul and what God was doing in Paul's life through this pain. Paul had a name for his uninvited companion—he called it his "thorn in the flesh." Anyone who has been impaled by a thorn knows that kind of pain. It is a graphic expression of the impact it had on him.

Paul begins 2 Corinthians 12 by telling about an experience he had that led to him receiving his uninvited companion. In his role as an apostle, God spoke to and taught Paul. Paul needed to fully grasp the truth of Jesus Christ. Apparently, he had some amazing revelation experiences. Having these types of experiences with God can lead some people to become proud, so Paul said that "because of these surpassingly great revelations ... in order to keep me from becoming conceited, I was given a thorn in my flesh, a messenger of Satan, to torment me" (2 Corinthians 12:7 NIV).

The text seems to imply that it was God who gave this to Paul, or at least allowed Satan to give it to him. Again, we do not know what this anguish was, but Paul's experience of it was that it was tormenting, and he called it a "messenger of Satan."

God Said No to Paul

Paul went on to say, "Three times I pleaded with the Lord to take it away from me" (2 Corinthians 12:8 NIV). Three times he asked and three times our Lord told him no, he would not take it away from Paul. Repeatedly, Paul went back to God, pleading for it to be taken away. But repeatedly, God denied the request.

Even the apostle Paul had personal prayer requests that were denied by God. Even the apostle Paul's personal journey necessitated suffering as God loved, shaped, and allowed Paul to be part of his greater purposes.

Just because God does not answer our prayers does not mean he does not hear us, nor that he does not care for us, nor that he is not powerful enough to bring about significant change in our lives. We must remember that God's ways are wiser than ours. He may be up to something that we cannot discern, and he invites us to trust him in the pain.

God's Wise and Good Purposes for Paul

Paul goes on to explain what God was seeking to do in his life through this chronic, unending pain. Second Corinthians 12:9 states the Lord's response: "My grace is sufficient for you, for my power is made perfect in weakness" (NIV).

Paul had been entrusted with spiritual authority, revelation, and responsibility. All that could have been enough to cause Paul to no longer rely upon God (see 2 Corinthians 1:9). Despite all God was doing through Paul,

Paul still needed to learn to rely upon God. In fact, all of us do. The Lord allowed this tormenting thorn in Paul's flesh to cause him to rely upon God's strength. The physical ailment was a concrete reminder that he was weak and needed God. And it was in Paul's weakness that God's great power could flow through him unimpeded.

If this is true for the apostle Paul, then it is true for us. We too must be reminded of how truly dependent we are on God. He knows we need to be reminded that we are utterly reliant upon him for breath, food, drink, life, and everything. *Paul learned that this thorn in his flesh was a provisional gift.* It taught Paul spiritual truths, kept him dependent on God, and allowed God to fully work through him.

Our uninvited companions are provisional gifts in our lives as well. It has taken me years to see this truth, let alone come to embrace it.

Paul's Response

Paul's response is remarkable here. He said, "Therefore I will boast all the more gladly about my weaknesses, so that Christ's power may rest on me. That is why, for Christ's sake, I delight in weaknesses, in insults, in hardships, in persecutions, in difficulties. For when I am weak, then I am strong" (2 Corinthians 12:9–10 NIV). Paul was learning what God wanted him to learn from this painful experience.

Paul had more than one hardship in life. While he carried about this thorn in his flesh, he had the other hardships that he also listed—insults, hardships, persecutions, and difficulties. He was learning that each of these adversities were allowed by God to draw him deeper into God's love and care. It was also the context in which God empowered Paul to do all he was doing. Therefore, Paul chose to boast even more gladly in his weaknesses.

God, at times and in various ways, allows us to endure painful experiences for the greater good. Earlier I mentioned that my sense is that God will never heal me of my chronic physical limitations, and yet he has used physical adversity to heal my soul. He is maturing me, drawing me deeper into his love, and giving me a voice in my weaknesses to serve others. It has been of necessity for me to endure this uninvited companion. It has been of necessity that he has allowed you to endure your uninvited companion too.

Reflection

» What hardships are you currently being asked to endure? Does your uninvited companion have a name?

» How do you find yourself responding to the notion that we must suffer to mature? Pay attention to your emotional reaction to this truth. Resist any urge to judge your responses; simply take note of them.

» Write out a brief prayer to God as you lean into your uninvited companion. Include any expressions of confusion, pain, loss, gratitude, and hope. How would you like to express your trusting response to him amidst your uninvited companion?

chapter 2

Sheltered in a Wise Father's Love

Storms can shred with shocking ease. When tornadoes or typhoons come our way, we rightly head for cover. On Palm Sunday, 1965, twin, side-by-side tornados roared down Highway 33 in Elkhart County, Indiana, causing incredible damage.[1] One set of my grandparents lost their home and their neighbors were killed, which left a huge impression on my young mind.

My other set of grandparents had a farm a few miles away. I was shown a set of doors that led down into the earth, called a "storm cellar," a place of safety when the world turned stormy. In much of America, tornadoes and hurricanes happen. It is best to be prepared with shelter.

We need the same protection in our life journeys—a safe place to hide when the heavens rage. It is not a matter of *if* but *when* the storms will hit. In a fallen world, storms happen. It's best to be prepared with a shelter.

Our prestorm preparation is our relationship with God. But who is this God we are dealing with anyway? What is this God, who allows storms, really like?

God's Glory from a Different Angle

We use the word *glory* in many ways. We speak of a loved one "going to glory," referring to him or her passing from this life into eternity. We say we "give glory to God" in that we acknowledge something true to who God is as we worship him. But glory is also used in a manner that describes what our God is like. When we speak of God's glory, we are speaking of that which is most true of him.

Let me give an illustration. Picture one of your favorite persons in your life. Okay, do you have that person in mind? How would you describe his or her glory? In other words, what makes him uniquely him? What makes you smile when you think of her? What draws you to her? This is how you experience core elements of his or her character and personality and who God created them to be. Their glory is their personality and their character, what makes them different from any other person. When God displays his glory, what do we see of him? What is he like?

"God, Show Me Your Glory"

One of those foundational moments in history is Moses engaged by God on Mount Sinai. In Exodus 33, Moses asked God to show him his glory. In context, this is an amazing request. Moses had already spoken with God at the burning bush; he had seen the ten plagues utterly destroy the Egyptian empire; he had led Israel through a parted Red Sea. And Moses had been on Mount Sinai dialoguing with God for forty days and nights. Yet Moses asked to see God's glory. What was Moses after here?

No doubt, Moses had clearly seen God's power and authority demonstrated throughout his relationship with him. This only heightened Moses's yearning to know God even more. He was not asking for more power displays; rather, Moses was asking to see his character, the core of who God is.

God's response to Moses's request is fascinating. God said to Moses, "I will make all my goodness pass before you and will proclaim my name, 'The

LORD,' before you" (Exodus 33:19). In other words, God said that he would show Moses what he was really like. Moses asked for *glory*, so God said he would show him his *goodness*. Same, same.

We pick up the interchange in the next chapter. Exodus 34:6 is a central revelation of our God in Scripture. It is a verse that is referred to throughout both the Old and New Testaments. God is about to display his glory, which is his goodness, but what is it that we shall be shown? In Exodus 34:5–6 we read, "The LORD descended in the cloud and stood with him there, and proclaimed the name of the LORD. The LORD passed before him and proclaimed, 'The LORD, the LORD, a God merciful and gracious, slow to anger, and abounding in steadfast love and faithfulness."

Those final two descriptors are what stop us in our tracks. Two Hebrew words are used to describe the core nature of God. First, he is abounding in steadfast, unconditional love; and second, he is true, unchanging, and faithful. God is love. God is faithful. This is God's glory. The core of his character is love and faithfulness, which make up the essence of who he is.

God's glory is who he is—and fundamentally, he is a God of love and faithfulness.

Even the description of what God did for Moses (and for us) is revealing. The text says, "The LORD descended ... and stood with him there" (Exodus 34:5). God is the God who always moves toward us. He gladly stoops down to our level. He comes alongside us and stands with us. He responds to our pleas. These are all expressions of his lovingkindness and faithfulness. That is to say that these are all expressions of God's glory.

God expresses his glory in an even more intimate manner—he calls himself our Father.

We Have a Father[2]

When you describe God, how do you describe him? Creator? Ruler? Redeemer? Judge? Savior? Lord? These titles are all true of roles that God fulfills. And it is interesting that each of these titles requires something outside of God in order for them to be fulfilled. For example, he needs someone to save to be a Savior; there must be a creation to lord and rule over. But God needs nothing outside of himself for purpose and fulfillment. What was God doing before creation?[3]

Scripture affirms that from eternity past God is Father. The concept of God as Father is not only a New Testament concept, but also an Old Testament one (see Exodus 4:2; Deuteronomy 1:31; Psalm 103:13; Isaiah 1:2; 63:16; 64:8; Jeremiah 3:19; Hosea 11:1). For all eternity, God has been loving and pouring his life out to his Son (see especially John 17:24). For all eternity, the Son has been the beloved of the Father and has responded to the Father in love. When we read of the numerous times the Father spoke from heaven about his beloved Son, Jesus never flinched. He knew well that he is beloved of the Father (see Matthew 3:17; 17:5; John 5:20). The Spirit is described as the love that flows between the Father and the Son, uniting them all into a single God.

The Father has so enjoyed loving his Son that he wanted other ones to love too. The Son so loves his Father and wants what his Father wants, and he also wanted others to be the Father's beloved so they too could know his life and love.[4]

The patristics (the early church fathers who came after the apostles in history) described the Father as a fountain that never ceases to flow, constantly pouring forth life and love and every form of goodness. The Son was sent to, amongst other things, reveal the Father to us and to save us that we might believe on him and be adopted as beloved children. One primary source for these early church fathers was the apostle John, who expresses this thought in the opening chapter of his gospel.

This Glory Walked Among Us

In his gospel, John picks up this same concept of the word glory from Exodus 34. In John 1:14, as he seeks to describe the Word that has become flesh and lived amongst us, John writes, "The Word became flesh and made his dwelling among us. We have seen his glory, the glory of the one and only Son, who came from the Father, full of grace and truth" (NIV). Those final two words—*grace* and *truth*—are playing off Exodus 34:6. John said that this one dwelling among them was the same one who revealed himself to Moses. The God who is love and faithfulness is also grace and truth. He is one and the same.

Glory in the Everyday

In John 1, John has given us a working definition of a way he will use the word *glory* throughout his gospel. We find the word used again in chapter 2. This was the well-known Cana wedding feast. As the story unfolds, the wedding party ran out of wine way too early into the festivities, and Jesus was encouraged to solve the problem.

Jesus proceeded to tell servants to fill five or six massive clay jars full of water. We are told by John that each of these jars held between twenty to thirty gallons each. That means there was somewhere between 100 and 180 gallons of water turned into wine. Upon the master of ceremonies tasting the next round of wine, he proclaimed it the good stuff. I did the math to get a better grasp of just how much wine this was—it was somewhere between 500 and 950 of the typical 750ml–sized bottles of wine. Even if this was a huge wedding of five hundred or more people, every person got his or her own bottle of wine! This is an extravagant amount of wine.

John concluded the story with this statement: "This is the first of his signs Jesus did at Cana of Galilee, and *manifested his glory*. And his disciples believed in him" (John 2:11). What is this glory Jesus manifested? What did the disciples believe in? Were they merely believing because of the display of power? We are reminded that displays of power did not seem to satisfy Moses; he wanted to see more. The disciples indeed saw more than power; they saw his glory. That is, they saw a glimpse of the heart of our God. They saw his love and grace represented in an absolutely absurd quantity of wine for a personal wedding party. They received a glimpse into the lavish bounty of this one's love. John writes, "They saw his glory." God is not stingy with his love, life, and goodness. He overflows with love and goodness toward us. The disciples were getting a small glimpse of who the Father was through Jesus's manifestation in the form of a ridiculous amount of wine for a wedding party. This is what the disciples caught a glimpse of, and this is the one they were willing to follow anywhere.

The Greatest Glory in a Shameful Death?

We skip ahead to John 12 to see another significant place where John uses the word *glory*. Chapter 12 is the final public statement of Jesus before he sequestered himself away with the twelve disciples in the upper room the night he was betrayed. Jesus declared, "'Now is my soul troubled. And what shall I say? "Father, save me from this hour"? But for this purpose I have come to this hour. Father, glorify your name.' Then a voice came from heaven, 'I have glorified it, and will glorify it again'" (John 12:27–28).

I have often heard it stated that the cross is the greatest display of God's glory. How can this be? The cross is a place of shame, public dishonor, a brutal means of a torturous death. How can this be glorious?

The reason the cross is the greatest display of God's glory is because it goes far beyond wine at a wedding in displaying Jesus's love, grace, faithfulness, and truth. Here God gives of his very self. The Father has displayed his name (i.e., glory) through Jesus many times in miracles and teachings ("I have glorified it"). Now he is going to "glorify it again," but this time more fully. Many will call it a foolish waste, but to those given sight, it is the most beautiful display of love, faithfulness, grace, and truth in history.

God's glory is an outlandish love. His love is always self-giving and self-sacrificing. On the cross, his glory was on full display. This is who our God is. This is his character at his core.

This glorious God of love and faithfulness is our storm shelter we run to when life gets hard. We need more than power displays; we need one in whom we can hide, who is love, faithfulness, grace, and truth. When life is turned upside down, we want to remember our Father's love for us. We are a forgetful people. Tough stuff can give us nearsightedness, causing us to lose sight of who our God is. We will be reminded that circumstances do not define God; it is God who defines our circumstances. It is too easy to assume that he is mean, vindictive, capricious, or punitive toward us.

But he is none of those; rather, he is love and faithfulness, grace and truth. The cross proved this is who he is. But when I compare who God is with some of the ugly stuff I see all around me, a tension begins to surface within me.

Paradox: A Lesson in Tensions

Here is a truth: We have a wise, loving Father. He is always pouring out his love, life, and care to us. He is faithful and he is true. Nothing messes with the goodness of God.

Here is another truth: Life is hard. It can be brutal at times. Yes, life is full of beauty, wonder, and joy, *and* it is also full of pain, evil, and grief. We all experience various kinds of pains. Some scar us for decades in one way or another, while others cut our earthly life short. These two truths form a paradox.

A paradox is two realities that coexist but seem like they ought not be able to do so. The two above stated truths *seem* like they cannot coexist, and yet they do. A paradox on this level creates enormous, unresolved tension. That level of tension can be disorienting at times.

Our God is a loving and wise Father, who, in his wisdom, at times allows us to experience various adversities. We walk this life with uninvited companions. He knows they are painful, *and* he also knows he can bring great good from them.

Pain is painful, for sure. And in the hands of a loving, wise Father, pain can also be gain. That is a novel concept in a culture that avoids pain at all costs. Our God does not avoid pain. Jesus did not avoid the pain of the cross; he walked right into it. He did this out of love for his Father and out of his love for us. The Father did not rescue his Son from the pain of the cross.

God knows pain is painful. In his wise and loving hands, pain can be used for great good.

God in Our Storms

Our God does not withhold his glory, but he lavishly displays it for the whole world to see. Our God's love is a self-giving, self-sacrificing, pursuant love. He is not a curmudgeon, doling out minuscule little pieces of kindness now and then. No, in his Son on the cross, he displays his love to the world. For those who would have it, he now pours out his love in our hearts by his Spirit (see Romans 5:5). This is our God's glory—he gives his very self to us.

This is how God *always* relates to us. He is always pouring out his love and life to us. He is always faithful, gracious, and truthful—even when life stinks. Our Father does not change when storms rage into our lives—and the storms *will* come—but he remains constant and unshakable.

When we are pounded by raging winds, we need a place to hide, a place to which we can run. Our triune God is our hiding place. The Father invites us to grow in his love. He has given us many gifts to teach us about his love for us. Paradoxically, he *gifts* suffering to us as one of those means. Yes, suffering is a necessary gift where, once again, God displays his love and faithfulness even in the darkest raging storms.

I learned this lesson the same way we all do. It is one thing to know biblical truth, but it is another to live through a life-altering storm and know God as a shelter.

Story: Allow Me to Introduce You to My Uninvited Companion

My uninvited companion crashed into my reality in my mid-forties. The storm was indeed as intense as I have ever experienced. In 2005, I contracted dengue fever while providing shepherd care for a church-planting team in remote Cambodia. I likely had dengue once before, as this case turned hemorrhagic. Dengue is a mosquito-borne virus similar to malaria. There is presently no immunization and no cure for it—you have to ride out the storm.

And a storm it was. But I was not going to let that experience slow me down. After all, millions of people contract dengue, so what was the big deal? I wore the experience as another badge of honor granting me further validation with cross-cultural workers all over the world. It eventually took me a full fourteen months until I was back to my "old self," which included a normal work routine and my usual athletic endeavors.

Two years later, Beth and I were back in Cambodia speaking at a gathering of workers from across that country. Again, I got sick. It started out as stomach stuff. As we flew back to the US, I felt awful the entire way. I hoped it would work through my system and that would be that. But it did not. As the next days passed, I began to feel other weird symptoms, like a tingling in my arm and growing fatigue. Eventually, Beth took me to an urgent-care facility close to our home. There, I had some sort of traumatic physical event. The staff thought I was going into cardiac arrest, so they got me into an ambulance and off to the hospital I went. Thus began an arduous, dark, confusing year of medical mystery.

Daily I experienced a constellation of symptoms—neuropathy in my extremities and face, vision problems, an irregular heart rate, incredible ringing in my ear, dizziness, short-term memory loss, and most debilitating was a crippling fatigue. I would sleep twelve hours, wake up, and have barely enough strength to get out of bed. I felt like my life was slowly ebbing away. Then began the panic attacks, usually in the middle of the night. I had never known such a disorientation.

I saw an infectious disease specialist, neurologist, cardiologist, and all kinds of *-ists*. The reports were nearly uniform—negative, normal, and neutral. For sure, there were many symptoms that could be measured, such as my irregular heartbeat. But no one had an answer. The fear raged on within me, panic attacks were not uncommon, nor were episodes of memory loss when

I had no understanding of what had happened to me. Furthermore, I was experiencing a prolonged season of silence from God. This became a long, dark, unfamiliar road on which I found myself.

I had numerous friends who encouraged me to go to Mayo Clinic, and after eleven months of symptoms, Beth and I went. I was poked and prodded for three days. The staff there are brilliant; in fact, I have seldom felt so medically well cared for. After all the testing, there was a theory put forth: I had contracted some unknown Asian virus and it had somehow "made the leap" into my nervous system. Due to the proximity of dengue, my body was not able to fend off the virus well, and I now have a dysfunction in my autoimmune system. As I was manifesting most of the symptoms, I was offered "probable chronic fatigue syndrome" as the only diagnosis.

It was comforting to have at least a theory. Yet there was no cure. No pills, no rehab, nothing was fixing it. I was introduced to my uninvited companion. A decade later, this companion still holds profound sway in my life. There are times a slow walk in the morning is no big deal, yet there are many times where sitting in a chair is exhausting. It took years of experience with these variable symptoms to begin to become familiar with them. The panic attacks have all but ended. Every decision I make, I filter through the grid of my diminished capacities. I used to run marathons, but now a public speaking gig can be dicey.

Looking back, it is easy to see that God was sheltering me through this storm. I often did not sense that in the moment because I was so overwhelmed with physical and emotional symptoms. Yet he was sheltering me through that first year of physical illness. He had far more of himself he wanted to show me.

At this point in my story, one year into becoming acquainted with my uninvited companion, I was being reoriented to a new way of life. I was only beginning to experience his love for me, but I had no idea how much further I was going to be invited into the communion that is the Father, Son, and Spirit. He was just laying the groundwork. Paradoxically, I was more deeply experiencing, through suffering, how profoundly loving and faithful God truly is.

Reflection

- » How has God displayed his glory—his love, faithfulness, grace, and truth—to you in your journey with him?
- » List the paradoxes you have experienced during seasons of difficulty in your own life.
- » How is God inviting you to be sheltered in his love as you weather life's storms?

chapter 3

A Livelier Response than Resignation

Ten years ago, when I was slowly recovering from what I eventually learned was a virus that had wreaked havoc on my autoimmune system, I asked God a very pointed question: "So this is what I get?" There was an accusatory tone in my question. "I go to crummy places in the world to care for your people, and this is what I get?"

Silence.

Followed by more ear-splitting silence.

The silence went on for over six months. I was anything but happy.

In a word, I was asking *why*. There was no answer.

In this dark, confusing season in my life, I was fighting through anger, resentment, and resignation. All of these are legitimate emotions, yet each one can leave us with a deadened heart. Resignation is a long way from embracing one's reality. God was seeking to enliven my heart in this dark time. But asking *why* was not going to get me there.

That Question *(You Know, the Big One)*

It is natural in dark times to ask *why*. Why did this happen to me? Why won't God take it away? This is such a natural, human question. We see this question asked in various ways as we read our Bibles. Even Jesus cried out this word from the cross: "My God, my God, why have you forsaken me?" (Matthew 27:46).

But as natural a question as it is, it is not helpful to get stuck on it. If we get stuck on the *why* question, it usually breeds fear and doubt.[5] Fear and doubt can only be tolerated so long before we find ourselves in the abyss of anger, bitterness, resentment, and heart-deadening resignation.

To this day, most of my *why* questions have not been answered. I don't think they ever will be. I have (almost) stopped asking that question at all (usually). But even if the question surfaces again, I do not stay there long. It does not serve me well, nor does it honor God to do so.

Cancer, car accidents, and cares of this life are seldom explained. The doctor report returns and suddenly we are thrust into a new world. We find ourselves having to live with realities we would prefer to just go away. God usually does not seem to tell us why; rather, he is up to something much grander than our cognitive understanding of our circumstances.

There is a wiser question to ask than *why*—it is *how*? "How do you want me to walk with you in this, God?" That question leads us down entirely different paths, paths that are relational and wise.

An Essential Trait of Maturity

No matter what we seek to accomplish, it requires a certain level of stick-to-it-ness. A musical instrument, a professional skill, an advanced degree, a marriage, a friendship, a means of income—each require we keep showing up and working at it.

Endurance is an essential character trait of maturity. It is noteworthy that the central New Testament passages on suffering mention the necessity of enduring. Even Jesus was called to endure. Note some of these passages:

> No temptation has overtaken you except what is common to mankind. And God is faithful; he will not let you be tempted beyond what *you can bear.* But when you are tempted, he will also provide a way out so that *you can endure it.* (1 Corinthians 10:13 NIV)
>
> For the joy set before [Jesus] *he endured the cross,* scorning its shame, and sat down at the right hand of the throne of God. ... *Endure hardship as discipline;* God is treating you as his children. For what children are not disciplined by their father? (Hebrews 12:2, 7 NIV)
>
> Consider it pure joy, my brothers and sisters, whenever you face trials of many kinds, because you know that the testing of your faith produces *perseverance.* Let *perseverance* finish its work so that you may be mature and complete, not lacking anything. (James 1:2–4 NIV)
>
> Blessed is the one who *perseveres under trial* because, having stood the test, that person will receive the crown of life that the Lord has promised to those who love him. (James 1:12 NIV)

I could list many more passages. Endurance, perseverance, and patience are all required to journey through the tough stuff of life.

Endurance is a central trait of a mature daughter or son of the Father. This trait is reflective of our Father's glory. Remember, he is faithfulness and he is love. This means that faithfulness endures in that it never changes. God's love, grace, and truth endure forever—they never change.

Like Father, like son and like daughter.

Left Hanging?

I began this chapter by recalling my own emotional struggle with relentless hardship. During this particularly dark time of my life, when I was being introduced to my uninvited companion, I was deeply angry at what God had allowed in my life. Not only was I experiencing acute physical symptoms, but these symptoms aroused all sorts of emotional distress within me. I was experiencing fear and anxiety like I had never known in my adult life. I was confused, felt helpless, lost, afraid, and I was angry about it.

However, over months that stretched into a year, I realized I was not fighting my new reality anymore. No, I had moved on to resignation. I had resigned myself to this. Hordes of doctors had poked and pinched me, and nothing had come of it but theories and more questions. But resignation is still an expression of a less than fully alive heart.

Eventually, God did answer my accusatory question of, "This is what I get for serving your people in tough places?" After six months of silence on the subject, he answered me one day. He simply said, "Yes."

God was inviting me into a different way of relating to him, living for others, and journeying in this world through the uninvited companion of suffering in my life. He was inviting me to endure with him through trials. He was inviting me to the bounty he was offering as he tended to me through suffering.

A Subtle Shift Takes Place Within

It was years into my journey before I noticed a subtle yet deep shift. God had always been there, though I had often not been able to discern his presence. As I was being invited to endure with this uninvited companion, I was being granted a keener sight. Passages on suffering that I had studied and taught on in the past were taking on new life. God was moving me on from demanding an answer to *why* to asking *how*.

I found myself praying prayers like, "Please, Father, you have to teach me how to walk this path with you. I do not know this way. I do not even like this way. Please show me your ways, that I may walk in them with you." That sort of prayer was opening me up to an entirely new chapter of relationship with God. This prayer was born on the street named Endurance.

Wisdom from Above

God encourages us to ask the *how* question—he is eagerly waiting for that very question. It is interesting that right after the James 1:2–4 passage quoted above, James encourages us to ask for wisdom: "If any of you lacks wisdom, you should ask God, who gives generously to all without finding fault, and it will be given to you" (James 1:5 NIV).

James 1:5 is frequently quoted as a prayer asking God for guidance on making a decision, as in the do-I-take-this-new-job-or-not type of question. However, the context for being encouraged to ask for wisdom is not to make a decision. Rather, the context is suffering. We are encouraged to ask for wisdom in knowing how to endure through various kinds of trials. The wisdom God is eager to extend to us is how to walk well with him as he guides us through the dark nights of enduring hardships of many kinds.

God is waiting for us to ask for help! He wants us to ask *how*. He loves it when we ask for wisdom on how to walk well with him when we find ourselves shaken by storms. This entire scenario plays into his deepest desires toward us.

Not About Fixing but About Relating

God's supreme desire for us is communion with himself. Our God is a relational God. Jesus repeatedly said he was in the Father and the Father was in him. For those of us who have been adopted as his children, we are now in Jesus and Jesus is in us; in Jesus, we are in the Father and the Father in us as we are united to him by his Spirit.

When we begin to ask the how question of God, we are leaning into this greatest reality. God yearns for communion with us. He longs to fully pour his life and love into us. He wants to give himself to us. He wants us to know that we are his beloved. The truth is that he wants this so much, and knows it is for our good, even for our very existence, that he will do whatever it takes to draw us there. That even includes allowing us to endure many hardships.

A Beautiful Life

God allowed—even gave—me this uninvited companion that I might come to know his love in ways I doubt I would have come to know through any other way. Paradoxically, it was through years of wrestling with my own frailty and illness that my heart had become more enlivened than ever before.

Yes, we have a wise and loving Father. He asks us to walk with him. The path will be stormy at times. It is a long, long path. It can be dark, scary, crushing, and confusing. And it is also the path that leads to life. Life is a person—he is a glorious God of love, faithfulness, truth, and grace. Thus, we are invited to endure various trials as he grows us in his love.

I was beginning to have a taste of the bounty that God extends to us as we walk with him amidst sufferings.

Story: The Prayer of a Broken Heart

Hannah was a housewife in the hill country outside of Jerusalem. Her's was a culture steeped in honor and shame values. It held women in honor *if* they provided their husbands with children. Sons, of course, were even a greater honor. Long before current medical technology, a barren womb was a burden of dishonor that women like Hannah endured without explanation.

The narrative of 1 Samuel 1, which tells of Hannah's struggle, is laced with words such as *distress*, *affliction*, and *bitter weeping*. This was Hannah's world. Her husband was a gracious man, gentle to her in her grief. He apparently did not shame Hannah for not producing children. But there was another player in the picture. Hannah's husband had two wives. The other wife, Peninnah, seemed to produce kids with humiliating ease. This was not a brief time of hardship for Hannah; the text says "so it went on year by year" (1 Samuel 1:7)—year after bitter year of weeping, deep distress, and another woman in the house who provoked Hannah.

We are given the cause of Hannah's deep misery. First Samuel 1:5 says, shockingly, that the Lord had closed her womb. Just in case we missed it the first time, the same statement is repeated in the next verse: "the LORD had closed her womb" (1 Samuel 1:6).

How can this be? Every fiber in us cries out, "Why? What did poor Hannah possibly do to deserve this?" We could easily go the way of Job's companions and lay the blame on some hidden sin in her life. But there is no indication that this is a punitive action being meted out by a grumpy God. With dead, cold clarity, we are stoically told God was the cause of this woman's deep brokenness. We are left wondering what God is up to.

Can it be true that this God of love at times causes deep pain? What are we to do with that?

The Divine Cause Conundrum

I have found myself wrestling over the mystery of divine cause in my own life. Frankly, I do not gain much help with the cause question. Did God cause my chronic illness? Did he allow it? I likely will never know the answers to those questions. I do not dwell there long. However, I have obviously come to some conclusions, of which Hannah has been helpful. If you carefully listen to my story, you will hear assertions that God took me into seasons of deep pain to bring about unfathomable transformation that otherwise (humanly speaking) would never have taken place. In other words, I have concluded, right or wrong, that God has caused my suffering to bring about a greater work in me. In the end, I confess the reality of mystery and submit my life to God's care and oversight.

Honestly, the journey has really stunk at times. Yet I like the fruit it has produced in me through the required endurance of this journey. I am not the same person I was before I was saddled with various forms of health crises. God has used the howling winds of suffering to soften my edges, ween me of many compulsions, and generally deepen me all over. I see life differently now. I sit with others in their pain, much more aware. I have become more attuned to my Father's love for me.

Is Pain "Bad"?

For some, to think that God causes pain is too bitter a pill to swallow. As I have engaged thousands of people in our pastoral work across many nations, I have seen a basic human assumption that pain is bad and to be gotten rid of at all costs. No doubt, pain is painful. There is little pleasant in physical, emotional, mental, relational, or spiritual pain. It hurts.

Yet pain, as we have seen, can be a means by which God brings about great work within us. I have not liked the pain I have been saddled with. I still would not mind if it would all just go away. Yet I know my pain has been for my good. In a way, I am truly grateful for it. I am being taught, like Paul and James were, to rejoice in adversities as God deeply transforms me. Furthermore, I realize that prayers took shape within me that I would not have otherwise uttered.

Prayers Taking Shape

If Hannah had a whole pile of kids, she would be praying the prayers of a worn and weary mother. You know, prayers like, "What were you thinking giving me all these kids?" But barren-wombed women do not know of such prayers. Hannah's prayers were far more desperate. In the darkness, sorrow, and emptiness of her soul's womb, something different took shape. Eventually, she gave birth to a prayer that changed the entire course of a nation.

One day, crying out to God, she told him that if he gave her a son, then she would give that son back to God in a life of service to him. God responded to that prayer. Hannah was graced with the birth of Samuel, who would become the greatest prophet in Israel since Moses and lead his people in deep spiritual renewal.

At this point, it could be tempting to consider some formulaic, negotiating-with-God principle. In the confusion of unremitting adversity, we could easily come up with some mutually beneficial trade options for both parties. "Tell you what, God—you give me my health back and I will go anywhere in the world you send me to serve you."

Such bartering with God misses the point of Hannah's prayer. Sure, she finally received a son, but she also would not have the privilege of raising that son, because he was to live his life from a young age serving God in the temple. There was still loss to be had for Hannah. The shift in Hannah's heart went from merely wanting a child for herself to wanting something that would be bigger than herself.

What if the hardships we find ourselves in today are not only for our benefit? What if God is doing something in us that will cost us much and immensely benefit others? What if we looked at life from that angle?

My Hannah-Like Prayer Moment

I remember clearly a Hannah-like prayer that was formed within me. This was not some well-crafted, long-thought-out prayer. It simply rolled off my lips, unrehearsed, one day. I was not prepared for what I said. It makes me wonder that Hannah's may not have been planned either.

My wife, Beth, was driving me home from yet another unhelpful medical appointment. I was simply too chronically exhausted to drive. My head was resting on the passenger window of our car. A tear rolled down my cheek and a prayer rolled off the edges of my heart: "Allow this to continue for as long as you want, to do whatever you want in my life."

Where did that prayer come from? I suspect in the recesses of my soul, where the Holy Spirit was shaping a deep, new form within me, such words took seed. I had never prayed such a prayer before. Up until then, I only wanted to be better. Fast. But the God of Hannah was birthing in me a posture toward him that had previously not existed. Like Hannah, a livelier response was being born in my heart.

God has answered that prayer. I am a different person than I was. He has not answered any prayers about getting physically better, yet he continues to use physical illness to ripen this soul of mine. What's more is that he has shaped me in ways that allow me to tend to others more sensitively. Like Hannah, God can use all our pains for others' gain.

Such prayers are one of the fruits of enduring through prolonged pain. What if God, in his wisdom, love, and mercy, is allowing us, yes, even causing us, to experience pain in our lives to shape some yet nonexistent reality in and around us? Does that make the pain any easier to live with? Certainly not. But it can take our engagement with God in profoundly different directions.

We can now be open to the paradigm of yielding to God in his redemptive purposes in us, rather than merely demanding he relieve us of our suffering. Hannah has shown us an entirely different response. This courageous housewife has shown us a beautiful, enlivened way to respond to suffering, even as the tears continued to flow over the losses she was asked to live with—years of barrenness followed by sacrificially giving her young son to be raised to serve in the temple and, eventually, for the well-being of a nation.

Reflection

- » Read 1 Samuel 1 and sit with Hannah in her distress. What in her story speaks to your own? God was present in Hannah's life during these barren years. How is he present in yours today?
- » As "year after year" passes in your life, what do you find God shaping within you? What prayers has he shaped in you that otherwise had not previously existed?
- » Write your own *how* prayer. Ask God how he is inviting you to walk with him and your uninvited companion.

chapter 4

Carving Out Capacity for Love

As I shepherd people in full-time ministry, I am constantly amazed at the gap between how we preach about God's love for us and our personal experience of that love. This has been true in my story.

There was a period of time when God was essentially silent in my life. After some months, I realized that after my morning time with him reflecting on Scripture, praying, and journaling, I more often than not headed into my day angry. Why was I so angry? What good was my time with God in the morning if my main takeaway was anger? This spiritual duress only added to the physical and emotional duress I was already experiencing. It was not fun. And I was angry about it. I couldn't understand what was going on inside of me.

Eventually two core lies began to be exposed. One of my lifelong lies is that I am on my own. No one is going to help me. Life is hard, so I need to figure it out on my own, or so went my thinking. Obviously, my circumstances confirmed the lie. I was sick, no doctors could help, and God was not rescuing me, so, of course, I was on my own. I was beginning to see how deep this lie ran.

The other lie was that silence is an expression of relational rejection. You know the line: if you don't have anything good to say, then don't say anything at all. Well, God was not saying anything, and so conclusions were being drawn, but from a faulty reference point. By being silent, God was actually loving me well. He was there, quietly doing a deep, loving, stirring work in my soul in places I did not know even existed. I could not feel him. I could not see him. I could not hear him. But with the grace of hindsight, I know he was very much present and active.

First, he addressed the lie of being on my own. He did this by helping me see that the lie existed within me. I was catching myself constantly giving into that line of thinking. A string of passages, books, and conversations slowly began to overwhelm that lie with the truth of Jesus's words, "I will not leave you as orphans" (John 14:18). I have a Father. I am an adopted son. I am called by name, taken, desired, indwelt by God, and, most importantly, I am never on my own. I do not have to figure life out on my own. I am well-provided and cared for. He guides and instructs.

Then he addressed the silence. As his reorienting truth began to seep into my soul in ways that were new to me, I realized that silence was not an expression of rejection; rather, it was just another way to be in loving relationship. God was comfortable being with me without having to clutter the space with lots of chatter. I was not so comfortable with that then, but now I love it. It has become an enjoyable space. These were not quick lessons learned; these insights came over many months and even years. He is still healing and teaching me.

These two lies, along with many others he is healing within me, are manifestations of how I do not experience the love of God. In fact, I am well practiced in bracing myself against God and his affections toward me. The fact is that I have an exceptionally smallish heart. I am a carbon copy of Dr. Seuss's Grinch, with a heart many sizes too small. I need someone to expand my heart.

God is relentless. His love knows no quit. He does not need us, yet he longs to pour out himself in our lives. He knows my Grinch-heart is too small, that my gaze is too near-sighted, and my desires are too self-absorbed. He seeks to expand those areas of my life. Once again, suffering is an instrument God uses to expand my soul's capacity to receive and experience God and his love. God was maturing me in the context of prolonged personal hardship. He does this redemptive work in all of us.

Paul, in Romans 5, expounds on this reality. Pondering this passage will grace us with understanding of what God is up to, in part, as we walk with him over long seasons of unresolved adversity. In the end, his primary concern is not our transformation nor our ability to do his work for him better; his first and foremost concern is to grow us in his love.

Hope Realigned

When we experience prolonged, unresolved pains in life, hope can take a beating. As we saw in the previous chapter, it's much easier to numb the heart by killing hope with resignation than it is to keep leaning into God and life. Romans 5:2–5 offers us profound insight into how God works this redemption in us through suffering:

> We boast in the hope of the glory of God. Not only so, but we also glory in our sufferings, because we know that suffering produces perseverance; perseverance, character; and character, hope. And hope does not put us to shame, because God's love has been poured out into our hearts through the Holy Spirit, who has been given to us. (NIV)

Paul says that hope will not put us to shame in the end. By that, he means that if we rely upon God and what he promises, then we will not be let down. He will come through. How does such a hope grow in us, and what does that have to do with God using suffering to grow us in his love?

Rejoice in Glory (in Suffering?)

In Romans 5:2, we are encouraged to rejoice in the hope of the glory of God. We have already considered the varied uses of the word *glory* in the Bible. Sure, this can refer to the hope of eternity, which is how I most often hear this verse translated. But more so, we can hope in glory as we defined it in chapter 2, namely in the character of God. Our God is love, faithfulness, grace, and truth, amongst so many other characteristics. We can rejoice in our hope in who God is because he will be true to who he is toward us, especially amidst suffering.

The previous chapters of Romans have just expounded on this very fact. Despite our utter depravity (see Romans 1–3), God has sought us out in Jesus, and we are offered the righteousness of God in Jesus through faith. Salvation is a gift freely given (see Romans 3–4). We now have peace with God (i.e., the Father) through Jesus (see Romans 5:1). Based on this staggering expression of mercy, grace, and love, we can now rejoice in the hope of the glory (character) of who our God is.

That's the easy part of hope. Those who have tasted of the Lord have indeed come to know that he is good.

Then Paul reminds us of the paradox in which we live. Life can be hard, so he says, "Not only that [i.e., we are to rejoice in the glory of God], [but] we rejoice in our sufferings" (Romans 5:3). Paul is encouraging us to equally rejoice in who our God is *and* in our pains. How can he say that?

The bridge to explaining what Paul is going to tell us is a short phrase that can get lost in all the big ideas of this passage: "because we know that ..." James uses the same phrase in James 1:2–3. These men can say they rejoice in suffering because they have come to learn a significant spiritual truth: something profound is going on in us as we endure through hardship. What we find is that they are not rejoicing in the pain but in what our glorious God does in us through pain.

This perspective is of utmost importance to hold on to when we find ourselves in the disorientating fog bank called suffering. What Paul is going to teach us here is a proverbial compass steering us back to true north when all else is disorienting.

Sequential Impact

Paul presents us with a series of causes and effects.

>Suffering *produces* perseverance.

>Perseverance *produces* character.

>Character *produces* hope.

Simply put, as we have reflected on so far, God's goodness provides ample opportunity to have a lively response to God, life, and others by leaning into him as we are called to endure hardships. As we persevere in our walk with God amidst pain, we are transformed. Our character is changed. We become like the one with whom we commune. Like Father, like daughter and like son. We have his Spirit within us, and we become like his Son over time. Suffering has a purging, clarifying impact on us.

As we are changed, something else takes deeper root in us—hope.

Hope is a dangerous commodity in this world. It opens us up to possibilities we did not know existed. It can also pile on the pain when life does not go as we had expected.

Hope is often based on expectations. We have expectations for our marriage (or having been married by now), for our children (or having had children by now), for our careers (or ... well, you know), our health, and on and on. But none of those are guaranteed in this uncertain world.

We are offered a hope that is sure and is not rocked by circumstances. That is why we hope in the glory of God—he is faithful and he does not change. He is always here. He is always true. As we walk with God on the long road called suffering, we come to know him in ways we never would have known. Hope is reborn within. Not hope in the stuff of life, as meaningful as it is, but a hope in God.

This hope does not disappoint; it is sure. And here is the punchline: this is what he is up to all along the way.

God's Expanding Work through Suffering

"And hope does not put us to shame [i.e., disappoint us or let us down], because God's love has been poured out into our hearts through the Holy Spirit, who has been given to us" (Romans 5:5 NIV). We come to know and experience in deeper ways the reality that the Spirit is pouring out the Father's love within us. The Spirit is what unites us to the Son, and through the Son we are bound to the Father. God the Spirit is in us, spreading abroad his love—all his life, goodness, and grace. This is what our hope is set on: God's love and its implications, despite our circumstances.

We have come full circle through suffering.

God's glory, who he is—namely, a God of love—comes into clearer focus as we grow in our communion with him *in the midst of* life's hardships.

Experiencing God's love is the fruit of a matured character, which is the fruit of perseverance, which is the fruit of suffering. Thus, Paul rejoices in suffering because he ultimately wants to know the Father's love for him in increasing ways.

These are significant spiritual truths that grant us keen insight into God's redemptive activity in us through suffering. God encourages us to endure through hard times. As we do so by turning toward him, he brings deep change within us. As we see this change, it encourages us and gives us concrete markers that he is present and active. Our hope is deepened, not in circumstances getting better, but in who God is and his purposes in and for us.

Through it all, what is being most significantly changed is our capacity to know the reality of the Spirit spreading abroad the Father's love within us. All this amazing growth happens in the context of suffering, Paul teaches. Thus, he can make seemingly outlandish exhortations such as rejoicing in our sufferings. We know that God has the last word and is up to beautifying our souls.

Story: My Struggle to Know God's Love

I am one of those shepherd-leaders who taught eloquently on God's love without knowing how far I was from actually experiencing it. Like many, my identity was firmly wrapped up in performance and what others thought of me. But I had a clarifying moment into this reality early on in my struggle with chronic illness.

I had a ministry engagement that I really wanted to fulfill. The reality was that there was no way I could navigate airports, airplanes, and all-day meetings with my level of chronic fatigue and other nagging symptoms. I dragged my feet for weeks, until I finally made the call. "I cannot make it," I told them.

"I have to cancel." When I got off the phone, I fell to the ground, and said to God, "I don't even know who I am anymore."

That was one of those moments when the words of my mouth revealed my heart to me. My identity was tied up in what I did, and when what I could do was massively diminished due to illness, I was lost. Who was I? The Father was rocking and reshaping my identity.

The Long Walk to a New Identity

God allowed me to live in this relentless struggle year after year to take me through a slow stripping and rebuilding process. A short-lived hardship would have been too easy for my personality to rebound from and carry on as before. There has been no rebounding from this one. Instead, I have been taken to the school of the Father's love. No recesses are allowed. I am being shown I have a different identity, one that allows me to do what God asks me to give my life to in much more meaningful ways.

It is a radically different posture to shepherd others from an identity based on performance than to shepherd others from the identity of being an adopted son of his love. Night and day. He knew that as I aged, I would need something more substantial than a performance-based identity to walk with him and serve others. But primary in all this was his desire to expand my heart so as to grow in knowing his boundless love toward me in Christ. In fact, he does the same loving handiwork in all of us.

Suffering's Bounty in My Life

It is a lasting impression upon me that as God has asked me to walk with him through chronic health struggles for the past decade, I am a changed man.

Supremely, I have come to know his love in ways that constantly take me by surprise.

God has graciously allowed me to live the Romans 5 passage. He has exhorted me to endure, and endure well with him. He has changed and continues to change my character. I am a different person. Many of my false hopes have been fully exposed. Thus, my initial experience was that of disillusionment. But as that slow stripping has taken effect, a deeper hope has also taken root in me. He has exposed the many ways I braced myself against his love and sought meaning in other places. He has expanded my heart to know his love. He is teaching me to receive his love, to see myself as a son of his love. *Much of this deep transformation has happened in the context of unresolved adversity.*

Can I say I rejoice in sufferings? Well, I don't want to suffer anymore, that is for sure. Pain stinks in whatever variety it comes in, *and* yet I love the fruit of it all.

Do I still feel anxious when my symptoms spike a new cycle? You bet. I can be reduced to bartering with God quickly! Yet he has repeatedly shown me that I am hidden in him. I am not on my own. He has me. I can rest in that truth.

Do I get weary of this and slide into distracting self-numbing at times? You know it. I am being taught there is no rest in my soul from consumeristic amusements. I am being taught that Jesus is the only one who can give me that for which I long.

I rejoice in what God has done in me through sufferings. In fact, I have gone from resignation to embracing my reality. My uninvited companion has become a gift. That is something I could not have imagined saying ten years ago. And all this is a work of the wise and loving Father toward one of his beloveds.

Reflection

» How have you personally experienced the reality of Romans 5:2–5?

» What false hopes are being exposed in your life right now?

» How are you experiencing the reality of the Father's love poured out within you by the Spirit? Think of concrete expressions of his love to you as of late.

chapter 5

A Quiet Strength Within

"Without faith it is impossible to please God ..." (Hebrews 11:6 NIV). Or to say it another way, we can bring immense delight to God when we trust him. Faith is essential to this journey of ours. But the focus of our faith is not on faith itself. This error shows up when teaching or thinking leads us to believe that, "If I only had more faith, then God would ____________________."

Our faith is not in our faith. We lean on a good, wise, and loving God. He is the one who is worthy of our trust. Our God cannot be manipulated either, for he needs nothing outside of himself. He has not set up a barter-and-trade economy. He doesn't scratch our back if we scratch his. He needs nothing from us. His economy is one of relationship expressed in love and grace. He offers himself to us freely. Will we trust him? Will we receive him?

A Genuineness Test

Our faith is shown for what it is when the going gets tough. It is easy to trust when things go well, but when circumstances do not meet expectations or hopes, then what? Will we still choose to believe or will we take our ball and go home unwilling to be a player anymore?

Our belief is not merely a cerebral ascent to some doctrinal statement.

Instead, it is a relational response—one of accepting or rejecting. Despite all that is going on in our lives, will we still seek to abide in Christ? To call out to God? To rely on him and not our own techniques to manage life?

Peter's Faith Was Slow Growing Too

Peter is a classic encouragement model about growing faith. His faith was supremely tested on the night Jesus was tried and sentenced, and he failed. He lied. He denied. He wept over it. But the Peter who wrote the two epistles in the New Testament is a transformed person. How do you experience the Peter of those letters? The passion and fire is still there, but he has an elderly, wise, authoritative tone about him. He speaks of a certainty. Though he fled suffering in the Gospels, he embraces it in his later writings.

Peter had been tried by suffering. Jesus worked wonders in Peter's life. Thus, Peter was a different man. He became an elder of the faith. This is something God longs to do in each of us. The church could use far more elders of the faith. The path to that level of maturity and relational influence is a costly and rewarding one.

A Boiling Cauldron

Peter began his first epistle speaking to the topic of faith. It is a well-known passage:

> In all this you greatly rejoice, though now for a little while *you may have had to suffer grief in all kinds of trials. These have come so that the proven genuineness of your faith*—of greater worth than gold, which perishes even

> though refined by fire—may result in praise, glory and honor when Jesus Christ is revealed. Though you have not seen him, you love him; and even though you do not see him now, you believe in him and are filled with an inexpressible and glorious joy, for you are receiving the end result of your faith, the salvation of your souls. (1 Peter 1:6–9 NIV)

The paragraph begins with a reference to "all this" in which we "greatly rejoice." Peter is referring to the living hope we have in the resurrection of Jesus from the dead and our eternal inheritance that is kept by the Father for us (see 1 Peter 1:3–5). Indeed, we greatly rejoice in these gifts, for they are firm and cannot be corrupted.

Yet our faith has room for growth. It's easy to accept good gifts, but will we trust the Gift Giver when the going gets tough? Peter writes that we experience all kinds of trials to prove the genuineness of our faith. Faith is a trait that will be tested. Your faith will be tried—you can count on it. The trying of our faith is as certain as the goodness of our God. We must not be surprised, because it will happen.

Peter then uses the analogy of gold purified over fire. As the gold heats up and melts, the dross comes to the surface to be skimmed off. The gold becomes more and more pure. Trials are like a boiling cauldron. The heat gets turned up in life and the boil is on. Cancer, parenting special-needs children, and losing a job are all boiling cauldrons we can find ourselves in. When Peter writes "all kinds of trials," he means any trying circumstances that encompass the breadth of the human experience.

Unwise Responses to Suffering

Minimizing and Dismissing

There are two extreme tendencies in the Western culture to suffering. One significant tendency is minimizing or dismissing:

- "I should be able to handle this."
- "I just need to try harder."
- "All I've got to do is figure out how and ________________."
- "It's not as bad as it sounds."

We might be dying inside, but if someone asks us how we are doing, we universally respond with one word: "Fine."

Western culture seeks to remove pain from life, so when pain won't go away, we have no idea what to do with it. It is not welcome. It is not embraced. It is not normalized. We have limited vocabulary for it. So we seek to squash it. And heaven forbid that we come across as weak, needy, or otherwise incompetent in some way.

It is important to note that the Word of God never minimizes the human experience. Our experience is always held up for what it is. It is always honored and acknowledged. Pain hurts. Fears are real. Distress happens. Even Jesus was "greatly distressed and troubled" the night he was betrayed (Mark 14:33). Trials are hard, and they do test us. We are invited to honor our own and the stories of others. We do this by transparently expressing our inner world to God and those closest to us. "I am afraid." "I am angry at God about this." "I do not know what to do. This has undone me." These and other similar statements are all honest expressions of the type of impact our trials have on us.

Overspiritualization Is Not Helpful

The other extreme, at least in the church, is to overspiritualize. We say some of the most damaging things to one another.

- "Oh, God must be preparing you for something great to give you this." Gee, thanks. I don't recall signing up for this.
- "It will work out for good." True, but I am not ready to hear that, and besides, I cannot see how this can be "good" yet.
- "If you have faith, then God will deliver you." You are telling me I have cancer because my faith is weak?

Again, we do not know what to do with loss, grief, sorrow, confusion, and doubt, so we slap all sorts of platitudes on them like whitewash on a stain. This is not only unhelpful, but it is disillusioning. God invites us to learn how to be with one another in our sorrows—to weep with those who weep. A primary way we become people who weep with others is by learning to weep over our own sorrows.

A Beautiful Sight

Peter tells us that our faith will be tried by the breadth of life. Emotionally, relationally, spiritually, professionally, financially—everywhere, there will be trials. The opportunity is to turn our face toward God and cry for help.

A cry of desperation is not a doubt act; it is a faith act. God does not expect us to be competent to handle all of life's challenges on our own. No, we need a Savior, and we need him again and again. Every breathing moment of my existence, I need to be saved. Every turning toward God is an expression of faith. When we are tried, he is waiting for us to wait on him so he can pour out his mercies on us (see Isaiah 30:18).

In 1 Peter 1:8, Peter speaks of not seeing Jesus and yet believing him as a tremendous act of faith. Peter is merely quoting Jesus when Jesus was responding to Thomas's post-resurrection faith.

> A week later his disciples were in the house again, and Thomas was with them. Though the doors were locked, Jesus came and stood among them and said, "Peace be with you!" Then he said to Thomas, "Put your finger here; see my hands. Reach out your hand and put it into my side. Stop doubting and believe."
>
> Thomas said to him, "My Lord and my God!"
>
> Then Jesus told him, "Because you have seen me, you have believed; *blessed are those who have not seen and yet have believed*." (John 20:26–29 NIV)

We are the blessed ones Jesus is referring to here. We have not seen him, yet we believe. As we continue to cling to him in faith and hope in the context of every imaginable human trial, we bring him great delight, honor, and glory. He is well pleased with us. And we are armed to journey well in this life.

What does a simple act of faith look like, especially when the dark clouds are rolling in? We cry out for help to God. We cling to him. We grab our Bibles and go to those passages he has used to encourage us. We call out the reinforcements—those friends and counselors who can hear us out, laugh and cry with us, pray for us, and help us with clarity in our clouded perspective. In short, we turn to God and ask, "How do you want me to walk well with you in the midst of this awful stuff?"

All these are beautiful, if not messy, acts of faith.

Story: Pushed to the Emotional Breaking Point

Paul begins 2 Corinthians with an eloquent description of how God graces us with his presence as we endure all kinds of trials. What we see in this opening paragraph of 2 Corinthians is that God allows sufferings to exist in our lives to shape a deep work within us. God does not always resolve hurts in our lives, but he always promises his presence for good purposes.

Up to verse 7, the passage is principled: God's presence is faithful in all our hardships. Thankfully, Paul gets practical. He goes on to share a time in his own life when he experienced the reality of the truth that God, by necessity, allowed extremely tough sufferings in his life. He shares that experience like this:

> We do not want you to be uninformed, brothers and sisters, about the troubles we experienced in the province of Asia. We were under great pressure, far beyond our ability to endure, so that we despaired of life itself. Indeed, we felt we had received the sentence of death. But this happened that we might not rely on ourselves but on God, who raises the dead. (2 Corinthians 1:8–9 NIV)

Interestingly enough, Paul does not tell us exactly what the circumstances were. We could cross-reference this passage with the book of Acts and come up with a short list of likely events. But Paul does not express the circumstances because, like his "thorn in the flesh" (2 Corinthians 12:7), I am not sure the circumstances are what is most important here. The impact of our hardships can be just as harsh as the hardships themselves. In this case, the impact on Paul and his teammates was death-like.

Paul uses strong emotive expressions to describe the impact of this unknown situation: "under great pressure," "far beyond our ability to endure," "despaired of life itself," and "we felt we had received the sentence of death." Paul is describing a time in his journey in which he was completely emotionally overwhelmed. In contemporary vernacular, we could say he was maxed out, at the end of his rope, and exceedingly rattled. Rightly so. He thought he was a dead man.

There is no indication of divine punishment, nor a lack of faith on Paul's part involved here. Paul and his colleagues were right where God wanted them to be, doing the very work God had told them to do. Yet this is what they were experiencing in the midst of that level of obedience to God and sacrificial service to others.

A common assumption is that experiencing hardship is punitive for our failings. Though the Father corrects us from time to time, he is not looking for opportunities to inflict us with pain every time we mess up. In the face of our failures, he responds with mercy. Equally true is the reality that, in God's love, he allows and sometimes orchestrates hardships to draw us deeper into communion with him. Paul and his teammates found themselves in the crosshairs of this paradoxical reality.

What was God up to with Paul? If he was not punishing Paul for some unknown sin, then why in the world would he allow the apostle Paul and his teammates to be pushed to the utter point of a death-like experience? And why does he allow us to experience the same? Verse 9 gives us the key. Paul says that "this happened that we might not rely on ourselves but on God, who raises the dead." Their faith was being tested and deepened in the form of dependence on God rather than on themselves.

Paul's confession is most comforting. Whether Paul knows it or not, he is in the process of writing a large chunk of what would become the New Testament. Furthermore, he is several decades into his walk with Christ, and he has become a preeminent leader of the early church. Yet he still needs to learn to rely on God. Apparently, this lesson of learning to rely upon God and not ourselves is a lifelong process for all of us. Even apostles.

God is our breath. When we wander away, it is to our detriment. He will not have that for his children. He wants us close and dependent on him, for he knows that our dependence on him is good for us. This means that at times he takes us into these death-like experiences to remind us that we are dependent on the resurrection God for our very lives. Apostles need to learn this lesson, and so do we.

Suffering was a necessity in Paul's life, not only to fulfill his apostolic calling, but even more so as an adoptive son of the Father. So is suffering a necessity in our lives, to purify our faith and to draw us deeper into reliance upon our good Father.

Reflection

- » How has God proven the genuineness of your faith? How has your faith been strengthened and tested?
- » In your dark times, who can you call upon to hold you in faith?
- » How has God reminded you of your utter dependence on him? How is Paul's experience of that lesson a comfort to you?

chapter 6

Catching Our Attention

The May 13, 2015, edition of *Time* magazine ran an article titled, "You Now Have a Shorter Attention Span Than a Goldfish." Gee, that sounds encouraging. The opening paragraph states, "The average attention span for the notoriously ill-focused goldfish is nine seconds, but according to a new study from Microsoft Corp., people now generally lose concentration after eight seconds, highlighting the effects of an increasingly digitalized lifestyle on the brain."[6]

We are a distracted lot. Forgetful too. As discouraging as our waning attention span is, our heart problem is deeper still. Indeed, our hearts are prone to wander. Hebrews 12 reminds us that at times our Father must discipline us as children as we wander, lest we wander further still. Hebrews 12:5–6 reads,

> And have you completely forgotten this word of encouragement that addresses you as a father addresses his son? It says,
>
> "My son, do not make light of the Lord's discipline,
> and do not lose heart when he rebukes you,
> because the Lord disciplines the one he loves,
> and he chastens everyone he accepts as his son." (NIV)

Is it just me or have you noticed how much more we cry out to God when life gets tough? When I cry to God, what I am usually after is relief. What I need, however, is more than just a rescue. I need a deep renovation. I need a sustained gaze on God, a willingness to obey at any cost. God yearns for more than dutiful allegiance.

Jesus's motivation gives us a glimpse of a love-driven focus when he says on the eve of his death, "I do as the Father has commanded me, so that the world may know that I love the Father" (John 14:31). Love is what prompted Jesus to obey his Father, even to the point of death. The Father desires to have the same driving force in us—a love-driven desire to obey.

Pain has a focusing impact on our hearts. Less important matters fade away. God has our attention. He is weaning us from that which distracts or otherwise harms us in our walk with him and others. As we lean back into the God who is always leaning toward us in the context of suffering, we are being, albeit slowly, transformed into all he has created and redeemed us to be in his love.

Being Weaned from Our Norm

In the beginning verses of 1 Peter 4, Peter explains that suffering has a purging and focusing effect on us. First Peter 4:1–2 states, "Since therefore Christ suffered in the flesh, arm yourselves with the same way of thinking, for whoever has suffered in the flesh has ceased from sin, so as to live for the rest of the time in the flesh no longer for human passions but for the will of God."

Jesus's earthly life was not comfortable. Peter spent a good portion of 1 Peter 3 explaining how Jesus suffered on our behalf, "the righteous for the unrighteous, that he might bring us to God" (1 Peter 3:18). His willingness to suffer was a profound act of love toward his Father who wanted us as daughters and sons. It was also an equally profound act of love toward us.

It is important to see that Jesus never obeyed out of mere duty. As we saw from John 14:31, Jesus responds to his Father's love by doing whatever the Father wants. Obedience is a response of love from the Son to the Father. Obedience is always an opportunity to express love to our God. This is exactly the love-driven obedience the Father desires in all his children. And suffering is a means of growing that love in us.

A Love in Need of Redirecting

Unlike Jesus, whose love was Father-directed, our love is often self-directed. Our desires are turned in on ourselves. Our bent is to relentlessly fulfill our passions in self-absorbed ways. This is not to our own benefit, as it leads to death. Our loving God knows this and seeks to purify our passions so they are love-for-God-driven passions. This is what Peter means when he uses the potentially confusing statement about "ceasing from sin."

To cease from sin does not mean that we become sinless—never failing in any regard. Rather, it refers to the act of choosing to endure in suffering rather than comforting ourselves. Our natural inclination is to bail at the first sign of pain. If we cannot avoid the pain, then we soothe the pain as fast as we can, however we can.

But the one who endures in suffering by seeking to walk well with God has most definitely acted in a way which shows that loving God by obeying God, not avoiding hardship, is a greater motivation for his or her actions. Thus, choosing to obey God even when it involves suffering has a morally strengthening effect on our lives. It commits us more firmly to a pattern of action where loving God through obedience is more important than our desire to avoid pain and be comfortable.

Yet we are master saboteurs of this love. We turn away from this great love for lesser loves. We give into our own self-absorbed desires. Left on our own, we would do this endlessly. God regains our attention and refocuses us through the galvanizing experience of prolonged suffering. He is seeking to awaken us from our stupor. He wants us to know his love and to walk in his love.

As we respond to that invitation in opting to endure these adversities by seeking how he wants us to walk well with him, his company with us transforms us. We become like the one we are with. As we continue this path with him, despite any pains, we are slowly but surely changed. We grow in his love, and that love drives us to want to do his pleasure, just like Jesus. Jesus so delights in his Father's love that he wants whatever the Father wants, regardless of personal cost. It is possible for that same love to grow in us. Suffering is one of the means God uses to do just that.

A Noble Life

There have been times when I felt dismayed of ever being changed. I have seen the same sinful response from myself toward others for so many years. I have impatiently cried out to God to change me. God is urgent about his loving, redemptive work; however, he is never in a hurry.

Today, through many years of relentless physical adversities (as well as the Word, wise counselors, and loving friends and other graces he has bestowed), he is slowly opening me to his love. I am grateful to see a depth being shaped in me toward God, others, and life in general. I am being taught to slow down, to listen, to see. He is growing in me a desire "to live for the rest of the time in the flesh no longer for human passions but for the will of God" (1 Peter 4:2).

When we find ourselves in prolonged trials of various kinds, the invitation offered to us is to turn to God and not to our old ways of responding to life. God is up to a deep work within us. He is inviting us to a more noble life. To repeat what I wrote earlier, choosing to obey God even when it involves suffering has a morally strengthening effect. It commits us more firmly to a pattern of action where loving God through obedience is more important than our desire to avoid pain and be comfortable.

Story: Life on the Back Side of the Wilderness

Moses was the greatest prophet Israel ever had. He was the recipient of amazing revelation from God. Soon after the Exodus from Egypt, Moses spent weeks upon a mountain alone with God receiving the Law. He was so immersed in God's presence that his face glowed. Later, he would continue in his deep communion with God by meeting with him in person in a tent outside the Israelite camp. Exodus 33:11 is one of the most extraordinary statements in the Bible: "The LORD used to speak to Moses face to face, as a man speaks to a friend." How did Moses come to such an amazing relationship with God?

Moses's Way or God's Way?

Moses grew up in a different sort of splendor. As a baby, he was taken in by Pharaoh's daughter. Acts 7:22 tells us, "And Moses was instructed in all the wisdom of the Egyptians, and he was mighty in his words and deeds." This was the summation of Moses's upbringing. In stark contrast, his kin were suffering under Pharaoh. In an arrogant effort to make more storehouses for grain that could not possibly be consumed, Pharaoh fiercely demanded the Israelite slaves make more and more bricks. Moses lived in plenty while his fellow Israelites harshly suffered.

There is so much of his story we do not know. Somewhere along the way, Moses came to know he was a Jew. And at some point, he came to think he could deliver his people. In Acts 7:25, Stephen tells us that "Moses thought his own people would realize that God was using him to rescue them, but they did not" (NIV). This is a peculiar situation in which Moses found himself.

Stephen is referring to the day Moses had come upon an Egyptian brutally beating an Israeli slave. Moses looked left and right, saw no one, and killed the Egyptian. He truly thought he could deliver the people. How did he get that idea? And what was his plan, to kill the Egyptians one man at a time? Obviously, there was a sizable gap between God's way and Moses's way of delivering God's people. How did Moses get from the place of implementing his own strategy of delivering God's people to becoming the amazing prophet and leader who did things as God told him to?

The Sands of Time

When we read the biblical narrative, it is easy to overlook the crucial element of time. In a matter of minutes, we can read a story in the Bible that covers years, even decades. This unfortunate reality causes us to miss crucial dynamics of the plot.

As we have already noted, we need many things in order to mature. Time is one of those central characters in God's story. We need lots of time to mature in our faith. Ideally, we never cease maturing, which is a part of God's design for our redemption. Again, God is seemingly never in a hurry. Think of all the major biblical stories:

- Abraham waited twenty years for his promised son Isaac.
- Joseph languished as a slave and prisoner in Egypt for many years.

- Hannah lived with the desolation of an empty womb year after year.
- There were fourteen years between when David was anointed to be king and when he was finally enthroned. Most of those years were spent on the run from a delusional King Saul.
- Noticeably, Jesus was born and remained unseen and unrevealed for approximately 90 percent of his time on earth—thirty of his thirty-three years.

It is not that God is not powerful to deliver us from our hardships, and it is not that he does not care either. He does care. He always sees. We might endure for years and years through painful hardships when God could easily change the situation. What is he up to? Why does he choose to work in this way?

The School in the Wilderness

Moses was about forty years old when he killed the Egyptian. When Pharaoh found out, he sought to kill Moses in retaliation. Moses fled into the desert wilderness. Very quickly, he went from a person in a privileged position to that of a fugitive wandering in the wilderness alone. No one cared who he was or where he came from. He was stripped of all power and influence. He could not even deliver himself, let alone an entire nation.

Thus began God's reformation process in Moses's life. For the next forty years, he would have a wife, children, and some sheep to tend to, but no other leadership role. He would live a simple shepherd's life for four decades. He was one of many nameless, nomadic shepherds in the wilderness north of Egypt.

I wonder what those days were like for Moses. It must have been a harsh transition from Pharaoh's palace to a shepherd's tent; from princely meals to subsistence living off the land; from being served by others to having to fend for himself. I wonder if it was forty years of silence from God. When God came to him in the burning bush, had he already spoken to Moses prior to that moment? We are not told. God's lessons were crucial to the future of his people and therefore had to be burnt deep into the fabric of Moses's soul and identity.

Moses had to learn that he was not going to deliver God's people by his own power or strength. God is the deliverer. Yes, he can use people like Moses, but it is God who does the work. Many years later, Isaiah would make the statement, "O LORD, you will ordain peace for us, for you have done for us all our works" (Isaiah 26:12). Somehow, all that we do in serving God is God working in us and through us. If he was not working in and around us, then nothing would be accomplished.

Jesus even modeled this for us. John records several times where Jesus made it clear that he could not do anything on his own. Jesus said that even the words he spoke and the works he did were not him but the Father in him speaking the words and doing the works (see John 5:19–20, 30; 14:10, 24, 31). Then, the night before he was crucified, when he was alone with the disciples, he made it clear that this truth is equally true for us too: "I am the vine; you are the branches. Whoever abides in me and I in him, he it is that bears much fruit, for *apart from me you can do nothing*" (John 15:5). We do our life's work just like the Son of God did his—in dependence on the Father through the Spirit.

It is in the harshness of wilderness experiences when we are stripped of our sense of false identity and false competency, and we are reoriented to this most fundamental reality of not being able to do anything without him.

A Slower Way of Life and Work

Another possible reason that God took Moses into the wilderness was to teach him to slow down. Imagine the environment Moses came from. Pharaoh was a hard-driving, demanding master. He wanted more and more storehouses, and he wanted them now. There were no days off, no Sabbaths for the Jewish slaves. The anxiety in their lives must have been extreme. Production had to be kept high, or else ....

Then Moses came along to deliver God's people. He did not wait on God but acted on his own. God was going to use him, but Moses was ahead of God—by about four decades. We live in a world where technology allows us to do more faster. But as we have seen, God is not in a hurry. He must teach us to slow down. To wait.

Are we aware that God waits on us? In Isaiah 30, Israel is under threat from the ruling global empire of Assyria, so they make their own plans to protect themselves. They enter a treaty with Egypt (ironically!) to receive protection. They don't look to God; rather, they look to their own devices.

In Isaiah 30:15, God says, "In repentance and rest is your salvation, in quietness and trust is your strength, but you would have none of it" (NIV). However, Israel rejected God's way. The following verses are rife with Israel fleeing, running, and executing their plans that would ultimately fail them. And our self-devised plans fail us as well.

Then God says this: "Yet *the LORD longs to be gracious to you*; therefore he will rise up to show you compassion. For the LORD is a God of justice. *Blessed are all who wait for him!*" (Isaiah 30:18 NIV). Indeed, God waits to be gracious to us in our hour of need. He invites us to turn toward him and to wait upon him as he patiently loves us. Time is a crucial element in the hands of our wise Father. He slows everything down to slow us down so he can gain our attention.

God's Slow Work in Moses and in Us

There are many lessons that likely shaped Moses over those forty years as he tended sheep in the desert. He probably learned patience, how to live in discomfort, and how to be gentle with the sheep and his family. Many have observed that this would be the same wilderness he would lead Israel through for another forty years. God was shaping Moses so that he could do his true work in him, in his way and in his time.

We have a small attention span—apparently about eight seconds' worth. God is seeking to awaken us, to regain our attention. Suffering is an essential means to do that. He is slowly, resolutely, lovingly shaping us through these adversities. He is a wise God. All his plans and ways are true and good. It is wise for us to slow down, to wait on him, to seek him, for he is longingly waiting for us.

Reflection

» As God has gained your attention through suffering, from what self-absorbed passions and lies is God seeking to free you?

» How is God inviting you to respond to him in a new love-driven obedience rather than out of a desire to avoid pain and be comfortable?

» Like Moses, how has God used your desert experiences to show you his patient, steady work? How would you like to wait upon him in this barren place?

summary of section one

Section One heightened our awareness of God's redemptive activity in our lives when we find ourselves in personal suffering. We have been confronted with the biblical reality that God has designed the redemptive process and created the human soul to necessitate suffering for maturation. This reality immediately confronts us with tensions.

Learning to embrace paradox is one key to walking in these tensions well. Our sufferings do not undermine God's love for us; rather, they are a context in which God lovingly and wisely draws us deeper into himself. Indeed, sufferings, along with many other provisions in life, are a means God uses to carve out greater capacity within us to know and receive his love.

Thus, how we respond to suffering is essential. He invites a trusting, reliant response toward him and a sacrificial companioning of others in their adversities. The one who walks well with God in his or her sufferings is uniquely formed to companion others in their sufferings. In the end, we find that God's loving work through suffering is not just for our own gain but also for the benefit of others.

Section Two will direct our reflection toward God- and other-oriented responses through personal suffering. The Hebrew word translated as *noble* in English is a beautifully-layered word. A noble person is one who is inclined with a willingness of acts that reflect the character of God toward others in sacrificially relational ways. Nobility is not self-generated. Rather, it is shaped in us by the one who is noble.

section two

Trusting Responses to Our Wise & Loving God Amidst Suffering

God shapes within us noble responses toward himself and others through our sufferings.

chapter 7

A Jesus-Oriented Perspective on Our Sufferings

We are not victims. The physical maladies I live with do not define me, nor do they define who God is. Rather, God is the one who defines my circumstances.

Whatever sufferings you have been asked to endure, whether caused by another, self-inflicted, or merely the result of living in a fallen world, do not define you. That which is profoundly disorienting and agonizing can, in the hands of a wise, loving Father, be an instrument of profound life-giving redemption.

Jesus's death on the cross is our supreme model when it comes to where we find our identity. The cross and all it involved did not define Jesus; rather, his Father's love for him defined him. He is his Father's beloved Son from eternity—long before he was incarnated or suffered. We too are defined by the Father's love for us; our sufferings in this world are always seen through the lens of that identity.

We are not victims; we are sons and daughters invited into a dramatic story of God's making. Suffering is merely one reality of that story—God's larger story, the one he is writing.

Paul's Outlook

Paul knew this well. His responses to his own sufferings are insightful for us as followers of Christ. Chained to guards in a prison, he wrote letters to fledgling churches he helped to establish and nurture. These churches were suffering as well.

The letter to the Philippians is one of those letters written during this time of suffering in Paul's life. It is intriguing that two core themes in the book of Philippians are suffering *and* joy, which is another paradox. These seem like they ought not coexist, yet coexist they do. Paul's perspective is a matured one; his is nobility on display. What shaped Paul's outlook?

Suffering in Christ

Paul writes the letter to the Philippians from a Roman prison. It is fascinating to note how he describes his experience. It reorients how he responds to the place in which he finds himself. Paul simply states that he suffers "in Christ" (Philippians 1:13). L. Ann Jervis, in her must-read book *At the Heart of the Gospel*, wonderfully captures the essence of Paul's outlook and message:

> The distinction is critical. Reckoning his imprisonment as being "in Christ" strongly suggests that Paul is not pointing a finger at anyone. That is, Paul is not interpreting his situation as one of persecution—his imprisonment may be caused by his commitment to the gospel, but he chooses to interpret and present his situation from a deeper level. His suffering is not shaped by his jailers but by Christ. In thus accepting his suffering, Paul does not accept victimization. He speaks rather as someone who has radically reversed the power dynamics of his circumstances. He is not the victim. Paul interprets the injustices he experiences in the context

> of being "in" Christ; other people and circumstances may cause afflictions, but Paul does not lay blame. He rather uses his energy to draw these difficulties into the sphere he now inhabits—the sphere of being "in" Christ.[7]

Jervis keenly observes that "Paul's suffering is not shaped by his jailers but by Christ." Paul chooses to see his circumstances from a deeper perspective. He is not merely in prison because others have unjustly treated him; he is in prison in Christ, for Christ, and with very real positive effects that we shall observe in this chapter.

Our personal sufferings are not merely shaped by our circumstances. We are invited to see life through the grid of being in Christ, and Christ being with us and for us. Our life is defined by him, not by what we experience in this world.

Our Realities Reframed

When I contracted a virus while serving others in Asia that eventually afflicted my autoimmune system, I had a choice in how I responded to the new reality I found myself in. I could take the angle of a victim: "This is not fair. I've been done wrong." But that is such a small and confining response to life's quandries. In reality, God was inviting me into a much broader and deeper awareness of himself and all of life.

Paul's perspective was shaped by his participation in the life of Christ. Our perspectives can take the same shape. Personally, God has helped me to see that my sufferings, painful and harsh as they are, are also a gift, for I am a better person because of them. What's more is that I do not experience them on my own; I experience them in Christ. For example, I find that when I share my story, I now use statements like "God gave me this." It's not that I know God afflicted my life with an incurable illness. Rather, I am expressing that I have experienced this adversity in Christ and in the Father's loving care and redemption. In the end, it has been a profound gift I would not trade for anything. This perspective has been shaped in me by God over many years.

In Christ, we have been invited to steward our uninvited companion and all the ensuing gifts that he has graced our lives with. Our sufferings are hurtful, yes, *and* they are also opportunities for a deepened life in God. Our realities can be reframed.

How do you see your uninvited companions? Are they something that has been done to you or are they something that has been extended to you? Your perspective makes all the difference in the world. It did for Paul. As Paul took this perspective, he could see some amazing ripple effects around him. Let's look at a few of Paul's observed gains from his personal sufferings.

Others Witness God in Our Lives

Paul states that the guards who he was chained to had all heard of the reality of the resurrected Christ. The guards were in fact a captive audience. Paul took the opportunity to love the ones who meant him harm. Others were getting a front-row seat to the presence of Jesus in this man's life. Paul wasn't griping; he was rejoicing. That caught the attention of the guards.

As we are taught by God to walk well with him in our own sufferings, we are in fact abiding in Jesus. Jesus is present with us, through whatever we may face. Over time, that presence overflows from our lives. It doesn't come across in some sort of pious spirituality, but rather in the normal messiness of our own struggles with the pains of life. In ways we never know, others sense and experience God in and through us.

I have been repeatedly surprised at the times someone has come to me and thanked me for exemplifying Christ to them. Are you kidding me? My inner world is fraying in concern over my physical symptoms. When I pray, God seems silent. I am utterly confounded by life's circumstances, and someone sees Jesus in me? Yet it is true. As we have noted, God is profoundly present in and through us as we suffer. His Spirit is upon us and tending to us. What's more is that he is allowing himself to pour through our brokenness to others in ways we likely do not know.

Others Are Encouraged to Endure in Their Own Sufferings

Paul states that other believers had become emboldened in their proclamation of the gospel due to Paul's response to his imprisonment (see Philippians 1:14). These fellow believers were willing to suffer for their faith because Paul was suffering for his faith.

As we choose to keep walking with the God of love in the midst of personal pain, we, by example, encourage others to do the same. The reality is that we all are facing various trials at any given time. These challenges run the range from everyday hassles to daily concerns for loved ones to life-altering circumstances.

It has struck my wife and me that what often encourages others from our story the most is when we share the hardships God has allowed us to endure. It is our weaknesses, losses, and brokenness that ministers to others. The lie that we need to have our act together in order to influence others distracts us from the truth that in our weaknesses God is strongest. Besides, everyone is struggling in one way or another, and it is helpful to hear how others are experiencing and responding to their struggles.

Joy and Gratitude Find Fertile Soil to Grow

Joy is also a major theme of Philippians. L. Ann Jervis once again is helpful at this point. She observes: "The paradox of joyful response to suffering is solved once love opens our eyes to who we are suffering in, who we are suffering with, and what we are suffering for. We suffer not in lonely isolation but 'in' Christ, with Christ, and with other believers."[8]

During some of my darkest hours, I have had to turn to these passages in Philippians. The fog bank of physical ailment had obscured my vision. Scripture reoriented me. I was constantly reminded that I am in Christ and that he is in me. He never changes and is always with me. He had a grand purpose for my life, even in my sufferings. In fact, he was suffering with me, and I was suffering with and in him. None of this resolved my circumstances, but these truths reoriented me and provided a larger perspective. Gratitude slowly took root within.

It is crucial to highlight the essential need of being in the Word during these times of suffering. Seasons of adversity are what I call "red-letter days," meaning they are opportunities to grow closer to God, to be shaped by him, and to move onward in his purposes. We do not want to miss out on these opportunities. Suffering is bad enough, but why compound it by not gaining all God offers us through it? His Word is a light unto our feet in these dark times.

Meditating upon and acknowledging the truths offered to us in God's Word makes room for deep thanksgiving. It is possible to be in pain and to be filled with joy at the same time. Whereas suffering is common to humankind, suffering with deep joy and confidence in a loving Father is a characteristic of a maturing son or daughter of the King. Paul knew this well, and he lived it in a foul Roman prison.

Our perspective on suffering is significant in how we respond to it. Paul grants us an exceptional model to emulate. The impact is like a ripple in a pond—not only does it stimulate our hope, faith, and joy, but it does so in others as well.

Story: The Greatest Act of Love and Courage

I have often reflected on how much a gift it is that we do not know what the next hour brings. If I received word from God that tomorrow I would be in a car accident that would not necessarily take my life but alter it, well, you know where you would find me tomorrow. I'd stay in bed all day long. I'd go nowhere near a car. In fact, God would have to drop a car through the roof of my house for me to be in that car accident. Like the rest of humanity, I am fairly committed to avoiding pain.

And yet Jesus knew his tomorrow. He knew when, where, and how his life would end. He knew what the Jews would do, and he knew what the Gentiles would do. He knew how his own disciples would respond. He knew it all—the pain, the shame, and the punishment for sin not his own. Despite knowing so intimately what lay before him, he walked right into it.

This is one the greatest displays of human courage. What enabled Jesus to do this? We will find that what drove Jesus can also be the driving force in our lives, no matter what comes our way.

The Father's Love

In the Gospels, Jesus is repeatedly identified as the Father's beloved Son. Jesus knew this; it was *the* orienting reality to his life. The needs of the world were not what drove Jesus; he was not need-driven. What motivated Jesus was his Father's love and his love for his Father in return.

In John 5:19–20, Jesus says, "Very truly I tell you, the Son can do nothing by himself; he can do only what he sees his Father doing, because whatever the Father does the Son also does. For the Father loves the Son and shows him all he does ..." (NIV). Jesus was directed by the Father who loved him and would not do anything on his own initiative. In turn, Jesus did everything because of his love for his Father. John 14:31 clearly summarizes this reality, when Jesus said "that the world may learn that I love the Father and do exactly what my Father has commanded me."

Everything Jesus did flowed from his Father's love for him. The cross was the supreme display of the love-driven response to his Father. But in all the hardships Jesus experienced, he was willing to endure because he knew he was loved.

Were the circumstances of Jesus's life distressing to him at times? Of course. He wept at Lazarus's tomb (see John 11), he was infuriated by the oppression of the religious system of that time, and on the night his betrayal and crucifixion was to happen, Mark records Jesus's inner world with these strong words:

> They went to a place called Gethsemane, and Jesus said to his disciples, "Sit here while I pray." He took Peter, James and John along with him, and *he began to be deeply distressed and troubled.* "My soul is *overwhelmed with sorrow* to the point of death," he said to them. "Stay here and keep watch." (Mark 14:32–34 NIV)

Even Jesus experienced deep distress, internal trouble, and overwhelming sorrow. These were not manifestations of doubt in his Father's wisdom and love; they were the impact of what he knew he was about to endure. Jesus's orienting reality toward his own suffering was the Father's love for him. His was a Father-oriented perspective toward suffering. And we can have the same orientation.

Our Father's Love for Us

Like our elder brother Jesus, we have a Father who deeply loves us. He uses *all* of life to draw us deeper into his love. Like his Son, he does not intend for us to be need-driven; he wants us to be driven by his love for us. Like Jesus who could do nothing on his own (see John 5:19, 30), so we too have been told by Jesus that we can do nothing on our own (see John 15:5). God uses suffering not as a punishment, but in love to draw us deeper into himself so, like Jesus, we can manifest this same love to a hurting world.

When we know who is with us, who is for us, and who we are loved by, and that in everything he has our ultimate good in mind, then the opportunity to have a trusting response, a receptive response, and even a grateful, joyful response is before us. Like Jesus, the Spirit can birth in us responses to sufferings with love and courage.

Reflection

» How do Jesus's and Paul's responses to sufferings stir you regarding your own sufferings?

» What do you sense the Father is inviting you to regarding a fresh orientation to your own sufferings?

» Reflect upon God's goodness in your life. List graces and provisions he has extended to you for which you want to express gratitude.

chapter 8

Embracing the Reality of Mystery

Much of what happens in our lives is confusing and disorienting. This past fall, I lost two friends only one week apart. Both were in their early fifties. One died suddenly of a heart attack, while the other finished his eight-year battle with a rare cancer. These were men in their prime with young families, men who were serving God and loving others. Fifteen years ago, my wife lost her mother instantly in a car accident. I have lost other friends to disease at young ages. Again and again, I have found myself disoriented by these events.

Making Friends with Mystery

> Mys·ter·y: 'mist(ə)rē; noun—Something that is difficult or impossible to understand or explain.[9]

This is an apt definition of the ways of God—something that is difficult or impossible to understand or explain. I do not want to give the impression that the conviction with which I have written this book means that I have a thorough grasp of the realities at hand. Not at all. I continue to wrestle with God in all these areas.

This past year, in the days after I received the news that my close friend Randy was gone in an instant, all the normal questions surfaced once again. "Why God? What good can come of this? What are you up to?" I simply do not understand. I am left not merely baffled, but deeply stunned and grieved. It seems like a mistake was made. Dazed, I once again wonder what happened.

I am a linear thinker. When I start to line up the truths I have been taught, it looks something like this: God is loving + God is good + God is always redeeming everything in my life + this suffering I find myself in stinks and I want it to go away *now* + God is not taking it away + nope, he is still not taking it away = I clearly do not understand God's ways.

I *clearly* do not understand his ways.

Suffering affords us the opportunity to become more aware of, and over time, more comfortable with the reality that we are not in control and that God has a wisdom and a way that are not ours. God is teaching us to relinquish control. And as we do, we grow in wisdom.

Let's look at a few passages that grant insight into the mysterious ways of our wise and loving God.

Loftier and Wiser

> God declared through Isaiah:
> "For my thoughts are not your thoughts,
> neither are your ways my ways," declares the LORD.
> "For as the heavens are higher than the earth,
> so are my ways higher than your ways
> and my thoughts than your thoughts." (Isaiah 55:8–9)

Indeed.

This passage has echoed in my soul for years. As I have already expressed, I have clearly seen the amazing transformative work God has done in me amidst prolonged personal hardships. And I have heard the same sort of testimonies from many others. I've also confessed that I do not like it this way. I do not like the pain. I am disoriented by the uncertainty of it all. *And* I have come to appreciate what his Word and his work have shown me about his deeper wisdom. There is much paradox in this pilgrimage.

God has a wisdom that we will never fully grasp. True wisdom is always expressed in love. Because of this, we can rest assured that he is not a cold and calculating God allowing hard stuff to happen and not caring about how it impacts us. Yet the reality remains that he has wisdom and ways we will never fully understand. He is God, and we are not.

I do not understand many of the losses I have experienced. But maybe God is offering me something far more substantial than a mental grasp of reality. Perhaps he is offering me himself in a loving relationship. Am I willing to give up my demand for explanations before I trust him and receive his loving care for me? It is our opportunity to trust his goodness, even if life experiences are painful, disorienting, and confusing.

Another Angle on Death

For example, God seeks to show us there is another way to look at the death of a loved one. When we lose a loved one or a wise leader or a good man or woman from our community, what is God thinking? Isaiah 57:1 says, "The righteous perish, and no one takes it to heart; the devout are taken away, and no one understands that the righteous are taken away to be spared from evil" (NIV).

I am often struck by our tendency to declare the death of a loved one who knows Jesus as "tragic." One possible implication of such a view is that it is far better to be in this world than to be with God, that this life is as good as it gets. But God does not seem to see it that way. When the righteous perish, God is not punishing them; he is caring for them.

We live in a fallen world that is full of pain. This world is not as good as it gets. Eternity is before us. Those who are covered in the righteousness of Jesus will see him and live in his presence forever. When we pass from this life, we are forever spared living amid the disorienting realities of this fallen world. It is those who remain in this world who have the hard path to yet walk.

Indeed, our God is good and wise. He is always up to good, even in the death of one of his own. Knowing the truth of God's benevolence, even in the event of someone dying, allows us to respond in trust and hope—and, yes, still grieve as we miss the presence of these loved ones.

God Has Made One As Well As the Other

There are other reasons we do not know all the *whys* of this life. We were not made to navigate life on our own. The truth is that uncertainties remind us of that constantly. Ecclesiastes 7:13–14 reminds us, "Consider what God has done: Who can straighten what he has made crooked? When times are good, be happy; but when times are bad, consider this: God has made the one as well as the other. Therefore, no one can discover anything about their future" (NIV).

This is one of those passages that reminds us that when times are bad, God might be the orchestrator behind those events. We cannot blame all that seems bad on sin, the lack of faith, or even on the enemy. It may be the sovereignty of God to lead us to new horizons. In his love, he often disrupts us from our own self-designed ways.

The fact that God does not show us what will happen tomorrow is his kindness. So when life is going good, celebrate. When life is hard, remember God has made both. It's in these hard times that we learn to remain dependent on him. Once again, I am reminded that despite the presence of "bad" stuff in my life, God is acting in a loving way toward me.

That Long Stripping Called Relinquishment of Control

In Jesus's relationship with Peter, we learn another important truth about God's work in us regarding the uncertainties of life. In John 21, we have the restoration of Peter after he dishonored his Lord, himself, and his community by denying Jesus three times. As we come to the end of this conversation, hear Jesus's direct words to Peter recorded in John 21:18–19:

> "Very truly I tell you, when you were younger you dressed yourself and went where you wanted; but when you are old you will stretch out your hands, and *someone else will dress you and lead you where you do not want to go*." Jesus said this to indicate the kind of death by which Peter would glorify God. Then he said to him, "Follow me!" (NIV)

Think about what kind of man Peter was in the Gospels. One of the best words I have heard to describe him is *impetuous*. Is there ever a time where Jesus asks the disciples a question and Peter is not the first to answer? One time Peter responded and Jesus said, "Blessed are you, Simon Bar-Jonah! For flesh and blood has not revealed this to you, but my Father who is in heaven"

(Matthew 16:17). A short while later (just the next paragraph in Matthew's narrative!) after a Peter-verbal-blurt-out, Jesus said to Peter, "Get behind me, Satan!" (Matthew 16:23). Later, Peter swore that he would die with Jesus, but then, within hours, he denied that he knew Jesus to protect his own life. One never knew what Peter was going to say or do next.

Jesus eventually told Peter that when Peter was young, he did whatever he wanted to do and went wherever he wanted. He was his own man living his own life. But as Peter followed Jesus, he was transformed. Eventually, as Peter aged, he would be dressed by others and led where he did not want to go. This process is called relinquishment of control. All of us must go through this painful transformation. God is stripping us of our insistence on having life go our own way.

During the early days of my battle with the virus that ravaged my autoimmune system, I was furious with God. I had a way of living life that I liked. I liked to go for long runs and bike rides. I liked the certainty of making work plans and not worrying if my body would crash on me. I wanted to do what I wanted to do, when I wanted to do it and how I wanted to do it.

Graciously, God has taken much of that level of self-determination away from me. There is nothing morally wrong with any of those desires on my part (to exercise and work freely), but the demanding, entitled self-determination that drove that lifestyle is what God was seeking to address. He knows it is good for us to be dependent on him, and it is to our detriment to live a self-determined life. Thus, in the long run, this stripping has been a gift.

Jesus's simple command to Peter and to us is, "Follow me."

Could There Be Another Way to View Our Reality?

By not knowing what tomorrow brings, we learn to completely trust God. As we walk with God and grow in his love, we begin to trust him more and more and learn to wait on him in the mysterious ways he works.

When we do not understand the hard circumstances that happen in life, we can be reminded that he is a wise God who does what he desires in ways we will never fully understand. He has a wisdom we will never fully grasp. We know he is a loving Father, so we choose to depend on him. Jesus gave his life for us, so we choose to follow him. The Spirit is within us, spreading the Father's love within as he brings to bear the graces of the one God in our lives.

In all this, God is making us familiar with the reality of mystery. We are not the master of our own fate, and we cannot possibly understand all there is to grasp. We are children who are dependent on God. He is God, and we are not. So we look to him in simple trust.

Story: When a Life's Effort Bears No Apparent Success

There are few guarantees in life. Despite our best efforts, sometimes it just doesn't go the way we hoped and dreamed it would.

Having raised three sons, I know a parent's fear of the "what-if's." There are far too many funerals for high school students in our community. We have dear friends who could not have been better parents, and yet their adult children have walked away from many of their foundational moorings. Other friends have invested the prime years of their life into a career only to have their position dissolved due to another corporate acquisition. And still others have been betrayed by their bodies after years of intentional decisions to live healthily, only to find themselves fighting cancer or some other disease. Some of us have walked with God, seeking to live as best as we understand

God wants us to live, and then our lives come unglued—betrayal, divorce, widowed, never married, dreams never realized.

Our culture defines success as accomplishing what we have set out to do. If our children grow up to be mature adults contributing to the good of society, then we are "successful" as parents. If we can acquire more and more comforts through financial independence, then we have had a "successful" career. If our church numbers demand a building expansion, then we are certainly deemed "successful" spiritual leaders.

But what happens when none of those supposed dreams come to be? Is there another way to define success? Or are we merely failures, duped by a slight of fate?

Jeremiah's "Failed" Career

When I was in graduate school, I had to read and do some exegetical work on every book of the Bible. There were some books I dreaded. Jeremiah was at the top of the list. It is all woe and misery and doom. What a drag. It was interesting though, that the further I go into this journey with God, the more I have come to appreciate Jeremiah. In fact, Jeremiah has become a hero of mine.

Jeremiah was called to be a prophet by God at a young age. For over forty years, his life was consumed by God's Word, and Jeremiah faithfully conveyed that message to God's people. Despite an entire life given to a role he never asked for, and despite doing what God told him to do, there was little to show for his efforts in ways that would be deemed "positive outcomes" in today's market.

God's own people rejected God's message and God's messenger. As a result, the southern kingdom of Judah was obliterated by Babylon, just as God had warned through Jeremiah. Did Jeremiah fail?

But Wait, It Gets Worse

In fulfillment of his role as a prophet, God forbade Jeremiah fundamental human expressions. Jeremiah was forbidden to marry. He was also forbidden to grieve at community funerals. All of Jeremiah's life actions, not merely his words, were to be a message to God's people. No celebrating the anticipation of new life; no grieving the loss of life.

There were numerous death threats against him. Even Jeremiah's own village and family sought to kill him. He became a near total pariah. Those who did respond positively to Jeremiah were a mere handful of Israelites and some Gentiles. Despite forty years of effort, Jeremiah did not see much fruit. No wonder we refer to him as the weeping prophet. He wrote the book of Lamentations after the fall of Jerusalem as an expression of his deep grief over all that had gone wrong with his own nation.

If one does the math through today's values, Jeremiah bombed, and bombed bad. He was an abject failure.

The Mysteries of Life

Maybe we need a redefinition of success.

Jeremiah can be held up as a beacon of faithfulness. Why? He did what he was told to do. He, like us, was not guaranteed the desired outcome. God did not call Jeremiah to change his people, but simply to convey his message to them. Jeremiah did that, and he did that faithfully. And we have his words in our Bible to this day.

Little can assuage the grief of a parent whose child has walked into a self-destructive lifestyle. That cute little boy or girl has grown up to live a life one could not have imagined. Torturous questions haunt our nights. How did we get here? What could I have done differently? Why did God not prevent this? Why will he not rescue my child?

The silence and pain seem to mock us.

The loss of a loved one leaves a void never to be filled by another. Heart attacks or a car accident alter the course of life. Widowed or orphaned is not a category we saw ourselves in. Parents do not want to attend the funeral of their own children. There must have been some sort of mistake. Could this have been prevented?

Two weeks before I contracted the virus that altered my life, I had completed a 120-mile ultra-bicycling event that took me over three mountain passes of eleven thousand feet each. I went from ultra-fit to ultra-fatigued. I could hardly walk to the bathroom. It took me five years, but I finally sold my bike. I couldn't ride it anymore. That part of life had to be let go of. It is easy for me to think, "If I had just not ____________, then this would not have happened." But that line of thinking does me no favors. It changes my reality not one bit. I'm once again invited to ask God how to walk with him in the reality I find myself in.

Comparing the loss of health to the loss of a loved one seems insignificant. Yet it is unwise to compare our pains. If it is painful to you, then it is painful. It is wise to not dismiss or minimize our sufferings. They are real, and they hurt. Just because it might not seem as bad as someone else's sufferings doesn't mean it is not suffering.

Success Redefined

Jeremiah was successful in that he did exactly what God asked him to do. And we are to do what we have been shown to do, leaving the results to God. Sometimes the results will be a bounty of beauty; sometimes it will be a barren wasteland.

I have done what God has shown me to in my calling and it has "cost" me my health. Yet the beauty God has born in me through this loss has been profound. God uses the confounding pains in our lives to draw us into his love and to usher us deeper into his purposes.

Jesus, by the world's standards, was a fool. But we know him to be the power, wisdom, and beauty of God. He gave himself for his own and most rejected him. We give ourselves for others, but we are not promised we will be received. Success is in the giving, the loving, the speaking, the going, and the showing up day after day—it is in the faithfulness—and the results are in God's hands.

Reflection

» Describe your response to the mysterious ways of God.

» How is God causing you to relinquish control in your life? What are you being invited to turn over to his control?

» What does faithfulness look like at this stage of your life? What is that requiring of you?

chapter 9

A Gut-Honest Cry to God

Western culture, in general, does not grieve well. In fact, most of us have few models of grief well-journeyed. We attend a loved one's funeral and the funeral home is, well, sterile and quiet. If there are tears, they are stifled as others scramble for the tissue box, saying, "There, there, everything is going to be all right."

If we shift our gaze to Eastern cultures, then we see images of men and women wailing in the street, giving full vent to shattered pain. Sadly, these images are displayed across the news apps on our mobile devices daily. We learn from others that grief can be expressed differently.

We see this biblically too. First Samuel 30 is a classic illustration. David and six hundred fighting men returned from the front lines of battle. Hungry and tired, they marched back into Ziklag, the Philistine town they were residing in, only to find it pillaged, burnt, and all their family members gone. Their collective response? They wept until they had no more strength to weep.

That must have been quite a picture—six hundred fighting men weeping over the loss of their families and their possessions. There was anger too. Some of the men blamed David and wanted to kill him for the situation. This is unbridled emotional grief in the face of acute loss. What's more is that God met these men in their expressed grief and delivered their families back to them.

Verbal and emotional expressions of loss and grief are manifestations of faith. God has designed the grieving process for our own wellness. When we deny it, dismiss it, or otherwise suppress it, the grief is still there. It will surface—eventually. If it is not expressed well, then it will be expressed in unhealthy ways. What's more is that we miss out on an opportunity profound loss extends to us, which is to venture deeper into communion with God and those closest to us.

How does one journey *through* grief well? When we have been pounded by life's storms and experience a storm of emotions inside, what do we do with that? When I am angry about life, maybe even angry at God, how does God invite me to lean into him? Is it even okay to be angry with God, or will he smite me?

Can You Really Say That to God?

God can handle our emotions. He does not need us to coddle him. He already knows more about what is bottled up inside us than we do. Despite this, many of us feel discomfort at the idea of so openly expressing to God deep hurt and raw emotion. Therefore, I will offer three biblical models: Jeremiah, Moses, and Hannah. Each of their circumstances are significantly different. Yet we will see that as they wrestled with God, God met them in merciful ways. Their voices can give us permission for our own.

Jeremiah's Complaint of Accusation: "You Deceived Me!"

Jeremiah is a true mentor for us in this world of grief, loss, and lament. Early in his role as a prophet, Jeremiah had been through a great deal of difficulty. God forbade him to marry. His own home town sought his life.

The message God asked him to proclaim was uncomplimentary to the recipients. Jeremiah was getting knocked around in this prophet gig. He had had about enough. In response, he let some intense accusations fly in God's specific direction:

> When your words came, I ate them;
> they were my joy and my heart's delight,
> for I bear your name,
> LORD God Almighty.
> I never sat in the company of revelers,
> never made merry with them;
> I sat alone because your hand was on me
> and you had filled me with indignation.
> Why is my pain unending
> and my wound grievous and incurable?
> You are to me like a deceptive brook,
> like a spring that fails. (Jeremiah 15:16–18 NIV)

Jeremiah essentially said, "Look, God, I have held up my end of the bargain and you keep letting me down." The last verse is particularly accusatory. Jeremiah said he came to God in need of care, like seeking out a brook in a dry land that had promised water. But upon finding the brook, there was no water. Jeremiah felt duped. He used the word *deceptive*, as if he just experienced a bait and switch from God.

Is it okay to speak to God in this way?

God seemed to think so. In fact, he had some equally strong words back to Jeremiah—he essentially renewed his call to Jeremiah, reminding him that if he did as God told him to do and not give into the pursuit of popularity, then

God would protect him. It is interesting that God's response to Jeremiah's angry outburst was not punitive, but affirmation of his prophetic call, some strong words reminding him of his identity, and a continued promise of provision.

Jeremiah 15 is one of many passages in which Jeremiah expresses how he feels undone by life and wrestles with God over it. Anger is not a sin—God gets angry. Anger is a God-given emotion. Where we mishandle anger is when we do not give proper voice to it in respect and honesty. Without appropriate expressions, anger builds within. Eventually, there will be a blow up, which is an expression of anger that is almost always hurtful to others.

As Jeremiah wrestled with God, God engaged Jeremiah in return. God did not turn his back on him; he did not mete out punishment. Rather, God leaned back into Jeremiah. Sure, there are some course corrections God gave to him, but he also reinforced his promise of presence and protection. Jeremiah was a better man for it. He went on to fulfill his prophetic calling.

Jeremiah's model has been so helpful for me. In my journal, there are some pretty fiery prayers. Sometimes I am bartering, sometimes venting, sometimes merely rambling directionless. When I go back and read some of those entries, I wince. Yet I have experienced the reality of God's mercy, his course corrections in my life, and his ongoing commitment to me.

God invites us to express what is going on within us. He is big enough to handle it. We are being far more true to our inner reality to express our anger than to cover it over with overspiritualized platitudes. An opportunity for deeper relationship is sabotaged by our resistance and fear of our own emotional messes.

Moses's Argument with God

Moses was eighty years old when he found himself staring down a bush on fire that was not consumed. He had lived forty years in the plush palaces of Egypt and forty years in the tents of a shepherd in the wilderness. That seems like it ought to be about enough life for one guy to have lived. Yet God had more for Moses.

The Exodus 3 interchange between Moses and God at the burning bush is fascinating. The conversation is lengthy, so I encourage you to look at it sometime. The more Moses argued with God, coming up with one reason after another why God had the wrong man for the job, God revealed more and more of himself to Moses. The end of all this back-and-forth is an amazing revelation of who this God is: "I AM WHO I AM" (Exodus 3:4).

Moses argued. God revealed more of himself.

Moses resisted. God pressed in more.

Maybe God is just waiting for us to lean into him with some honest words, to really let what is in our hearts find voice. Moses was respectful, shoes off, knees on the holy ground, but he was far from compliant. The more Moses pushed back, the more God revealed himself. What if God wants us to come to him in our resistance and express what is truly in our hearts? When was the last time you had a good, healthy argument with God?

Hannah's Cry of a Deeply Afflicted Soul Poured Out Before God

We have already looked at the story of Hannah, but I would like to go back in the context of grief and lament as she provides such a marvelous, if not pain-filled, model for us. As one slowly reads through 1 Samuel 1, the number of emotional words is striking. In my ESV Bible, I have the following words circled (verse numbers in parenthesis): wept and would not eat (7), weep (8), sad (8), distressed (10), wept bitterly (10), affliction (11), troubled in spirit (15), and anxiety and vexation (16). That is quite a long list of anguishes. We are reminded that this went on year after year for Hannah (see 1 Samuel 1:7).

Hannah did not clean this all up when she engaged God. In fact, she brought to God the full load of her grief. She said to Eli the priest, "I am a woman troubled in spirit ... pouring out my soul to the LORD" (1 Samuel 1:15). It was in the context of pouring out her troubled soul to God that God heard her and she conceived Samuel.

Hannah cried out. God listened.

This is our example. That is what God is after and invites us into.

When we experience a profound life crisis, God draws ever nearer to us. He waits for us to do as Hannah did—pour out our souls before him. He is present to receive from us. He is here to tend to the raw ache of our soul.

If God can handle Jeremiah's accusations, Moses's argument, and Hannah's distress, then he can handle ours as well.

The Road to Maturity

Lament, sorrow, and grief over profound loss is invited because that is how God has designed us to respond to hurts. Each are essential for maturing—emotionally, relationally, and spiritually. When directed toward God, each are unique expressions of a mature faith. Our God is here. He is Father. He sees, knows, and cares. He is loving enough and powerful enough and caring enough to hear us out. He invites us to draw closer in all our messiness. Our turning toward God and giving voice to these hurts is an expression of faith. We believe he is here, he cares, and he mercifully receives us in our brokenness.

When we do not give adequate expression to our pains, they build up within us. Bitterness, doubt, fear, isolation, and other compounded hurts build up like a volcano. They will come out eventually, and almost always they will leak out sideways in harmful ways to self and others. These are immature responses to life hurts.

Giving voice to our pains is one of the ways we walk with God. This entire path of suffering is not meant to lead to isolation. Remember, God's greatest desire is to draw us deeper into communion, to grow our capacity to know and receive his love. Having it out with God is one way we do that.

He is leaning into us. He knows what is inside of us. He hears our secret thoughts fermented on our beds in the night hours. Jeremiah, Moses, and Hannah were each walking their walk of faith with God as they wrestled over life's injustices and sufferings. Each had a different path to walk, a different role to play in the larger story. Voicing their angst was one means of walking the path of faith.

Story: Jeremiah's Remembering

Despite these three biblical examples, there may be some people reading this who feel uncomfortable with all this encouragement toward grief and raw emotion. Aren't we supposed to rejoice in all things? Of course. Yet we are to be a people of deep joy and faith amidst the realities of a fallen world. Otherwise, our "rejoicing" rings exceptionally hollow and overspiritualized. It is walking well with God *through* suffering and its resulting impact on us that turns up the soil of our hearts for the seeds of true joy in Christ. The one who has been through the valleys of darkness and knows God's loving care will give rise to a true, lasting, and God-oriented joy.

How does this process work? How do we move from the initial hurt and expressing that to God to a more settled place of faith? Once again, we will rely upon Jeremiah for guidance.

Jeremiah wrote an entire book that is a lament. The book of Lamentations is his response to God's judgement on his people for rejecting him and his word. Jeremiah lamented over the pain of it all. As we will see, it was through the voicing of lament that Jeremiah is brought to remember that God is loving and faithful.

Love and Faithfulness

Lamentations 3:22–23 is an often-quoted passage of great encouragement to many: "The steadfast love of the LORD never ceases; his mercies never come to an end; they are new every morning; great is your faithfulness." Great hymns of our faith have been written from this passage. But do we know that this passage is smack in the middle of a complaint of all the pain that Jeremiah and the people of God have experienced? Jeremiah came to this expression of God's faithfulness *after* he expressed his lament.

Chapter 3 is a graphic description of pain's impact. We will pick up the passage in verse 16. Jeremiah cries out:

> He has made my teeth grind on gravel,
> and made me cower in ashes;
> my soul is bereft of peace;
> I have forgotten what happiness is;
> so I say, "My endurance has perished;
> so has my hope from the LORD."
> Remember my affliction and my wanderings,
> the wormwood and the gall!
> My soul continually remembers it
> and is bowed down within me. (Lamentations 3:16–20)

Once again, Jeremiah does not hold back in his expressions to God. He simply expresses in a vivid manner how he has experienced life. Furthermore, he understands the sovereignty of God and clearly states that God is the cause of his anguish. He both portrays the pain and the impact of that pain on his person—physically, spiritually, and emotionally.

But Jeremiah does not stay with the pain. He doesn't allow himself to be a victim or to wallow in his pain. And this is why our cries of lament are so important. We do not want to be stuck in our grief forever; rather, we want to move *through* the anger, sadness, and hurt. But it can't be rushed and it must be tended to. Only after we have allowed grief its process can the hope begin to surface.

Jeremiah has been in this game for a long time, decades of hard-fought ministry years in which the primary response he received was rejection. His is not a quick Band-Aid of overspiritualization. His is a hard-earned faith and hope. And it is his expression of hope in the context of lament that we received the beautiful words that we sing in our churches today.

What was the hinge between Jeremiah having no hope in the Lord (see Lamentations 3:18) and declaring God's faithfulness in verse 22? Note verse 21, "But this I call to mind, and therefore I have hope."

Remembering

Jeremiah remembers.

After giving full voice to the impact of his life circumstances, Jeremiah lifts his gaze off those circumstances and *fixes it on God*. He remembers that this God is the same one who revealed himself to Moses on Mount Sinai in Exodus 33–34. He uses the exact words that God uses to describe his glory to Moses: "steadfast love and faithfulness." Jeremiah remembers that God has not changed.

God defines our circumstances. Our circumstances do not define God. Jeremiah remembers that greater reality and gives voice to it.

God indeed invites us to fully express our hurts to him—even if they are unjust and unfitting of God. This is a pathway to renewed, proven, strengthened faith. Jeremiah models this well for us, as do so many others who have walked with God through the ages.

Our Remembering Stirred

Suffering has a disorienting effect. It can feel like a thick fog obscuring our vision and way forward. We can get stuck there. Lost. Expressing the full impact of life's pains is the initial way forward. This can be done in private prayer, writing out a prayer of lament, or pouring out our souls to a trusted friend or mentor.

As we do this, we find that God uses that expression to lead us to remembrance. What we experience is not the sum total of reality. God is. He is still loving, faithful, gracious, and true. He is present. He is a Father who loves us as his adopted children. He will be with us and see us through. Like Jeremiah, over a lengthy time of wrestling with God, we are moved from the place of grief to the place of true joy. This is not a smooth pathway, but it is the wise one we walk.

Reflection

- Write out a prayer of lament in your own words. Put to paper a description and impact of your sufferings. Give expression of your emotions to God. Let him see your heart. Trust in faith that he is with you and will hold you in your pains.
- Remember how God has met you and others you know in the past. What did he show you of himself then? How is that true in this situation as well? Give expression to this experience.
- How can lament, gut-honest prayers, become a more common expression of your faith journey with God from now on?

chapter 10

Recognizing God's Presence in Our Suffering

Earlier in this book, I made several references to the silence I experienced during the early days of my illness. Though I can now look back and see God's loving hand doing a deep work in me to open me and draw me into his love, at the time the sensation of God's absence simply piled on top of the physical challenges I was facing. On top of all the physical discomforts, God seemed to have up and left.

I often describe the experience in the following manner: It felt like I had been riding down the road of life with God, and then one day he pulled the car over and told me to get out. So I did. Then he drove off. I looked in every direction and had no idea where I was. All I saw was a barren, featureless terrain I had never been to before. This barrenness went on to the horizon in every direction. I sat down and waited for God to return.

And I waited.

I cried out to God in anger and confusion. The silence was simply overwhelming. It was one of the most confusing, disorienting, and disrupting times of my life. What was God doing?

I recently heard a sermon that helped me see God's mercy in all this.[10] His withholding the sense of his presence and love was a mercy to me. At that time, I had a nearly exclusively performance-based sense of identity. If I was loved, it was because I earned that love. If he had allowed me to feel his love in those days, it would have only affirmed my faulty thinking.

With hindsight, I now know I was being reoriented to learn of God's presence and love with me even if I did not hear him or see him or sense his activity in my life. He does this same work in all our lives. Second Corinthians 1 is one passage that gives us insight into this reality.

Experiences of dry spiritual times are common amongst God's people. God is up to a unique work in us during these wilderness seasons. He is teaching us not to rely upon our feelings and circumstances. God has not left. His love remains. These supposedly barren chapters in our lives are where we grow in a deeper awareness of God's presence and activity in and around us. In the end, they are truly a mercy, severe as they might be.

Assured of God's Presence

Paul begins his extremely transparent second letter to the Corinthians with a most paradoxical and yet reassuring passage:

> Praise be to the God and Father of our Lord Jesus Christ, the Father of compassion and the God of all comfort, who comforts us in all our troubles, so that we can comfort those in any trouble with the comfort we ourselves receive from God. For just as we share abundantly in the sufferings of Christ, so also our comfort abounds through Christ. If we are distressed, it is for your comfort and salvation; if we are comforted, it is for your comfort, which produces in you patient endurance of the same sufferings we suffer. And our hope for you is firm, because we know that just

> as you share in our sufferings, so also you share in our comfort. (2 Corinthians 1:3–7 NIV)

What stands out in this passage is the repetition of two themes. The first theme is that of comfort. Depending on the version you read, your Bible might use the word *comfort*, *mercy*, or *compassion*. Ten times in this short passage, Paul refers to this word.

The Greek root is *parakletos*, which means to comfort with a sense of coming alongside. It is the same Greek root Jesus used of the Holy Spirit in the upper room recorded by John. Jesus called the Spirit the Comforter or Helper (see John 14:26) who would be sent to us. Our God is a God of comfort and compassion. This comfort takes the form of coming alongside. In a word, it is *presence*. Amidst our pain, God offers his presence.

The second main theme in this paragraph is suffering. Again, your version may have slightly different words such as *hardships* or *adversities*. What Paul is referring to is the normal pains of life. The words he uses are generic and inclusive—any form of suffering falls within what Paul is referring to here.

Put these two truths together and what we have is Paul telling us we can be grateful that we have a God who comes alongside us in all our pains. Once again, we are bumping into that paradoxical tension we began the book with—the mutual presence of a loving, comforting God, and the presence of personal suffering.

When I am in pain, the comfort I want is the resolution of that pain. I want it gone. I want solutions. Sometimes God does in fact bring resolution to the trial we are experiencing, but often he does not. What he does promise is his presence. God's mercy, his compassion and comfort, is his presence with us in the midst of any type of hardship we may be living with. These are two realities we can be certain of as his children: times of hardships and God's presence in the midst of those hardships.

We also see the element of endurance mentioned in this passage (see 2 Corinthians 1:6). In other words, it is not abnormal for this tension of God's comforting presence *and* unremitting pain to coexist over an extended time in our lives.

We will have hardships in this world—that is a certainty. Jesus himself told us plainly in John 16:33, "In this world you will have trouble" (NIV). However, for the follower of Christ, we also have an equally real certainty—God's abiding presence. He comes alongside to grace us with whatever we need to endure well through hardships as he draws us into deeper communion with himself. He loves on us, tends to us, strengthens us, and allows us to display the resurrected Christ for the world to see.

A Better Offer

Frankly, this passage was a confounding one to me during the time of sitting in that barren and silent place. God was not speaking to me. I could not sense his presence. I did not have the discernment at the time to sense his abiding presence and work, but he was there all along. Herein lies an important spiritual reality: We often want from God what he can do for us, more than we want God himself. In my case, I just wanted all the pain to go away—and fast.

But God's primary longing for us is not for our comfort; it is for our communion. He is not merely extending his gifts to us, but he is extending himself. His primary desire is always relational. Suffering is but one means he uses to catch our attention and draw us deeper into himself. It was in this barren landscape that I was being awoken to the greater gift he was extending to me than the mere removal of suffering.

I wanted resolution. He invited me to an enduring companionship with him in the midst of suffering.

I wanted explanations. He offered his presence instead.

He was using all the disorienting, painful stripping of my inability to solve my own problems to invite me deeper into his loving presence.

A New Recognition

There are spiritual truths we will otherwise never learn unless we find ourselves in similar barren places. Our life situations are as varied as could be, yet God is up to something beautiful in each of us. What is common to all, though, is his unbridled commitment to draw us into his loving presence. This is one of those unforeseen gifts of our sufferings.

As we lean back into his quiet leaning into us, a masterful transformation takes place. For me, I am now far more comfortable with the times of silence in my walk with God. I will always prefer he speak and speak loudly. But when he doesn't, I am reminded of a time in my life when he showed me that in the silence, his strong presence was real.

How about you? What invitations has he and is he extending to you in your trials? These invitations will primarily take the shape of relationship. Sure, there are going to be character deficiencies he will address in us. We are reminded that character is always revealed primarily in the context of relationships. Relationship first, and then transformation flows from that. We become like the one with whom we abide.

Responsive to God's Presence

There are some concrete ways we can be responsive to God's abiding presence in our times of suffering. Let's consider some essential practices during seasons of adversity.

The Word: The Objectifying Source for Us

The Word is a primary shelter for us. When we find ourselves lost and confused, then we need even more time in the Word. This is not time for catch-as-catch-can devotionals. We require searching, wrestling, pondering, nourishing times in the Word on a daily basis.

I have a dear friend who has found herself in a prolonged season of organizational chaos. It has been depleting as the discouraging months have piled up. She concluded that she needed to have her "quiet times" in the evening as well as her usual morning routine. The evening sitcoms on television were simply not providing the water her soul was thirsty for. As she leaned back into God with this doubling down in her time with him, she made space in her soul to be available to whatever God was doing in and around her. This is a wise response to a season of trial.

In my work with ministry leaders all around the world, I have repeatedly found the thematic reality of what I have dubbed "spiritual anemia." We simply do not adequately take nourishment in our spiritual lives. This significantly takes form in a massive lack of engagement with his Word. Some of us are naturally inclined to rigorous exegetical study. For others, that sounds like going to the dentist. These folks do much better in a guided study around a table of friends and a hot mug of coffee.

Whatever works for you, *make sure you show up*. Every single day. The Spirit will grace you with growing spiritual insight that leads to life through extended time in his Word.

Simple, Honest Prayers

Simple prayers are also helpful to center us in a whirlwind of pain. I learned from my spiritual director to pray one simple prayer. It is so simple, I am not sure how I missed it. He will simply ask me, "How have you invited Jesus to be in that with you?" Initially, that was met with a deer-in-the-headlights look. Gee, why had I not thought of that?

We can invite Jesus into the middle of whatever we find ourselves in. The reality is, he is already there. But by asking, our gaze is redirected off our pains to the One who is always gazing upon us.

Showing up daily to spend time with God is one of the main ways we express fidelity to him. His fidelity is certain, but ours tends to waffle. In these dark times, we are addressed by him in his Word and then respond in personal conversation (prayer). Again, this cannot be simply done on the fly. We are invited to carve out extended time to be with him.

What's more is that we can schedule a day or weekend away for more extended times alone with God. This is what he is eagerly waiting for. Extended trials invite extended time with God.

Due to our tendency toward self-determination, I want to emphasize that showing up for time in the Word and prayer does not earn anything from God. We are already graced with his presence and his love. We are already adopted ones. We cannot atone for our sin and brokenness. God has already dealt with that in his Son on the cross. Our spiritual practices are always a response to God's movement toward us. The Word and prayer are both means of grace the Spirit uses to draw us responsively to Jesus's invitation to abide in him.

The Wise Practice of Reflection

Life is a whirlwind. The to-do list mutates in exponential swelling. What is severely needed during dark times, though, is more space to reflect. The Word, especially the book of Proverbs, is replete with examples and admonitions to consider what God has been showing us. Life, seen through the objectifying sense of the Scriptures, is a gold mine of wisdom—if we take the time to reflect, listen, and learn. Just as we need more time in the Word, so we need more time in reflective prayer.

Community and Counselors

Another provision is advisors. This can take the form of pastors, clinical counselors, spiritual directors, mentors, and a group of intimate peers. Turbulent seasons are the time to call in the relational reinforcements. I meet as regularly as I can with a spiritual director. This person, even though he lives half a continent away, has been a profound source of perspective, wisdom, and guidance in the featureless landscape of personal trials as we connect over video calls.

Do What Your Kindergarten Teacher Taught You

There are piles of writings on the subject of managing stress. We were taught many skills in kindergarten. You know, like eat healthy snacks, take a nap, share, and go out to play during recess, really are life essentials. What brings you joy? Painting? Woodworking? Gardening? Exercising? Baking? One of mine is fly-fishing. What is yours? Now is a good time to go out for recess—not to distract and numb yourself, but to gain a fresh perspective on the grandeur of God's immense goodness and beauty toward you. Sleep. Lay off mindless numbing online. Go for a bike ride. Share what God has given you with others. These simple practices protect us from over self-absorption and refresh us.

Becoming Wise Ones with Eyes to See

One of the riches we find in the mine of suffering is that God is always there wooing us deeper into his love. Slowly and steadily, we are graced with the ability to see God's presence. God is always the initiator; we have the opportunity to respond.

For those who lean back into his leaning into them, they will become wise men and women. For those who take him up, by faith, on his offer of his presence with their own presence, they are the ones who grow in his love and wisdom. Wise women and men of an enduring faith in the abiding God amidst the raging, lashing winds of life's storms are most needed in these days. We simply cannot have too many wizened souls in our churches, communities, and organizations.

Story: A Look Back—He Was There All Along

Joseph's story is one of the more iconic ones in the Bible. From his childhood dreams wrapped in a coat of many colors to slavery and imprisonment to the height of the Egyptian empire, Joseph saw many highs and lows. Our familiarity with his story can unduly soften our remembrance of just how hard it was for Joseph at times.

Joseph's first blow came at the hands of his own brothers in the form of betrayal. Clearly, Joseph was brash and insensitive when he declared that, in his dreams, his immediate family would all bow down to him. Being the second youngest of the brood meant that, socially and culturally, he was destined to do his family's bidding, not the other way around. Another layer in the story is Jacob's dysfunctional favoritism toward Joseph, which bred jealousy and hatred amongst the brothers. All this reached a boiling point when Joseph was sold into slavery.

What Joseph experienced being sold to a passing caravan was all too common. There was an ancient interstate between the northern kingdoms of the Middle East and Central Asia to North Africa and back. Human trafficking was commonplace. Joseph was sold into a vibrant market of commodity trading. His life would never be the same again; his eyes would never see his own homeland again.

Despite this traumatic change of events, we read of his early successes in Egypt. Joseph showed tremendous resiliency as he rose through the ranks of his master's residence. But that did not last long. Betrayed once by brothers was a horrible experience; to be done wrong again by false accusation from his master's wife was another brutal blow. Joseph was cast into the dank, violent death-hole of an Egyptian prison where he was forgotten for many years.

Through these years of betrayal, being bartered like any other commodity, owned like livestock, and slandered for his attempt at purity and fidelity, what did Joseph experience of God? We are not told what, if anything, he knew of God's presence with him. We as readers are graced with the narrator's words breaking through the story, repeatedly declaring, "The LORD was with Joseph ..." (Genesis 39:2, 21, 23), "the LORD caused all he did to succeed" (Genesis 39:3), and "whatever he did, the LORD made it succeed" (Genesis 39:23). The emphasis of these statements stands out to the reader like neon signs in a dark night. I wonder if Joseph saw any of these lights himself.

Clearly, he attributed his success to God. But was there any other form of consolation than circumstantial blessing? We are not told.

A Larger Reality Than Experience

This passage is a reminder that even if we cannot sense God's presence, he is with his own. Joseph had some circumstances go his way and others go against him. He did what he thought he was to do—obey God—and sometimes even that backfired.

Is God capricious? No. As we have seen, we, just like Joseph, require hardships to mature. Clearly, Joseph was an intelligent and skilled man. More than that, God was with him and had a specific destiny for Joseph to fulfill in the history of God's people. Despite that high calling, Joseph still had to be honed and wizened. That wizening came in the form of some of the harshest life happenings in the human experience: betrayal, slavery, and imprisonment.

The severe blows we have experienced are painful and, we are reminded again by Joseph's story, elements of redemption in our lives through God's wise, loving presence. Those who have lived long enough and allowed their hearts to not be embittered by such hurts can gain a perspective that Joseph gained. During confusing life events, perspective is like water in a desert landscape. Joseph's perspective reflects the wisdom God grew in him, a wisdom born of suffering, that blessed the nations.

Lifetime Perspective

Years later, Joseph found himself exalted to one of the highest positions in the Egyptian kingdom. He had been delegated authority to manage the nation's entire food reserves. Amidst a massive regional famine, his brothers came to

Egypt for food lest the entire family starve. Thus, the backdrop is set for one of the most dramatic scenes in Scripture—Joseph's brothers bow down to their younger brother, just as Joseph had been shown years ago through a dream.

When Joseph finally revealed his true identity, obviously, his brothers were shocked, then fearful. Will their now-powerful brother seek revenge? Joseph's words of assurance are staggering in his breadth of understanding of God's providence over his life events. This stunning interaction plays out in Genesis 45:

> Then Joseph could not control himself before all those who stood by him. He cried, "Make everyone go out from me." So no one stayed with him when Joseph made himself known to his brothers. And he wept aloud, so that the Egyptians heard it, and the household of Pharaoh heard it. And Joseph said to his brothers, "I am Joseph! Is my father still alive?" But his brothers could not answer him, for they were dismayed at his presence.
>
> So Joseph said to his brothers, "Come near to me, please." And they came near. And he said, "I am your brother, Joseph, whom you sold into Egypt. And now do not be distressed or angry with yourselves because you sold me here, *for God sent me before you to preserve life*. For the famine has been in the land these two years, and there are yet five years in which there will be neither plowing nor harvest. And *God sent me before you* to preserve for you a remnant on earth, and to keep alive for you many survivors. (Genesis 45:1–7)

"God sent me ahead of you." This is an amazing perspective that Joseph gained. It was more than mere theological ascent. He now had the power to do to his brothers what they had done to him. But he saw a larger story. He knew that God's hands were somehow involved in the events that played out in his life. Like what we read of Paul in the Philippian prison, Joseph did not play the victim; rather, he proclaimed the providence of God. Of course, he acknowledged that they sold him into slavery—the facts are the facts. But the purposes of God are seen by Joseph.

The one who has learned to live in the tension that God is loving and wise and he uses suffering in one's life for greater good (even suffering inflicted at the hands of others who should care for us), receives eyes to see beyond the circumstances to God's greater purposes for one's life. What's more is that God's purposes in suffering can, in part, be for the benefit of others.

Joseph was sold into slavery by his brothers. He now saw that God's purposes for those many years of pain was to save the lives of many, including the very ones who had caused the pain.

Jesus did the same for us. He came to save the ones who had caused the problem in the first place. His suffering was for our gain; his death is our life.

Our sufferings can be used by God for far greater purposes as we trust him to do in us and through us as he sees best. Our scars can bring healing to others. Like Joseph, some of us have been deeply hurt by family members. Betrayal, abandonment, abuse, and neglect from ones who ought to have protected and provided for us leaves immense scars across the contours of our lives. We are shown by Joseph that we have a choice in how we respond to such life experiences. We are not victims. God was with Paul in his prison and Joseph in his slavery, using those events for great purposes. Their perspectives were shaped by God, not by their circumstances.

God can do the same work in us today. What others meant for harm, God will use for good. We can ask why God allowed these things to happen, but we will seldom receive an acceptable response to that question—and it changes nothing of what we experienced. We can rather ask the wiser question how—how does God invite us to walk with him in the presence of such scars. What we see is that he is with us through it all.

Like Joseph, God has been with us in every dark, painful time of our lives.

Every.

Single.

One.

He is always with us. Even in the slime pit of an Egyptian prison.

Like Joseph, we can be taught by the Spirit to see that our hurts can be redemptive not only in our lives, but in the lives of any one we meet. Looking back, we see that God has been there all along the way and has born amazing fruit in our lives.

Reflection

- » How has God grown a deeper sense of an awareness of his presence in you, even in the silence and darkness of suffering?
- » What are practices that would facilitate you leaning back into the One who is already leaning into you? Who can you process this with and gain perspective from?
- » What lifelong perspective is God granting you in your sufferings?

chapter 11

Becoming Carriers of Comforting Presence

The news headlines are filled with stories of suffering from all over the world. Each of us has a different capacity for responding to the pains of others, whether or not they are known personally by us. Compassion fatigue is a reality.

There are many possible responses as you hear others' expressions of suffering. When you find yourself at the receiving end of someone else's pain-filled tears, how do you respond? Some lean in. Others experience a deep desire to flee. Some try to offer suggestions to the cause or the solution to the problems at hand (like Job's friends did). To the degree you are unwilling to hold the paradoxes of your own life well, that is the degree you will be handicapped in doing that with and for others.

One of the greatest gifts we can offer others is to allow God to mature us to walk well with him in the midst of our personal adversities as he draws us deeper into his loving communion. As we walk well with God in our adversities, he equips us to walk this same walk with others. In this way, our sufferings are not only for our own benefit, but they can also be for the sake and benefit of others.

Our best model for responding to others in pain is our Father himself. In the previous chapter, we noted Paul's teaching in 2 Corinthians 1 on this subject. What we saw was that the Father's promise is an abiding, comforting presence with us as we endure with him through personal pains. That is our cue. If what God extends to us is presence, then that can be the greatest gift we can extend to others as well.

But first we must acknowledge our tendency to offer anything but a quiet, listening presence.

Fixoholics

There are powerful driving forces within us that cause us to respond to others' pains and the paradoxes of life in ways that are less than helpful. We will reflect on two here.

First, we like to be needed. Personal insecurities and misplaced identity in performance fosters within us the need to be needed. But, who people need most is Jesus. We have been given the opportunity to bring Jesus to others and others to Jesus. As we shall see, our loving presence is the means of offering Jesus to others.

Second, humans tend to be fix-it junkies. Our drive to not look incompetent in the face of life challenges is a potent reality that prompts us to offer solutions to others' problems. The US culture, for example, drills into us that we can overcome anything if we just work hard enough at it. However, God is committed to stripping us of the illusion that we can make life work on our own. A case in point is Jesus's words to Peter in John 21:18–19 about relinquishing all control of his life.

Attempts at fixing, or helping others fix their pains, is unwise. We really do not want to (nor can we) fix people or their problems. God really can handle them. No matter how enormous our life messes are, they do not come close to outstripping God's competency to be, well, God. God will deliver us when the time is right. One of the ways he brings care to us is through one another, but not to fix one another.

There is a crucial warning here we must heed as we sit with others who pour out their wounds.

Could We Actually Be Working Against God?

If it is true that God has designed the redemptive process such that we reach greater depths of maturity, in part, through suffering various afflictions, then there are huge consequences for how we respond to others in their suffering. If I were to simply seek to help a person find a solution to his or her pain as quickly as possible, I just might be undermining the redemptive work God wants to do through a time of patient endurance.

That ought to stop us cold in our fix-it tracks.

Let me rephrase that. If God's design for a friend is for him or her to learn to walk well with God through a season of adversity, and I seek to help my friend solve his or her problems, then I may actually be working against God's intentions for my friend. That is an alarming thought indeed.

Emulating the Father's Model

As we have noted several times, what God offers us in our pain is not necessarily solutions but presence. Sometimes God delivers us from pain; sometimes he does not. But he is always with us.

Paul said that God "comforts us in all our troubles, so that we can comfort those in any trouble with the comfort we ourselves receive from God" (2 Corinthians 1:4 NIV). In this context, the comfort we receive from God is presence. As he graces our life with his comforting presence, we become stewards of that very presence. We carry that same gift of his presence into the lives of others who need comfort.

A Theological Course Correction

God is not like Santa Claus. Each year Santa bestows his gifts on us, but we never get to be with Santa. God is not interested in being an aloof gift-giver. We do not promote deism—the idea that God is a detached, indifferent force. No, our God is a Father who is present and pursues his children. His care for his children is specific and personal, for he calls each by name. He offers himself to us. We are now graced with his very presence through Jesus. Furthermore, we are invited to do the same—not merely offer "gifts" as we remain relationally aloof. Rather, we offer ourselves.

The Greatest Gift We Have

Companionship is the greatest gift we can offer another who is in pain. In the presence of one who is experiencing difficulties of any severity, our primary gift is not facilitating a remedy for the problems at hand, but rather that of being a journey mate through their personal hardship as God's purposes are explored.

Please reread this last sentence—it is crucial.

What all of us long for when life is harsh is love and accompaniment. Our greatest opportunity is to be a companion through personal hardship as God's redemptive purposes are explored. There is no greater gift we can offer someone in the midst of deep, lasting suffering than our simple, abiding, enduring presence.[11]

No Expertise Required

There is so much pressure in our world to have answers to any and every problem at hand. But as we have seen, answers are not what people need. And yet, we don't just want to sit there like a stump with nothing to offer. Counseling or theological degrees are not necessarily required to be of immense comfort to others. So what are some possible responses when a friend pours out his or her laments to us?

Being Seen and Heard

We all long to be heard, seen, and known—even more so when life is turned upside down. When we are seen by others, it is a profound gift. I know I am being seen when a friend observes some aspect of my life he could not have otherwise known unless he keenly watched and listened to me. He connects the "dots" of my story. It is also not presented to me as a showy know-it-all manner, but with gentleness and with a tone of curiosity. One might say, "I imagine that must be hard for you when ____________," or "When I listen to you, I begin to wonder ____________." It amazes and encourages me when others truly invest themselves with a deep, particularized listening and watching presence.

Sorrow with Those Who Sorrow

In almost any conversation that involves the tears of another from life's blows, we can simply offer a gentle "I am so sorry." In that moment, we are reaching across the divide of the other's sense of isolation into their pain and offering sorrow for their sorrow. When we share our pains, seeing another person moved by our reality can cause us to feel as though the weight is being borne together. It can melt some of the sense of loneliness. Companioning with one another in our sorrow is a profound kindness. Loss, sorrow, and grief is a courageous response to life that we want to facilitate by providing permission and a safe space.

No Advice, Initially

Being sensitive to the circumstances at hand is essential. If a person is in the initial stages of reeling from a freshly inflicted wound, there is often no capacity to receive any truth at that time. Indignation, fury, lament, and confusion need a space to be vented. Now is not the time to correct theological distortions. Rather, it is time to create a safe place to allow pain to find space and voice. Really, our answers or corrections have no weight here. A safe, permission-granting presence must be extended. The Lament and Imprecatory Psalms are classic models for the messy expression of pain and confusion.

Welcome the Tears

Furthermore, tears need space to flow. Often people are uncomfortable with their tears. Ours is a culture that has neither given permission nor guidance in grieving. I have told many people that one of the best ways we can honor life's hurtful experiences is with tears. The tears of others are most welcome. Our own unforced tears can be an immense comfort as well.

A Consoling Embrace

Depending on the situation, a physical touch can be comforting too. Caution is important here, as overstepping appropriate physical boundaries will only compound the confusion a person can be experiencing. In the least, we can sit for as long as is needed to simply enfold them in the presence of our deep concern.

Perspective Offered When Sought

In time—and that length of time is difficult to define, for we all grieve at different paces—there can be pertinent offers of perspective and truth. Even if a person is asking *why* questions early, we want to resist the temptation to offer answers. Remember, God often does not answer the *why* question and we need not attempt to either. Besides, intellectual grasping of *why* does little to remove the pain of the reality we find ourselves in. Much wiser is to lean into the impact of what others are experiencing. God will meet us in our hearts long before he meets us in our heads. We can simply ask questions like, "What is that like for you?" and "How do you feel about that?" But even then, we are not coercive so much as inviting. It is up to the other person to accept invitations.

How do we discern when to say more? Again, it is wise to err on the side of caution here—we rarely have the opportunity to share our story without others telling their stories or trying to help us clean up our messes. What we are seeking to do is discern where Jesus is in this person's life. As the sheer ache begins to subside, some gentle questions of where he or she is experiencing Jesus can be offered. I always start with questions and leave any counsel for later. We are on sacred ground in these raw conversations, and we must tread lightly.

Many times, I have sat with another person as he poured out his heart to me. I said little other than short expressions of sorrow or asked a few simple questions about impact. It is amazing the number of times people thank me for being "so helpful." In reality, I did not offer any counsel or advice—I simply listened and received their story. That is all they needed that day. Listening, receiving, and accompanying is truly the greatest help we can offer to others.

How We Journey Our Own Stories Is Crucial

Throughout this book, we have looked at God's loving purposes toward us in our sufferings. How we respond to God's offering of himself and his transformative presence amidst our sufferings is critical for our growth in abiding in Jesus. Through that growing communion, we are transformed. We are slowly and steadily taught how to hold the paradoxes of our lives well. He creates greater space within us for the reality of mystery in this fallen world. He grows in us a loving, joyful endurance, even as we grieve the losses in this life *and* celebrate the profusion of gifts. Our lives are immeasurably deepened by the presence of the Father, Son, and Spirit in and with us as we endure adversities with him.

We then become stewards of these magnificent gifts. As we are taught by him to walk well with him amidst our adversities, he is also shaping us to walk well with others in their adversities. The image of two friends with arms over each other's shoulders as they limp along this rough-and-tumble pilgrimage as God showers them with love and mercy is a beautiful and biblical one.

An Enduring Presence

We must be forewarned, though. Sometimes the enduring presence of unresolved pain in a loved one's life far outlasts our endurance to journey well with them. It takes tremendous deliberation and dependence on God to hang in there with others. God has allowed me the privilege of having others hang with me through years of my unpleasant life hardships. I doubt I would have made it without the grace of others with me in this journey.

I have a dear friend who has for much of his life dealt with the weight of depression. If you were to hear his childhood story, you would be staggered by what he endured. I marvel that my friend is not only upright and functioning, but ministers to others, including me, in profound ways. In the early days of our friendship, as he began to let me into his inner world, I told him these simple words: "You will not scare me away."

My friend, naturally, was skeptical. You know the line of thought: "Once you know what I am really like, then you will be looking for the exit from my life."

My friend and his wife have navigated many deep waters with Beth and me over the years. We have sat with one another through many highs and lows. Because we have cried together, our laughter together is all the richer.

I have a theological degree. I have taught on a theology of suffering all over the world. But in times of pain, my friend did not need any of that. What he needed was a companion. He needed a friend, someone who saw beyond the manifestations of his scars that ran the breadth of his life. Really, that is all I had to offer. I have my own scars that run the breadth of my life. I have my own fears. I have my own staggering failures; my own batch of regrets. My friend did not need my expertise; he needed my accompaniment.

Presence is what God offers each of us, and presence is what each of us can offer each other. There is no greater gift we can offer another than companionship. It is simple and yet the richest, sweetest gift we can give. It is what the one sitting across from us in their tears longs to know—"Am I still lovable as I implode all over my world?" Our response can be the same as our Father's: "Yes, you are his beloved. He is here, and so am I."

Story: Taking a Hit for the Benefit of Another

In the vocation of shepherding souls, I am regularly reminded by God to lay my life down for others. I am repeatedly asked to sacrificially receive the hurts and grievances of others as I hear their stories and walk with them through the deep, dark valleys of life. But this role is not only for the "professional." We are a gift to each other in this journey.

Each of us is invited to live a far more noble life than an existence of self-preservation. Ours is the opportunity to lean into others at our own personal cost. But is it wise to risk our own well-being for others? That is a bit of a loaded question. To say that it is unwise to risk personal well-being for others' gain would be to essentially admit that Jesus's actions were foolish. And in the eyes of the world, the cross remains foolishness and weakness. Scripture holds up the illogic that risking our own well-being for others is actually the very expression of wisdom, strength, and love. There are numerous examples of saints suffering for the sake of others. I would invite us to focus on a little-known character named Epaphroditus.

A Little-Known Hero

Epaphroditus is one of the many names that shows up in fringes of Paul's letters. We know nothing of his background or profession. From Paul's comments in the letter to the Philippians, it appears that the Philippian church had sent a letter and a personal care package of sorts to their imprisoned shepherd. Epaphroditus was the one sent out to find Paul and to be the carrier of the church's gifts. His efforts are described in Philippians 2:25–30. We do not know if Epaphroditus had an exact location of where Paul was in Rome or if he had to search through that huge city to find him.

Sometime during his visit with Paul, Epaphroditus fell gravely ill and nearly died. Paul's description of Epaphroditus's courageous ministry is freighted with descriptive terms that are instructive to us. Before we look specifically at that text, let's remind ourselves of the context of Philippians 2.

In Philippians 2, we read of a string of people who have suffered for the well-being of others. First and foremost, we read of Jesus's descent into glory. He became a man, a servant of humankind, and eventually sentenced to death itself on behalf of humanity. Because he suffered the greatest of all, he received the greatest glory of all (see Philippians 2:6–18).

Then in 2:20–21, Paul shifts the focus to his apprentice Timothy. He says of Timothy: "I have no one else like him, who will show genuine concern for your welfare. For everyone looks out for their own interests, not those of Jesus Christ" (NIV). Timothy is held up as an example of someone who does not look out for his own interests, but lays them aside for the interests of Christ. By inference, he does that by laying aside his interests for the needs of others.

After the examples of the Lord Jesus and the well-known Timothy, Paul then mentions the little-known Epaphroditus. This is what Paul says about him:

> But I think it is necessary to send back to you Epaphroditus, my brother, co-worker and fellow soldier, who is also your messenger, whom you sent to take care of my needs. For he longs for all of you and is distressed because you heard he was ill. Indeed he was ill, and almost died. But God had mercy on him, and not on him only but also on me, to spare me sorrow upon sorrow. Therefore I am all the more eager to send him, so that when you see him again you

> may be glad and I may have less anxiety. So then, welcome him in the Lord with great joy, and honor people like him, because he almost died for the work of Christ. He risked his life to make up for the help you yourselves could not give me. (Philippians 2:25–30 NIV)

Paul states that Epaphroditus ministered to Paul's needs, and in the process, he nearly died for it. He risked his own life for Paul's interests. Because of that attitude and action, he is held up to us as an example of self-sacrificing for the well-being of others.

A Gambling Man

The Greek in this paragraph has a rich word to describe Epaphroditus. The phrase "he almost died" is a single Greek word with a long history—*parabaloni*. In society at the time, it meant to put yourself at risk for another person. It could be used in a legal setting when a person would give a character witness for one accused of a crime. Essentially, the one giving the witness was aligning him- or herself with the accused and could find himself or herself on the wrong side of the legal system. Later, in the Middle Ages, there was a monastic order that took on the ministry of tending to the terminally ill who had been cast off by family and society. They called themselves the *parabaloni*.[12]

To be a *parabaloni*, is to put oneself at risk for another's gain. And to do so is to join in a magnificent fraternity of Christ-followers down through history. A mature Christ-follower is willing to walk well with God (i.e., endure in faith, hope, and joy) when his or her own personal pilgrimage gets difficult. Even more, a mature follower of Christ will willingly step into circumstances that could cost him or her significantly as he or she tends to the interests of others. This is what courageous Epaphroditus did when he set out from the relative comforts of his own home and community and pilgrimaged to the enormous, dank city of Rome to tend to Paul's needs.

Leaning into Others at a Personal Cost

When we set aside our own comforts to tend to the needs of others, we imitate not only Epaphroditus but Jesus. This can take the form of listening attentively as another pours out his or her pain-filled story. It is sticking with a friend who has failed and is now living with the awful consequences. This self-sacrifice takes the form of enduring with others as they endure suffering. Presence is what God offers to us, and a listening, caring presence is the gift we offer to others. This is, in the end, a culmination of a trusting response to God as we experience our own sufferings.

There is immense benefit from God's redemption of adversity. We are shown his love, matured, transformed, purified in faith as we are invited into an enduring walk with him. This all finds full expression in the self-giving, self-sacrificing acts of enduring with others in their pain. Like Timothy, we are encouraged to look out not only for our own interests but the interests of others. Like Epaphroditus, we can risk our own well-being in the care of others when God has clearly shown us to do so. In all these responses, we emulate Jesus. Our lives become a message of consolation, hope, and love to others in a world that includes sufferings.

Reflection

» Who has companioned well with you in your own pains?

» Who in your sphere of relationships could use accompaniment through personal trials? How can you accompany them as they wrestle with their uninvited companion?

» Consider how God has tended to you and journeyed with you and your uninvited companion. How can you emulate God's care to you as you seek to provide a caring accompaniment to others in their sufferings?

Conclusion

We have come a long way in our reflections on suffering. Our lives are laced with dual companions—one is the God of eternal life, and the other is the impact of a fallen world. He is constantly beckoning us deeper into himself, that we might hold these paradoxical tensions well. He knows. He sees. He hears. He is with us. One day, he will come to us forever and we will leave our uninvited companions behind for good. No more pain. No more tears. Until that day, it is our opportunity to do something here that we will not be able to do in eternity—trust him and walk with him in the midst of suffering.

May this simple writing effort be a significant encouragement to you to live a noble, courageous life in the love of God for the sake of others, regardless of life circumstances. May you continually experience the bounty our Father extends to us, even in suffering. May you do what only you have the opportunity to do on this side of eternity: to know his love and steward that love to others in the midst of uninvited companions in life.

And after you have suffered a little while, the God of all grace,
who has called you to his eternal glory in Christ,
will himself restore, confirm, strengthen, and establish you. To him be the dominion forever and ever. Amen.
1 Peter 5:10–11 (NIV)

Reflection

» We wrote an opening prayer at the start of this book. Write another prayer reflecting your heart to the Father as your conclusion to this book.

Resources

Below are recommended books and resources further exploring the Triune God and his redemptive ways toward us in suffering. These resources have been profoundly significant to me in my journey with God through the joys and pains of life.

- *Delighting in the Trinity: An Introduction to the Christian Faith*, Michael Reeves
- *Enjoy Your Prayer Life*, Michael Reeves
- *Formed for the Glory of God: Learning from the Spiritual Practices of Jonathan Edwards*, Kyle Strobel
- *Called to be Saints: An Invitation to Christian Maturity*, Gordon T. Smith
- *At the Heart of the Gospel: Suffering in the Earliest Christian Message*, L. Ann Jervis
- *A Grace Disguised: How the Soul Grows through Loss,* Gerry Sitser
- *Raging with Compassion: Pastoral Responses to the Problem of Evil*, John Swinton
- *A Severe Mercy*, Sheldon Vaauken
- *The Roots of Endurance: Invincible Perseverance in the Lives of John Newton, Charles Simeon, and William Wilberforce*, John Piper

- *Trauma and Resilience, A Handbook,* eds. Frauke Schaefer and Charles Schaefer
- www.tendingscatteredwool.com, a blog by Scott E. Shaum

Notes

1. You can see a picture of these twin tornadoes at https://en.wikipedia.org/wiki/1965_Palm_Sunday_tornado_outbreak

2. I am indebted to Michael Reeves's writings, particularly *Delighting in the Trinity: An Introduction to the Christian Faith* (Downers Grove, IL: InterVarsity Press, 2012), for the shaping of my thoughts on these and other Trinitarian understandings of God.

3. Ibid., 21.

4. Ibid., 28.

5. I am indebted to John Swinton, *Raging with Compassion: Pastoral Reponses to the Problem of Evil* (Grand Rapids, MI: Wm. B. Eerdmans Publishing Co., 2007), for some of these insights into our response to evil and pain. For this thought, see pages 84–85.

6. Kevin McSpadden, "You Now Have a Shorter Attention Span Than a Goldfish," May 13, 2015, *Time*, http://time.com/3858309/attention-spans-goldfish/, accessed July 14, 2017.

7. L. Ann Jervis, *At the Heart of the Gospel: Suffering in the Earliest Christian Message* (Grand Rapids, MI: Wm. B. Eerdmans Publishing Co., 2007), Kindle Locations 502–507.

8. Ibid., Kindle Locations 777–778.

9. Google search definition of *mystery*, https://www.google.com/#q=definition+of+mystery, accessed July 17, 2017.

10. Ken Ross, "Straining on Tip Toe" (Sermon, International Anglican Church, Colorado Springs, CO, June 18, 2017). You can listen to this sermon at http://www.springsiac.org/wp-content/uploads/2017/06/StrainingOnTiptoe.mp3.

11. Some of this material first appeared in *Trauma and Resilience, A Handbook*, eds. Frauke C. Schaefer and Charles. A. Schaefer (Condeo Press, 2012), 17–19.

12. Fritz Reinecker and Cleon Rogers, *Linguistic Ket to the Greek New Testament* (Grand Rapids, MI: Zondervan Publishing House, 1980), 555.

About the Author

SCOTT E. SHAUM has served as a church planter in Hong Kong amongst the Cantonese-speaking, blue-collar workers of that city and on the pastoral staff at Grace Community Church in Detroit, Michigan. Since 2003, Scott, along with his wife, Beth, have been itinerant shepherds of cross-cultural workers with Barnabas International (BI). Currently Scott is serving as director of staff development with BI, as well as providing public speaking, shepherd care, spiritual direction, and coaching to workers globally. Scott and Beth have been married for thirty-two years and have three adult sons and one daughter-in-law (whom I womped in the most recent game of Settlers of Catan). They are ever being drawn into the Father's love amidst their personal physical adversities *and* the beauty he has showered upon their lives.

Scott has been previously published in *Tender Care*, eds. Reagan Wilson and David Kronbach, and *Trauma and Resilience*, eds. Frauke C. Schaefer and Charles A. Schaefer. Scott also writes at tendingscatteredwool.com. You can contact him for speaking events at sshaum@barnabas.org.

Printed in Great Britain
by Amazon

Child's Play QUILTS

MAKE 20 Stash-Busting QUILTS FOR KIDS

Stacey Day

stashBOOKS®
an imprint of C&T Publishing

PUBLISHER Amy Marson

CREATIVE DIRECTOR Gailen Runge

EDITORS Monica Gyulai and Liz Aneloski

TECHNICAL EDITOR Julie Waldman

COVER/BOOK DESIGNER April Mostek

PRODUCTION COORDINATOR Tim Manibusan

PRODUCTION EDITOR Jennifer Warren

ILLUSTRATOR Linda Johnson

PHOTO ASSISTANT Mai Yong Vang

STYLE PHOTOGRAPHY by Lucy Glover and
INSTRUCTIONAL PHOTOGRAPHY by Diane Pedersen and Mai Yong Vang
of C&T Publishing, Inc., unless otherwise noted

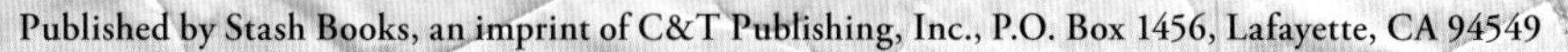

Published by Stash Books, an imprint of C&T Publishing, Inc., P.O. Box 1456, Lafayette, CA 94549

Library of Congress Cataloging-in-Publication Data

Names: Day, Stacey, 1984- author.

Title: Child's play quilts : make 20 stash-busting quilts for kids / Stacey Day.

Description: Lafayette, CA : C&T Publishing, Inc., 2018. | Includes bibliographical references.

Identifiers: LCCN 2017039229 | ISBN 9781617456138 (soft cover)

Subjects: LCSH: Patchwork--Patterns. | Quilting--Patterns. | Children's quilts.

Classification: LCC TT835 .D395 2018 | DDC 746.46/041--dc23

LC record available at https://lccn.loc.gov/2017039229

Printed in China

10 9 8 7 6 5 4 3 2 1

Dedication

This book is dedicated to my family: I am everything because of you. I love you.

Acknowledgments

They say it takes a village to raise a child. The same is true for writing a book.

Thank you to Amy Dame, Paul Krampitz, Miriam March, Stacey Murton, Jade Prosser, Arita Rai, and Matt Wheeler for your help with the quilts. Your efforts and talents are greatly appreciated.

Kim Andersson, Amy Gunson, Gillian Smith, and Anne Sullivan—thank you. For all I can think of and everything else I can't.

Thank you to Aurifil, Dashwood Studio, Free-Spirit Fabrics, Moda Fabrics, Timeless Treasures Fabrics, TinLizzie18, The Warm Company, and Windham Fabrics for providing the supplies and materials to bring my vision to life.

Finally, thank you to my readers—my fellow quilters—for your support in picking up this book. Having people with whom I can share my ideas and knowledge makes all the effort worthwhile.

TIP **Baby Quilt Safety**

We make beautiful quilts with the intent of them being used, so it makes sense to ensure that they are used safely. It is recommended that babies under the age of six months sleep only on their backs, with nothing in the crib that could accidentally be pulled over their faces and become a suffocation hazard. This includes quilts, blankets, and sheets—even stuffed animals and crib bumpers. For more information on safe sleep for babies, check out the websites included in Resources (page 126).

Contents

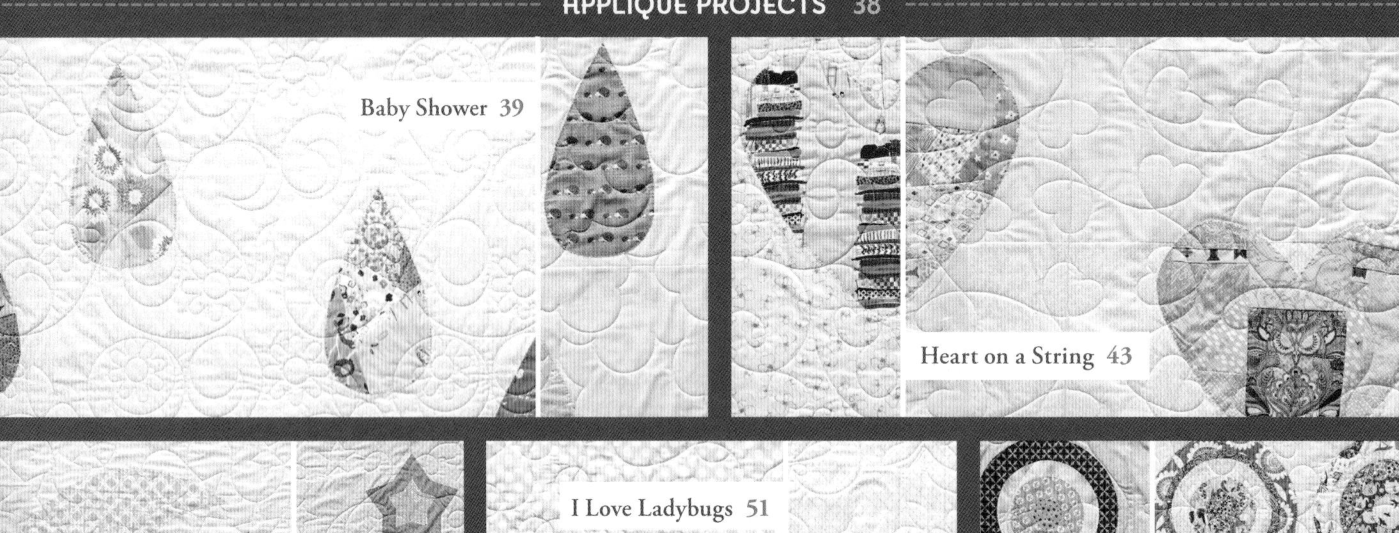

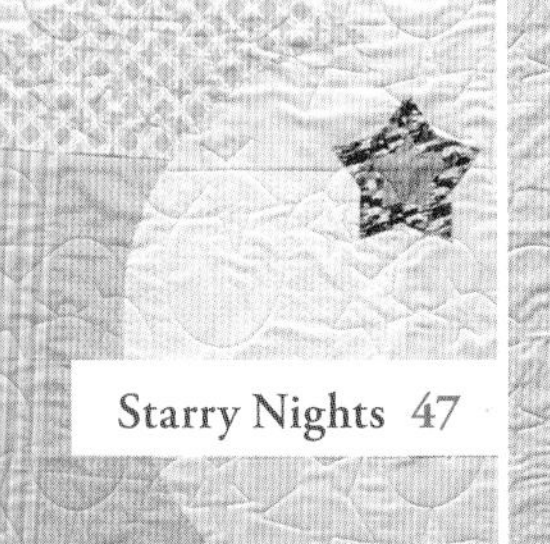

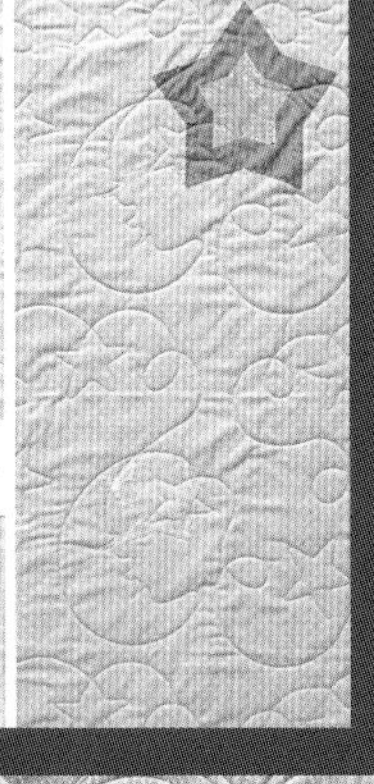

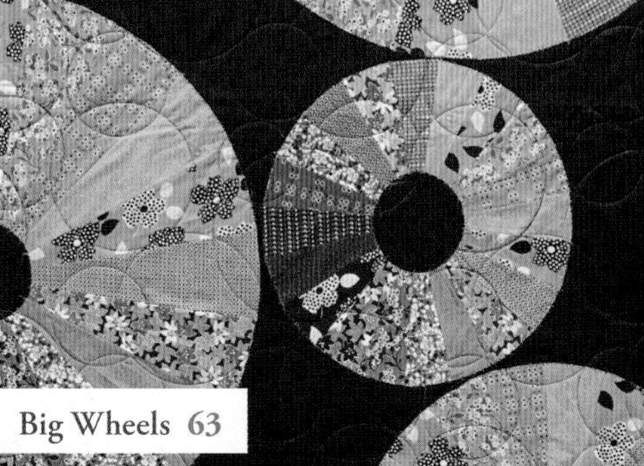

Glow 67
Twinkle Twinkle 71
Diamonds Forever 75
Rainbow Brights 79
Bows Peep 83
Prism 87
Apple Blossom 91
Fishbowl 97
Butterfly Kisses 101
Beaded 105
Pinwheel 109
Swish 115
Fox Hunt 121

OH, BABY!

Have you noticed that once one friend, coworker, or relative announces they are expecting, it seems like everyone else you know quickly follows suit? While making baby quilts to gift, I found myself making the same thing over and over. I wished for a collection of simple stash-friendly projects that would be easy to start (and finish!). I made my own wish come true.

It is a tradition in my family that every baby gets at least one new quilt made just for them. My family is large and spread wide, so we don't always get to see each other. There are new little cousins and second cousins that I have never met and may never get to meet. For us, a quilt is a hug you can send—a reminder that we love and think of one another even though we are far apart. It is a big reason why I love making baby quilts.

Another reason is the fabric. I get to use all the cute and fun prints that inevitably end up in my stash: birds on a wire, fluffy bunnies, and dapper foxes donning monocles and hats. But I discovered that many patterns called for pieces of fabric larger than the small cuts and fat quarters many of us buy. So I sat down and started sketching out options for stash-friendly quilts.

I played with designs, fabric options, and sizes with the goal of utilizing smaller cuts and even scraps. However, I still wanted quilters to have the option of using new yardage to great effect (because we all love buying new fabric!).

The quilt designs grow and mature as you get deeper into the book. If you promised a quilt to a pregnant friend but don't get around to it until the first birthday (or later), you will find an appropriate design. With my first son I learned how babies see color and contrast and how to safely use quilts in the crib. These concepts were solidified with my second son, and I experimented with different batting, binding, and backing options.

All the lessons I learned are here. I hope you have just as much fun making the quilts as I did presenting them. Create beautiful quilts with confidence, knowing that they will be loved and cherished for years to come!

Color and Fabric

Pick What They Love, Love What You Pick

Choosing fabrics and colors for baby quilts can be a fun yet challenging experience. Parent preferences, child preferences, and nursery themes may all be considerations. Traditionally, gender played a large role in color and fabric selection, but these days many parents are of a mind that no color is off-limits. And a plethora of adorable children's prints are available in a variety of neutral colors.

I made all the quilts in this book using warm and cool colorways. At first glance these palettes may read as gender-specific, but in reality they are favored color wheel combinations.

BABY COLORS

The idea of gender-based colors is relatively new. For a long time, boys and girls were dressed identically in white dress-like garments with hats, high boots, and curled hair. It wasn't until the early 1940s that gender-specific colors and clothing became popular. But at that time, blue was for girls and pink was for boys! Pink was considered a strong, bold color suited for boys, whereas blue was seen as soft and delicate—the perfect expression of femininity. In the late 1970s, the colors were switched to what we now consider "gender appropriate."

Warm colors

Cool colors

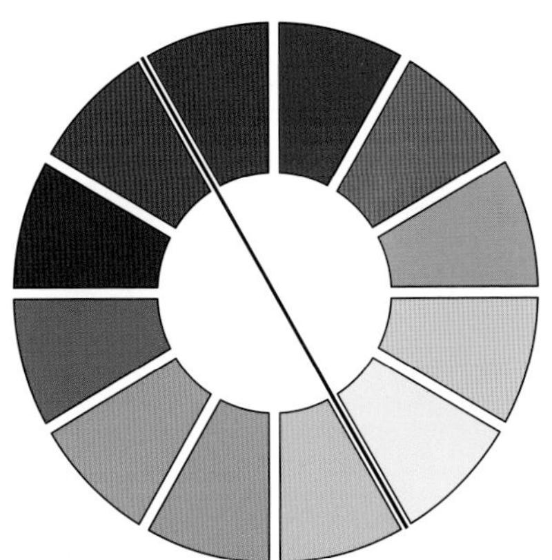

In this color wheel, the cool colors (clockwise from green to violet) are on the left of the black line and the warm colors (clockwise from red-violet to yellow) are on the right.

Baby quilts and fabrics are often very soft and muted, but they don't have to be. Research shows that babies are drawn to *contrast*, the difference between darks and lights (also called *value*). The larger the difference between two colors, the higher the contrast. High-contrast quilts such as *Bows Peep* (page 83) are exciting and visually stimulating. Quilts with low contrast, such as *Glow* (page 67), are softer and calmer. Contrast may be created between the background and feature prints, the feature prints and supporting prints, and even the background and binding.

Bright or dark colors against a contrasting background will play up the shapes of the pieces within the blocks. Colors that are muted or that match with the background will blend together; the emphasis then turns to the composition of the overall quilt and how well the colors play together.

Contrast between colored fabrics is best demonstrated in a grayscale picture. Take a photo of a selection of fabrics and convert it to a grayscale (or black-and-white) image on your computer or phone. It's easy to see dark and light this way.

There is a lot of contrast between the group of fabrics on the right and left, but within those groups there is very little contrast. The darker elements of a quilt stand out against the lighter elements, creating obvious focal points.

A high-contrast palette yields a visually exciting quilt, with the emphasis on whichever colors stand out the most against the background.

Here is a wider range of contrast, but it is not as pronounced. This is a soft-contrast selection.

Newborns can only focus within an 8″–12″ range, so anything outside that range appears blurry and indistinct. Similar colors blend together, but bright primaries capture attention. It isn't until about five or six months of age that babies start to really notice color differences. Around eight months, they start to pick out different shades of the same color, starting with brighter hues and moving toward pastels. Look at the grayscale contrast examples to get a sense of how babies see things—it's easy to understand why high contrast captures their attention.

With this in mind, you can have a lot of fun with baby quilts. Don't feel limited to pastels or low-volume prints. Pull bright primary colors from your stash; play up the contrast between the shapes and background. Stark contrasts will draw a young baby's attention, while multiple prints of a similar color will help develop the senses. As sight develops, small details of a quilt will become visible.

For background fabrics, I recommend practical choices. We make these quilts hoping they will be loved. And they will be! But baby and toddler love involves a lot of dragging, snuggling, wrapping, playing, drooling, and chewing. Even older children will kick bedding to the floor and ball up quilts only to launch them from a balcony. I recommend low-volume printed backgrounds—such as marbled textures or tonal prints—in off-white, gray, and ivory. These tend to hide stains, survive frequent laundering, and hide wear better than white. I also use colored backgrounds, but I make sure that there is enough contrast in the quilt for the main design to be visible (see *Rainbow Brights*, page 79; *Fishbowl*, page 97; and *Butterfly Kisses*, page 101).

Exploring the Color Wheel

More on Color

C&T Publishing has some wonderful books on color theory. If you need some extra help or want to dive deeper into the wonderful world of color, see my favorites in Resources (page 126).

It's likely that you can make the quilts in this book using fabric and scraps already in your stash. If you are sewing for older children, let them have a hand in choosing colors. My son developed a strong attachment to orange, so many of his quilts feature orange prints. Choosing colors makes older children feel part of the process, and even babies and toddlers will show preferences if allowed to play in a random pile of fabric or scraps.

When I pull fabrics from my stash to begin a quilt, I usually start with a favorite fabric (typically the one that inspired the quilt in the first place) and then build my palette around that print or color. I have some go-to combinations when it comes to color. Each is eye pleasing and, when combined with the concepts of contrast, yields a successful quilt every time.

Combining Colors

ANALOGOUS COLORS

My go-to method for creating harmonious quilts is using three *analogous colors*—adjacent colors on the color wheel. Analogous colors typically appear together in the natural world, match and blend well, and are pleasing to the eye. They are a surefire way to create visually appealing quilts.

It's important to consider contrast when working with analogous combinations. Because the colors flow seamlessly from one to another, adding contrast can provide emphasis to parts of a quilt, whereas a lack of contrast creates a soft visual without an obvious focus.

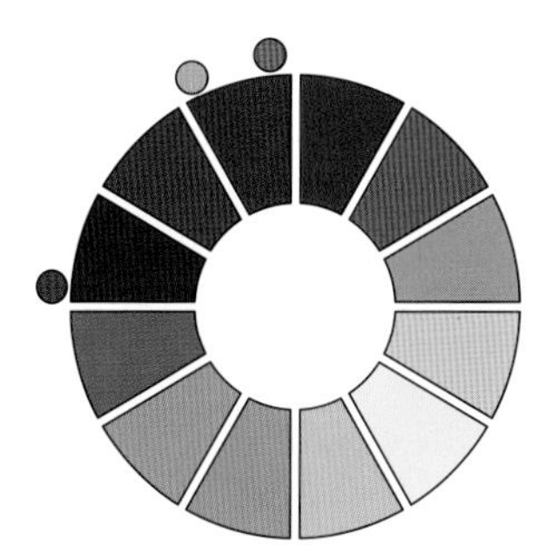

Analogous color wheel

In this analogous scheme, the colors blend harmoniously from one section of the color wheel to the next. There is just enough contrast to create depth and interest. (This is the same group of fabrics from our second grayscale example.)

In this analogous color scheme, fewer fabrics and more contrast between the colors energize the fabric selection.

COMPLEMENTARY COLORS

Complementary schemes pair colors on opposite sides of the color wheel. The opposition makes them visually striking, though sometimes they can be off-putting because there is nothing to mute the intensity of the colors. Red and green are an excellent example of this. To lessen the intensity but still provide the energy that comes from complementary pairings, use a color that is slightly off the pure opposite.

Blue and orange are complementary colors. By using a yellow-orange instead of a pure orange and a range of similar contrast colors, you have a group of fabrics that is exciting without being overwhelming.

Another way to lessen the hit of complementary colors is to provide contrast.

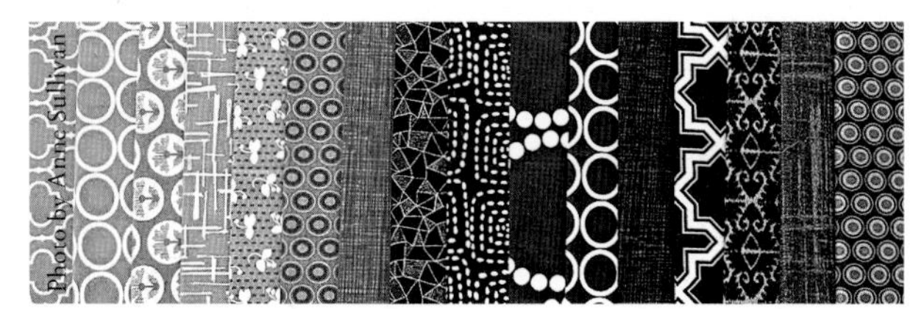

Blue and orange are opposite, but there is a stark contrast between the two hues. (This is the same stack of fabrics used in the first example of grayscale contrast.)

A quilt from these colors would be exciting but not overwhelming because the emphasis would be on only one of the hues—navy, if paired with a light background, or orange, if paired with a dark background. You could also use one color as the background and the other for the block sections to make a stunning two-tone quilt!

Beaded is an excellent example of both these concepts.

The cool version of *Beaded* (page 107) features blue and orange opposites that are intense but reined in by the use of contrast, which creates focal points.

In the warm version of *Beaded* (page 105), a pure medium green is combined with a color slightly off the exact opposite—pink—to lessen the intensity.

SPLIT-COMPLEMENTARY COLORS

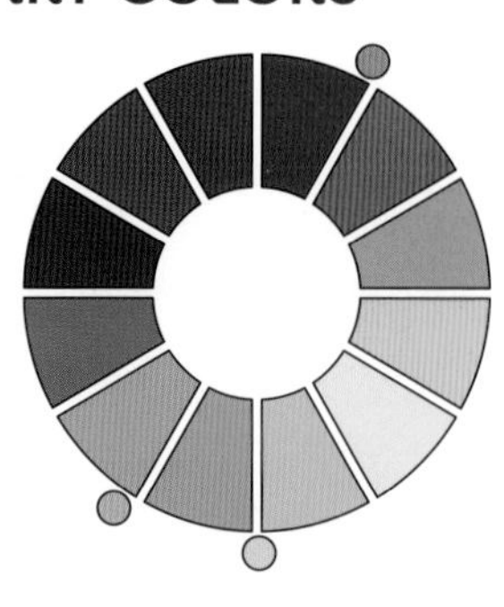

When I want to make a quilt with a lot of impact, I use a *split-complementary color scheme*, which refers to an analogous color grouping with the addition of a color that is directly across the color wheel—a *complementary color*.

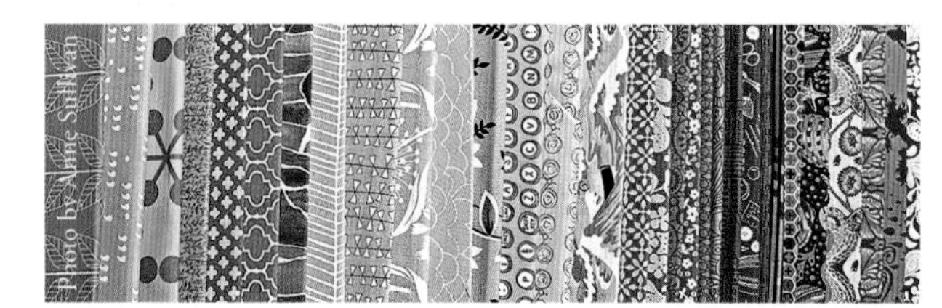

Green and aqua are analogous colors. Red is the complement to green.

In these palettes, the analogous colors create harmony while the complementary color adds zing.

The warm version of *Pinwheel* (page 109) is a good example of a split-complementary color scheme.

It is very important to make use of contrast in a split combination so that the eye has a place to rest in a vibrant quilt or a focal point to draw it into a muted quilt. Sometimes the complementary color can be a bit too intense, so using a color just one step to either side of the complement can rein it in.

ALL-OR-ONE COLOR

Finally, I use an all-or-one approach when I make a quilt, with all the colors (rainbow) or a single color in various tints and shades (monochromatic).

Rainbow quilts are always a hit!

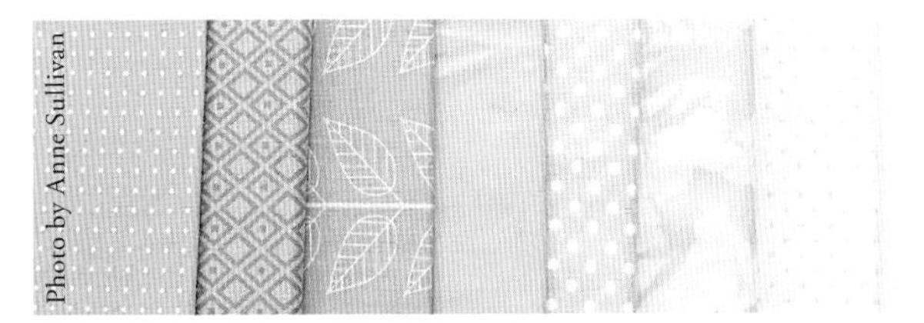

A single-color pull is most successful when there is contrast among the fabrics, creating a gradient effect from light to dark.

Full-spectrum quilts can have very little contrast, making the scheme smooth and easy on the eyes, or quite a bit of contrast to highlight a particular color or section of the quilt. Monochromatic quilts *must* have contrast in order for the elements of the quilt to be seen, whether it's a single light print with a single dark print or a large selection of prints.

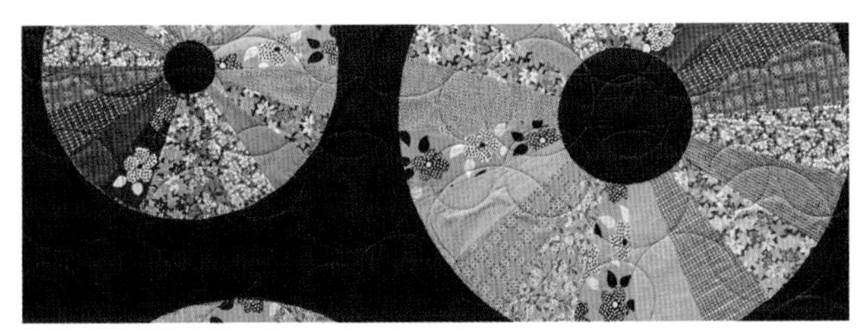

The warm version of *Big Wheels* (page 63) is a smooth gradient. No one section has more emphasis than the other.

TIP

Yellow Is Special

Technically yellow is considered a warm color, but it is so versatile that it can be used anywhere to add a splash of life or to create a successful color story. I used yellow in both my warm and cool quilts. Don't be afraid to use yellow—it goes with everything!

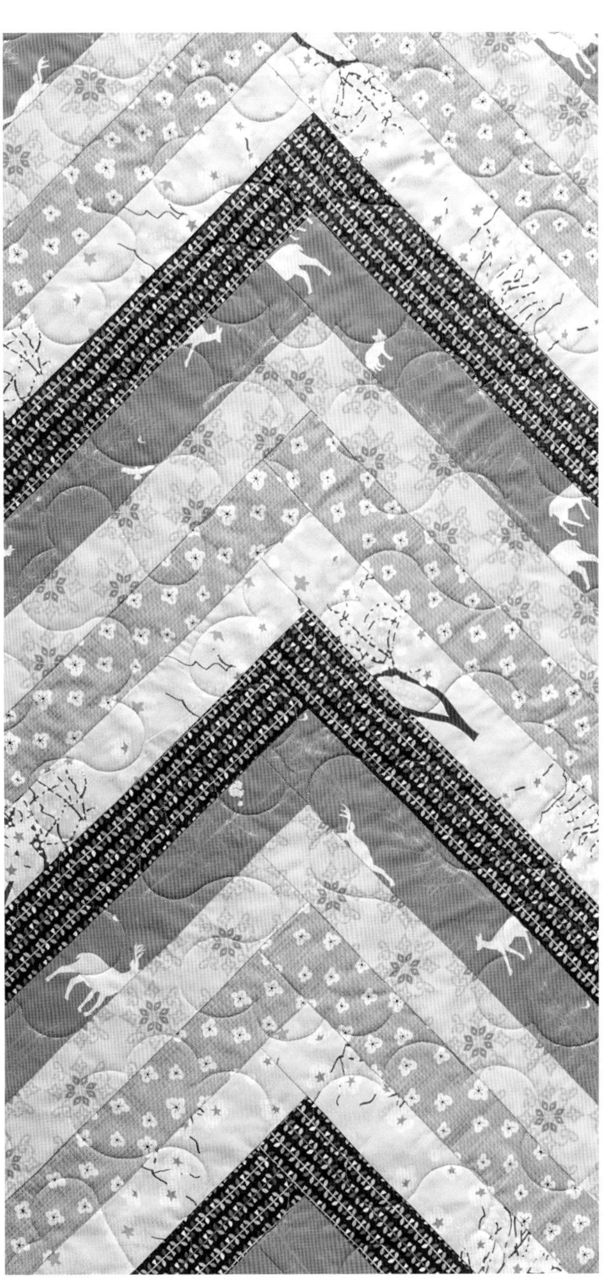

The warm version of *Rainbow Brights* (page 81) highlights the deep blue-violet, creating a visual barrier between the rainbow sections.

Maintaining Your Stash

Quilters tend to have impressive fabric stashes—full of yardage, small cuts, precuts, and scraps. But we are often pretty terrible about organizing and storing our beautiful collections properly, rendering these stashed resources inefficient and often unused.

Organizing Fabric

Once upon a time, all my fabric was kept in colored or opaque bins and organized in two categories: batik and not batik. Fabric would make it in the door and get placed in a bin. There was fabric layered upon fabric—buried, poorly folded, and hard to find. It was a mess. Every time I tried to dig through it, the mess got messier, with new stuff working its way to the bottom and older pieces being forgotten under a mound of fabric.

For many quilters, space is an issue. I am lucky enough now to have a room dedicated to my craft, but for many years I didn't have the space to set up a permanent sewing station. So I got creative with my storage and came up with efficient solutions. From dressers and under-the-bed drawers to bookshelves and bins, I have tried it all.

THE BATTLE OF THE BINS

The first step on the road to fabric organization is taking the fabric out of closed bins. I know that for most people bins allow for easy storage, but having used bins for years, I can attest to the fact that once it's in the bin, it's forgotten. When I finally pulled everything out of the bins, my stash was not what I had pictured. I discovered huge holes in my color wheel and way too much of certain colors that I never actually used, in addition to fabrics I had no idea I owned!

If you absolutely must have bins, choose shallow clear ones that are 10″ deep or less. These are typically sold for under-bed storage. The clear plastic keeps the contents visible, and the shallow depth allows them to fit at the bottom of a closet, under a couch, or in other small spaces. Fat quarters fit in smaller shoebox-size bins if you want to keep them separate from full-width fabric cuts.

If you have a dedicated space, whether it is an entire room or a corner of the dining room, a shallow bookcase is perfect for storing fabric. I recommend shallow ones to save space and to prevent stacking fabric behind fabric. You can find small bookcases or cube shelving that takes up the same amount of space as a plastic bin. This way you can see what you have on hand, fabric stays folded, and you can even store your machine on the shelves or on top of the bookcase when not in use. Ideally, the height of the bookcase would depend on the wall space available.

This bookcase lives in my sewing room and keeps thread in easy reach. This unit is dedicated to neutrals and fabric collections that I don't want to break up. I can even make space for small bins that contain everything I need for upcoming projects.

SORT BY COLOR

To make finding fabric easy, organize by color. Sorting by color makes the most efficient use of space and time and can reveal some distinct purchasing trends. After I started to use the rainbow as an organizing principle, I learned I was consistently very low in warm reds, oranges, and yellows and had an overabundance of bright greens, teals, fuchsias, and red-violets.

Break up collections and matching fabrics unless you have a plan to use them together. I find that pieces are more likely to be used if they aren't with their collection mates.

My beautiful, well-balanced rainbow stash. To the left is a small DVD-size bookshelf that is home to fat quarter bundles. It keeps them close at hand without getting lost in the main stash. These are usually new bundles, bundles with a specific project in mind, or ones that I just can't bring myself to break apart.

TIP

Charmed, I'm Sure

2½″ precut squares and strips, charm square packs, and 10″ precut squares inevitably find their way into any quilter's stash. Thankfully they are pretty easy to store. I keep a section dedicated to precuts and simply stack them according to size. In the case of 2½″ precut strips, I stack them with their tags facing out so I can remember what collection I have. I usually don't break up precuts because there are plenty of ways to use them as a group and they store much better as a package. Small decorative cube shelving is perfect for stacking and storing your 2½″ precut squares so they don't get lost, and small spools of thread fill in any remaining space. A functional and fun storage solution!

Organizing by color and storing fabric as visibly as possible provides a lot of design freedom. And it's much easier to keep a stash neat, tidy, and well-balanced when you know what you have on hand.

TIP

Keeping Order

After a purge or cleanup, I start out enthusiastically putting back fabric the way I found it to keep things neat. But I tend to lose steam over time. So one day a year I spend the evening with a friend folding fabric, drinking cocktails, and catching up on life.

FOLDING FABRIC

Whether you put fabric in bins or on shelves, visibility is key. I like to stack my bundles from smallest to largest and place my fabric so the fold is visible, revealing the greatest surface area of each print.

Before: Raveled edges and indistinct columns make it hard to grab a piece of fabric without messing up others.

After: The stacked fabric is neat and tidy and makes good use of space.

To make the most of whatever storage space is available, do some math and fold your fabric thoughtfully. It's easy to do, and while it takes a little time at first, it's a breeze to maintain.

TIP

Prewash

There are two schools of thought about prewashing fabric. There are those who wash every piece before adding it to their stash and those who don't bother. I normally do not prewash my fabrics because I find it easier to work with fabric that is fresh and crisp off the bolt. But baby quilts are an exception. I prewash fabrics for a baby quilt to eliminate any concerns about shrinking or bleeding—for the recipient and for me. It does add some time to the start of your project, but a quick wash cycle with a tiny amount of detergent and a tumble dry could save you potential heartache later on.

Tutorial: Folding 101

1. Measure the width of the storage space, such as a bookshelf or a stacking cube. Decide how many columns of fabric you want. Divide the total width by the number of columns and subtract a ½″. For example, my cube shelves are 13½″ wide, and I divided them into 2 columns, each 6¾″. Subtract ½″ from that, and the final folded fabric width is 6¼″.

Storage space: 13½″

Half of space 6¾″

Folded fabric width 6¼″

Calculate the finished width of your stacks.

2. Measure the depth of the space—to the wall, the back of the bookcase, or the bottom of the bin or drawer—and subtract 2″ from that measurement. My shelves are 12½″ deep. Subtract 2″ from that, and the final depth is 10½″.

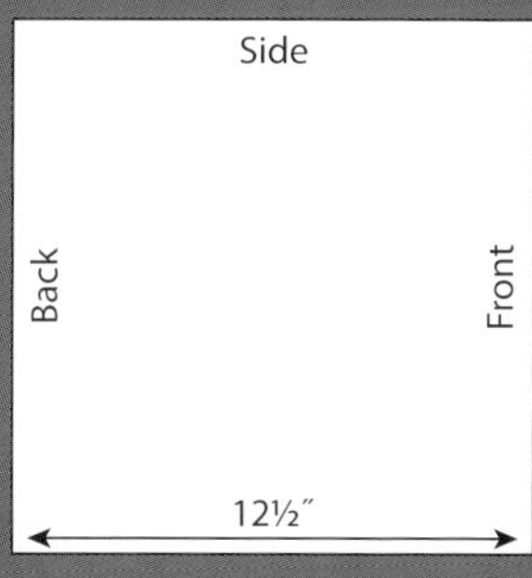

Subtract 2″ from the depth of your storage space.

3. Cut a piece of cardboard to the final measurements. In my example, the cardboard is 6¼″ × 10½″.

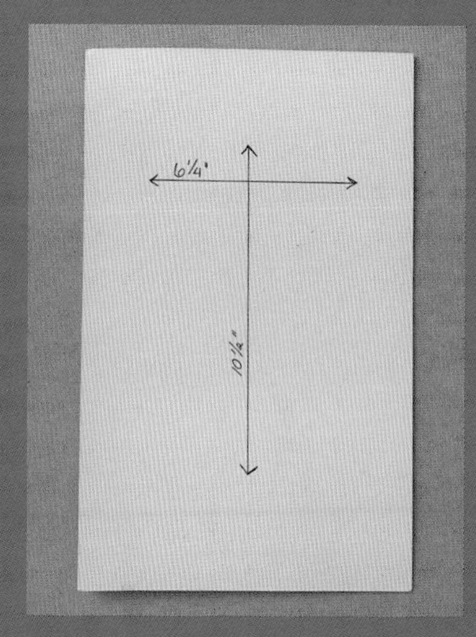

Fold the Width

1. Place a piece of fabric with the cut end facing you as if it was just cut from the bolt—right side out with a single fold and the selvages together. Place the cardboard so the shorter edge is parallel to the width of the fabric and centered, with the fold of the fabric to the left and the selvage to the right.

2. Fold the fabric to match the width of the cardboard by bringing the right side over the top of the cardboard first until it is snug against the right side of the cardboard and matches (or overhangs slightly on) the left side of the cardboard. Bring the left side over and fold it back on itself like an accordion, doing so as many times as needed while keeping the fabric as flat as possible when you are finished.

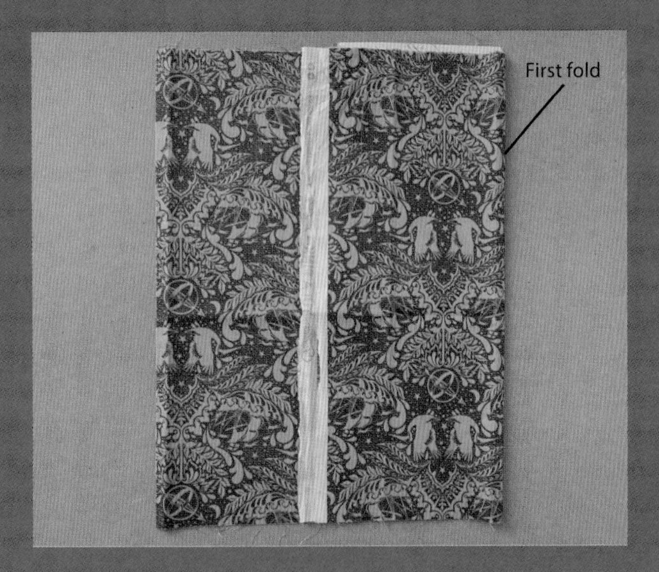

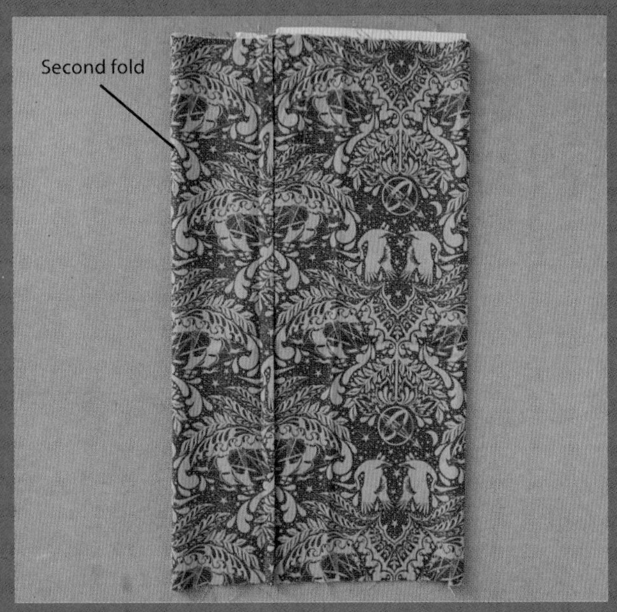

FOLD THE LENGTH

1. Place the cardboard on top, matching the width of the cardboard to the width of the fabric.

2. Start folding the fabric down the length of the piece, flipping the cardboard over and over until the entire length has been folded around the cardboard piece. Remove the cardboard.

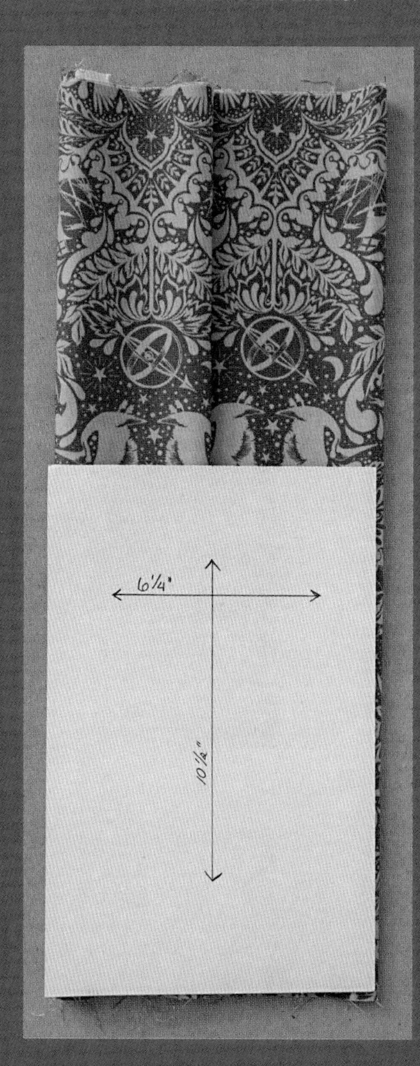

Repeat

Fold all the fabric pieces that need to fit in the same-sized space with the same piece of cardboard. Stack the folded fabric on the shelf (or in the bin or drawer) by color or your preferred organization method. It's helpful to turn bins and drawers on their sides when loading them with the folded fabric pieces.

Building a Working Stash

KEEP WHAT YOU LOVE

During the process of organizing your stash, you are going to handle every piece of fabric you own. This presents an opportunity to do some serious thinning. I'm not going to lie: Purging fabric is hard—*super hard*. But it is also completely worth it.

Remove fabrics to make room for things that are more likely to be used. Eliminate fabrics that may have been well priced but aren't well loved. Take away things that you maybe *sort of* like and create more room for prints to love.

Set Some Free

While folding stash fabrics, ask yourself some important questions. When did you buy it? What was its intended purpose? Does it still match your taste and style? And the big question: Will you ever use it? If you answer "no" to the last question, then it's definitely time to remove that piece from your stash.

Keep bins or bags at arm's reach for discards. *Do not* go through them again, because the fabric will just end up back in your stash. Having an iron-willed friend nearby really comes in handy for this task. (Ask me how I know!)

My stash after The Purge of 2013

PASS IT ON

After you have a big bin of fabrics removed from your stash, the next question is what to do with them. There are many options. You can sell them online or on Instagram using #thegreatfabricdestash, but that is time consuming. You need to have a PayPal account, and it may require lots of trips to the post office. Sometimes it isn't worth it.

When I did my major purge, I opted to give away everything. I found a local charity that makes quilts for cancer survivors and their families. I also took bins to my quilt guild for my sewing mates to rummage through. It was fun seeing prints for which I had no use appear in finished quilts the next month!

Consider giving to senior centers, schools that teach sewing, or organizations that routinely make charity quilts. There are lots of options out there for unneeded fabric to be used and loved by someone else—keeping it out of a landfill.

Photo by Stacey Day

Purged fabrics ready for donation. I gave the majority to a charity called Victoria's Quilts. The rest went to my grandma's guild, where it was divvied up and made into quilts for their local women's shelter.

SMART BUYING

With your stash sorted, consider what you have and what's missing. Do you have lots of one color but not much of another? Are you heavy in busy prints but light on blenders? Is your purge bin full of a specific style or color? Determine what you have, how much you have, and what you were buying that you weren't using. Taking a good look will make future trips to the fabric store easier and more productive.

I have a system for deciding how much yardage to purchase. When I find a print or solid that I think is perfect for backgrounds, I buy it in 3- to 5-yard lengths. (3 yards will generally make a lap-size quilt, and 5 yards is usually enough for a queen.) I buy prints I love in half-yard cuts. If I *really* love it, I will take a yard or more, especially if it's a blender in a color that I use frequently or a print that makes a great binding.

If it's cute but I don't have an immediate idea of where I can use it, I'll buy a fat quarter. I try to find fat quarters that have the collection information on the selvage, so if I end up loving the print I can find more of it. I try to find fabric for backings in the clearance or sale sections. Often shops will provide a discount if you finish the bolt.

If you tend to buy small cuts of a lot of fabrics (like I once did), consider instead purchasing larger pieces of fewer fabrics. You will still be buying the same amount of fabric, but you will be limiting the number of prints you have. You may find that you are more likely to buy things you love and use rather than just buying fabric for the sake of buying fabric. This approach will keep your stash under control and functional.

To keep my stash manageable and to save money, I wait to go fabric shopping until there is a sale on fabric. Most of our favorite shops will have a big sale at least once a year. That's when I make larger purchases of favorite prints, whole collection bundles, and background fabrics.

TIP Having large pieces of background fabric gives you so much flexibility in the size and number of quilts you can make. And you always have enough left over to make scrappy backgrounds when you want them!

ORGANIZING SCRAPS

For years, I tossed scraps into a bin under my cutting table and immediately forgot about them. When the bin got too full, I would try to find someone who used scraps and bribe them to take mine. It wasn't until I started sorting my scraps that I found uses for them. The key to scrap sorting is finding what works for you.

Sort by Size

My grandma cuts irregular pieces into squares and stores the squares in bins by size. When she makes scrappy quilts, she reaches for the size she wants. Cut the squares into the nearest ½″ measurement (2″, 2½″, 3″, and so on). Label the front of each bin clearly with the size. This method works well if you have the space to store a dozen bins dedicated to different square sizes and don't mind having all your colors mixed together.

Sort by Color

I prefer to keep my scraps sorted by color. I still use that large bin under my cutting table, but instead of just tossing scraps in haphazardly, I keep large plastic ziplock bags in it. Each ziplock bag is dedicated to a color, and I put each scrap in the designated bag after I'm done cutting. When I want to make a slab, all I have to do is grab the relevant color bag and start sewing. I keep very basic color bags: red, orange, yellow, green, blue, purple, pink, black, white, and gray. I throw the in-between fabrics, like busy prints, into whatever bag seems to fit best.

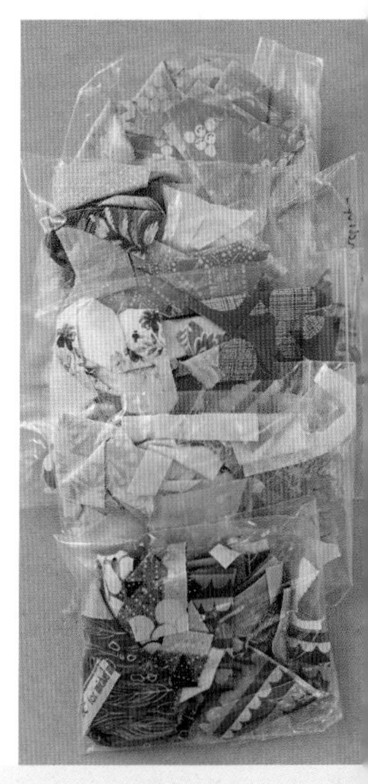

Slabs

For the projects in this book, a "slab" is a large piece of usable fabric made from many small similar-hued fabric scraps. Anything can be turned into a slab: 2½″ precut strips, 5″ charm squares, or scraps. You can even sew together scrap pieces of the same print to make a usable piece!

Slabs are perfect for large appliqué shapes and scrappy backgrounds. They may appear busy when viewed up close but will read as a single color from a distance. They can be orderly and geometric or improvisational and randomly pieced. Most of my slabs are made with squares and strips because that's what I have in my scraps. Yours might feature lots of irregular pieces.

Scraps don't have to be tiny pieces. A fat eighth with a corner removed, a narrow strip, leftover squares from a large project—all these can be used for making slabs.

Large scraps are perfect for large appliqué pieces, like the moon in *Starry Nights* (page 47), which was made from leftover pieces of fat quarters.

However your slabs turn out, they can replace single fabrics in a project.

Improv Slabs

Improv slabs are simple and easy to make, and they are great when you have a lot of scrap pieces. Sew together fabrics of similar tone and hue in random order, pressing the seams open as you go. Start by sewing together the smallest pieces of fabric, much like a Log Cabin block.

After making a center unit, trim the edges even with the raw edge of the shortest piece of fabric. You can trim on angles or on straight lines to preserve as much of the scrap fabric as you desire. The piece does not have to be square. Keep sewing, and build the slab until it reaches the desired size.

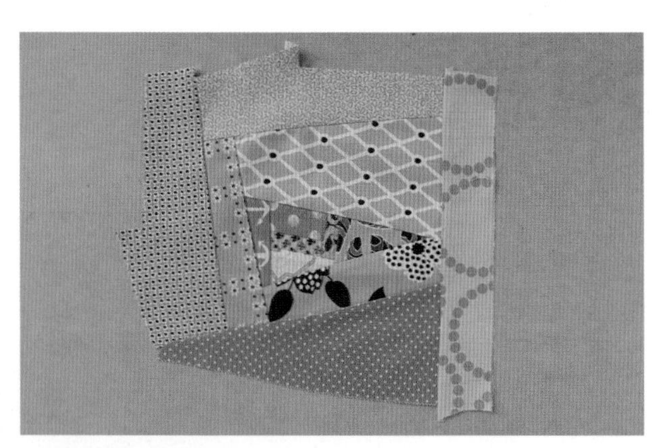

A standard Log Cabin–style slab—these are the easiest to make. Keep sewing round and round with increasingly larger scraps.

Small or large, a slab can be any size you desire.

If you have lots of small cuts and not a lot of longer scraps or strips, make multiple small slabs and trim them to roughly the same size; then sew together the small slabs to make bigger ones. I like to use 3″ × 6″ rectangles for super small scraps. They don't take long to make, and a 3″ × 6″ rectangle is a versatile size to sew together to create larger slabs. Sew scraps into slabs ahead of time, or make them as you go.

Most of the time a slab will have irregular edges. Depending on how you want to use your slabs, you can either square them up in order to piece several together or leave them as is for cutting out appliqué shapes. Either way, make sure there are no gaps or blank areas in the middle of your slab.

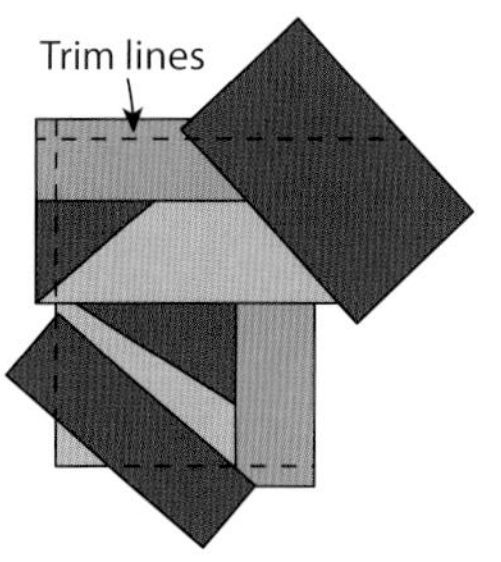

The dotted lines show where this slab needs to be trimmed in order to eliminate gaps and keep the edges square. Some areas will require more trimming than others, and that's normal. Keep the trimmings to start new slabs, or add them back in.

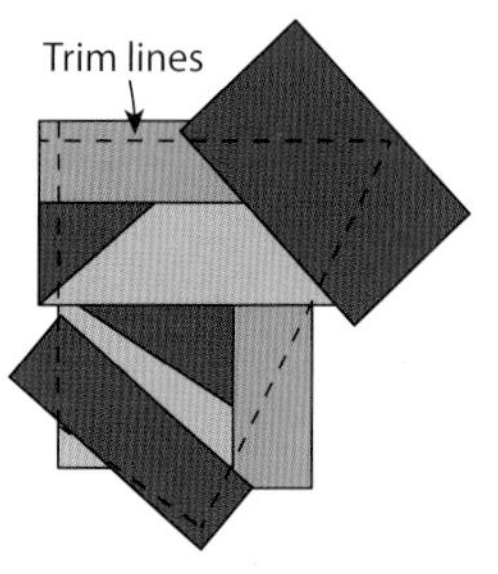

If you are cutting appliqué pieces from a slab, check that the template will fit within the ideal usable area of the slab. If you need to make it bigger in order to cut the template pieces, keep adding strips. The dotted lines illustrate where you would need to trim in order to avoid gaps.

Planned Slabs

Planned slabs take more time but are well worth the effort. Sew the slab into the shape of a template that will be used. Usually planned slabs are designed around a specific feature fabric, such as the owl motifs in *Heart on a String* (page 43) and in the *Baby Shower* quilts (page 39). I had been hoarding those owl pieces for a very long time. By making them the focal print in a slab, I was able to use them in a functional and beautiful way.

Get Crazy

Most of my slabs end up very geometrical; that's just the nature of my scraps. Yours might be more crazy pieced, full of random shapes and sizes. Mix colors to make rainbow slabs, fussy cut small or large prints and artfully arrange them inside a slab, or even print small pictures on printable fabric and incorporate the images into a slab. Have fun and mix it up! There is no wrong way to make a slab.

Making Planned Slabs

1. Trace or draw the desired shape on paper.

2. Press the scraps that will be used.

3. Place the feature scrap inside the drawn lines of the shape where you want it to appear. Arrange scraps around the piece, filling and overlapping the drawn lines of the shape.

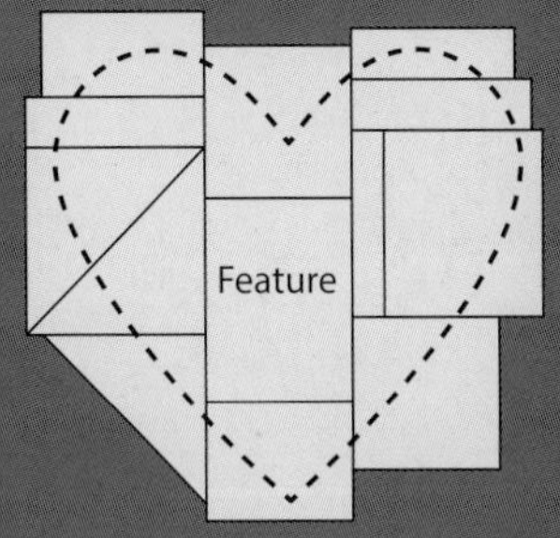

By arranging scraps beforehand, you can see where you will have areas of overlap and plan out the most efficient piecing order around the feature print.

4. Sew together the scraps in sections, fitting and trimming the pieces as you go. Periodically check to make sure that the focal print is still roughly where you want it in the slab. You may need to add additional scraps in some places to compensate for fabric lost to the seam allowances.

5. Cut out the template.

Finished planned slab from the cool version of *Heart on a String* (page 43)

Background Slabs

Background slabs are intended to be the background of a project, often taking the place of a single fabric. My background slabs are usually low-volume neutrals—cream, white, tan, and gray. Background slabs are usually constructed from fewer and larger pieces and are quick to make.

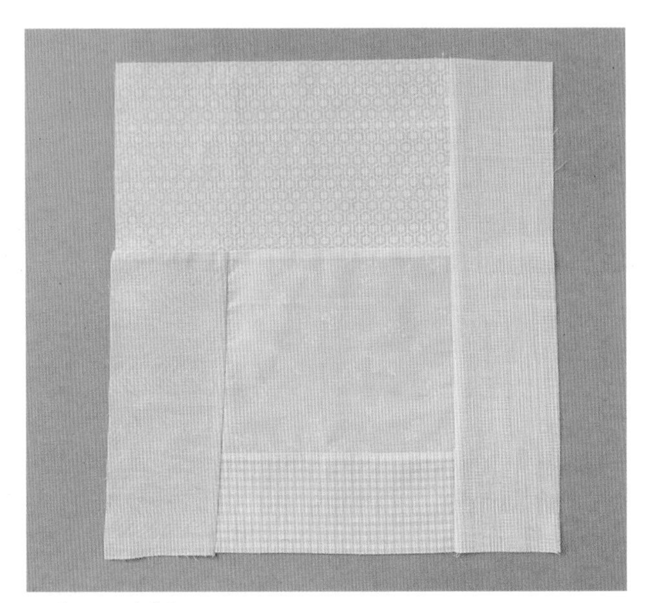

Background slabs are easy to construct.

I make background slabs 12½″ × 12½″ square because a 4 × 5 grid of 12½″ squares makes a perfect 48″ × 60″ baby quilt. That block size is also ideal for quickly increasing the size of a quilt in even increments. To make the backgrounds for the applique projects in *Child's Play Quilts*, I often combined 12½″ square slabs with single-fabric squares to create texture.

Background fabrics are the only scrap fabrics I sort by size. If a scrap includes the full width (selvage to selvage) and measures at least 9″, I fold it and put it back on the shelf with my other background fabrics. If it is less than 9″, it goes in the scrap bin to be cut and pieced into slabs. If the background scrap is not a full width of fabric, I will cut as many 12½″ squares from it as possible. I keep such squares in a dedicated bin for background squares. The rest is scrapped and turned into slabs.

Tools and Techniques

Quilter's Toolbox

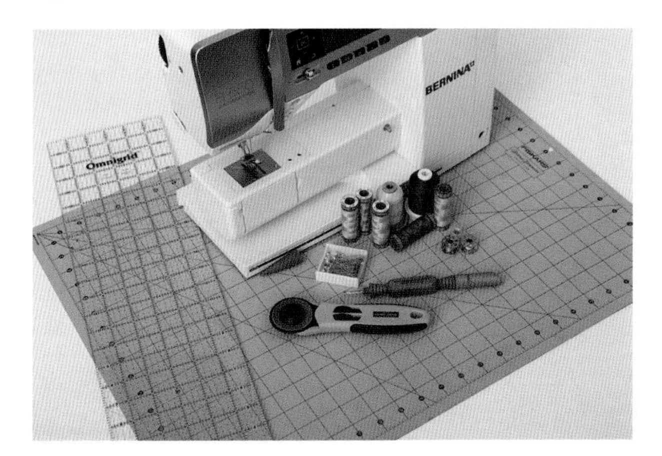

SEWING MACHINE

All you need to make these quilts is a machine that can sew a straight stitch and a blanket or zigzag stitch. There are lots of extra features that are nice to have—such as a wide throat (the space between the needle and the body of the machine), a ¼″ foot, and a walking foot—but the stitches are the most important aspect of a machine.

MACHINE NEEDLES

My favorite needle sizes are a 75/11 for piecing and a 90/14 for quilting and binding. Larger needles penetrate thick layers more easily. Opt for quilting-specific needles when possible. They are built differently and will produce more accurate stitches and straighter seams.

PINS

I don't often use pins, but when I do, I prefer slim glass-head pins. I have melted too many cheap plastic pinheads under the hot steam of an iron! Appliqué pins work best because they are a little bit thinner and have sharper points, so they leave fewer marks in your fabric. A great alternative to pins, especially for bindings and holding thick layers together, are Wonder Clips. I use Clover brand.

Tutorial: Perfecting a ¼″ Seam

When piecing, it's essential to sew a precise ¼″ seam, or the quilt won't fit together as planned. Whether you are using a standard foot or an official "¼″ foot," measure the width of your seams before getting to work.

1. Place a piece of clear tape in front of the foot, just to the side of the feed dogs.

2. Place a clear acrylic ruler under the needle so that the ¼″ line is just to the left of the needle, and mark that on the tape with a fine-tip permanent marker. Let the mark dry completely.

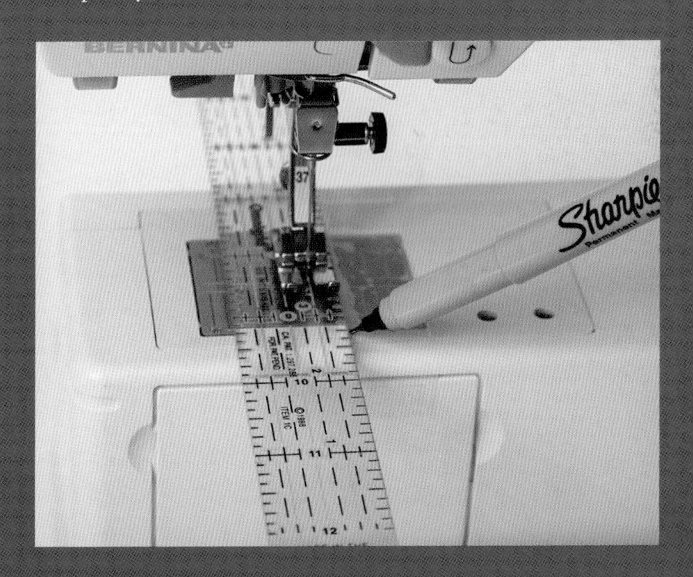

3. Cut 2 scraps 4″ × 2¼″ and sew them together along a long edge, lining up the raw edges with the drawn line.

4. Press the square with the seam allowance to one side, and measure the total width. If it measures exactly 4″, then you have a perfect scant ¼″. If it's less or more than 4″, replace the tape and test again until it's perfect.

ROTARY CUTTING SUPPLIES

A rotary cutter, acrylic grid ruler, and a self-healing cutting mat are a quilter's best trio. I use a 45 mm rotary cutter for straight cutting and a smaller 28 mm rotary cutter for curved shapes. Gridded rulers come in lots of different shapes and sizes. My go-to favorites are an 8½″ × 24″ long ruler and 6½″, 12½″, and 20½″ square rulers. I use the big one primarily for squaring up finished quilt tops. If possible, stick to one brand for consistency in the grids.

SCISSORS

A good pair of fabric scissors is the best tool for cutting out large appliqué pieces. Smaller shears that are sharp right to the tip are good for cutting out small appliqué pieces. Set aside a pair of scissors for cutting out templates and trimming paper. I have different-color handles for mine so I know which is which (and the family knows which is off limits), but it's handy to clearly label them.

IRONING

Most irons will tout the fact that they are lightweight, but heat, steam, and pressure get the best results. So while heavy irons may seem inconvenient, they actually allow you to press well with the least force on your part. Adjustable steam settings are a must, especially for paper piecing, since steam will warp the paper and can transfer the printed lines onto the ironing board. If you have the space, I recommend an extra-wide ironing board. The increased surface area allows you to press large blocks all at once or press larger sections of a finished quilt top.

THREAD

The types and varieties of thread available to quilters are enormous. Most of us already have our favorites, but here are a few tips and tricks to choosing the ideal thread for a project.

Fine weight My favorite piecing thread is Aurifil 50 weight. This fine thread contributes to the accuracy of scant ¼″ seams. I use the same fine-weight thread for stitching appliqués when I want the stitches to be invisible.

Medium-weight If I want the stitches to be more decorative and noticeable, I use a 40-weight or 30-weight thread. I will also use a thicker thread for quilting the tops and binding.

Heavyweight If I am doing any heavy decorative hand stitching or embroidery, a 12-weight thread is ideal. It is almost as thick as embroidery floss, but I find it twists less as I stitch and has a very nice sheen to it.

APPLIQUÉ TOOLS

Freezer paper I prefer freezer paper to plastic for making appliqué templates because it is super affordable, wide, and long—just pull the length you need from a roll! It's also easy to stick pieces together to make larger templates.

Marking pen Use a marker that won't run or bleed, such as a permanent marker, to trace the templates onto the paper.

Temporary spray adhesive Spray glue can hold large appliqué pieces in place without pins. Make sure the spray you choose is specifically designed for paper templates. I recommend testing on scraps before using it on your main fabric.

Quiltmaking Techniques

CUTTING FABRIC

To save time when cutting out projects, layer multiple fabrics on top of each other. This is especially effective when you are making large projects from lots of small fabric cuts. Make sure each piece is pressed and wrinkle free. Line up the folds of full yardage or the selvage edges when using fat quarters. Trim the raw edges straight across the width; then proceed to cut the pieces. Use a sharp, new blade, and cut no more than four layers at a time to prevent the fabric from slipping under the blade. When cutting a lot of pieces from a single fabric, match the raw edges on either side of the fabric to be sure of cutting four layers at once.

CHAIN PIECING

Chain piecing is a time-saving technique. To chain piece, sew together a pair of pieces; then—without cutting the thread—feed the next pair of pieces through the machine like an assembly line. Repeat until all the pairs have been sewn together. Chain piecing can be utilized everywhere during your quilt construction, even when paper piecing. It's much quicker than sewing each individual block before starting the next. I use it for almost everything I make!

NESTING SEAMS

Nesting refers to sewing together blocks so that the seams in each block face in opposite directions, creating a ridge. The ridges press against each other and prevent the fabric from slipping out of alignment when you sew. Once these blocks are sewn together, the seamlines match perfectly. I use nesting in place of pinning as a time-saver and only press the seams open when there will be a large group of seams meeting in one place. Follow the pressing directions given in each project to keep seams flat and nested.

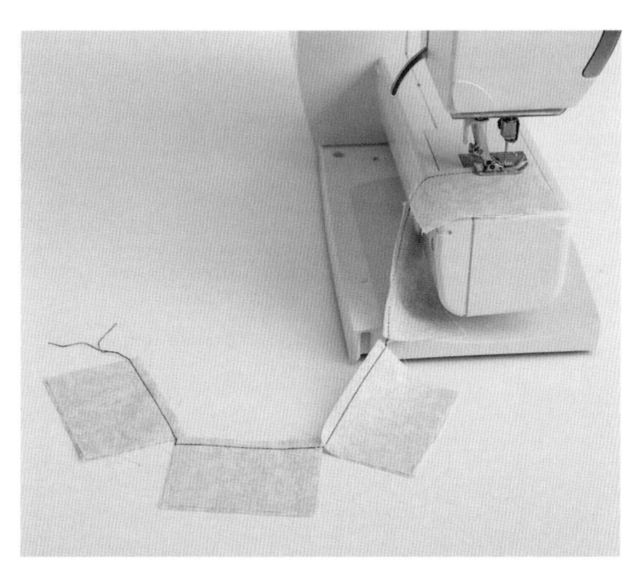

Chain piece whenever possible to save time.

Nested seams help keep blocks flat and aligned.

RAW-EDGE APPLIQUÉ

Simple and easy, raw-edge appliqué is the primary appliqué technique used for the projects in *Child's Play Quilts*.

1. Cut a piece of freezer paper large enough to cover the required pattern. To make the paper wider, overlap the shiny side of the added piece by ¼″ onto the paper side of the first piece and press the overlap with a warm iron.

2. Place the freezer paper over the master pattern with the shiny side down, and trace the pattern exactly as shown. Cut out the template around the drawn line using paper scissors. (*Note:* The patterns *do not* have seam allowances unless there is an overlapping edge, and those are marked with dotted lines.)

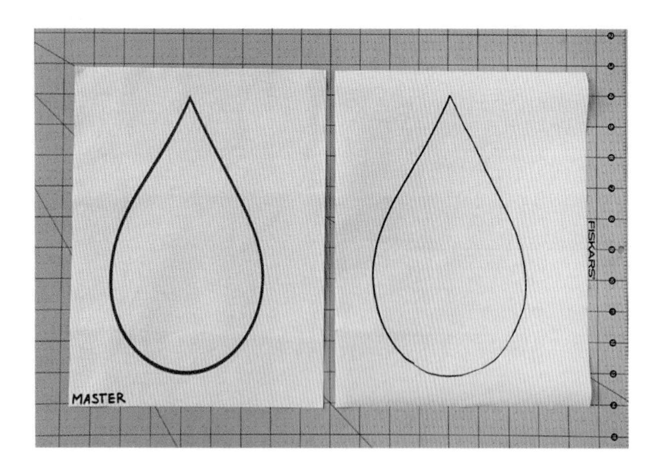

3. Place the fabric right side up on the ironing board, and press well to remove any wrinkles or folds. Set the iron on medium-low heat. Place the template on top of the fabric, shiny side down, and gently press. The template will adhere to the fabric.

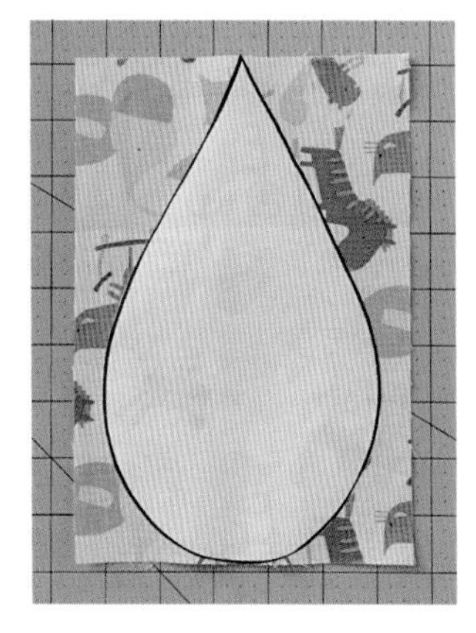

4. Using a small rotary cutter or fabric scissors, cut around the template. Gently peel the freezer paper from the fabric piece. Repeat until all the template pieces have been cut.

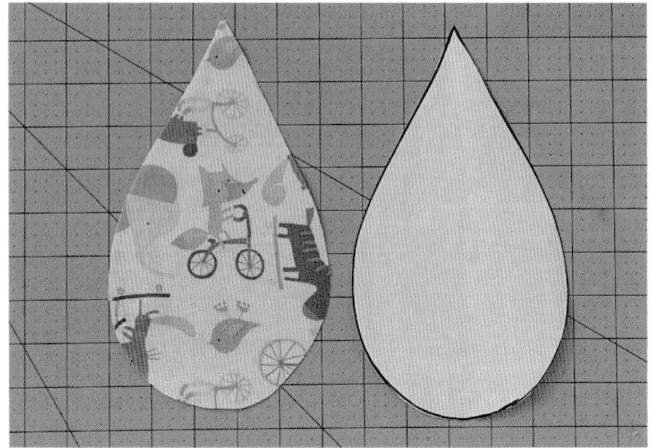

5. Pin the fabric pieces right side up to the background fabric or block. If you choose to use a light temporary adhesive spray, spray the wrong side of the fabric and then place it on the background fabric.

6. Sew the fabric piece to the background with a blanket stitch or a small zigzag stitch using matching or invisible thread.

APPLIQUÉ STITCH TIP

A blanket stitch is traditional, but my preferred finish for raw-edge appliqué is a small zigzag stitch done with a matching thread. Set the machine to the zigzag setting, decrease the stitch length to 1.5–2 mm, and increase the width to about 0.8 mm or 0.9 mm. Sew a test piece to check the zigzag, and make any adjustments. The fabric should feed evenly without the stitches bunching or the fabric beneath the thread pulling.

APPLIQUÉ THREAD TIP

Variegated thread is your best friend when it comes to raw-edge appliqué because it can reduce the number of thread changes needed for projects such as *Whirling* (page 55), which have a lot of different colors that need to be stitched down. I like using monochromatic (light-to-dark) and multicolored (rainbow) spools.

BORDERS

A couple quilts in this book have borders. The measurements and sewing order are included in the project instructions, but it's always wise to measure a top before adding borders to a quilt. Some length or width may have been lost during the squaring-up process.

1. Find the center of the quilt top. Measure across the width and record the measurement.

2. Trim the completed top and bottom border strips to match this actual measurement of width. Sew the borders to the quilt top and bottom as directed in the pattern. Then measure the length of the quilt top, including the borders just added, and cut the second set of borders to this measurement. Sew them to the sides of the quilt as directed in the pattern.

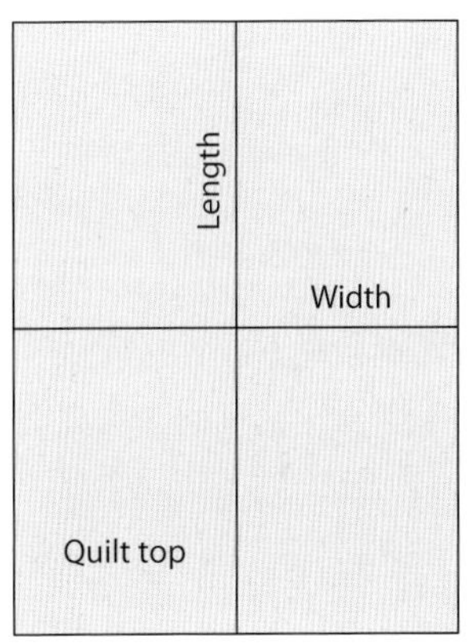

CURVED PIECING

Don't let this section scare you! Curved piecing is fun and easy. My favorite curved sewing method is the three-pin method.

1. Place the convex (outside) curve right side up on your worktable.

2. Clip the seam allowance of the concave (inside) curve ⅛", and place it right side down on the first piece, matching the centers of each piece. Pin the curved pieces together at the center; then pin together the ends at the seam allowance.

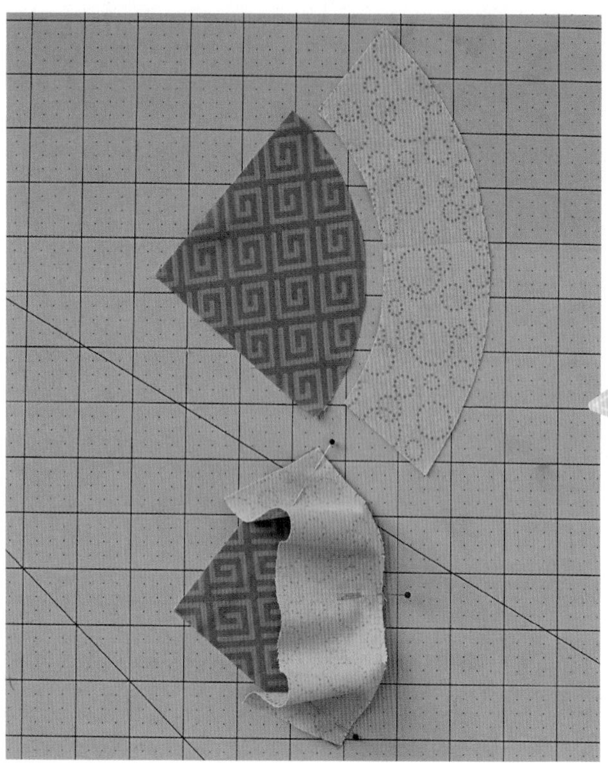

Pin together the opposing curves with three pins.

3. Sew a straight seam for ¼". Then start easing the concave curve to the convex curve as you sew, carefully smoothing out any puckers and keeping the raw edges aligned with the machine foot. Sew straight again for the last ¼".

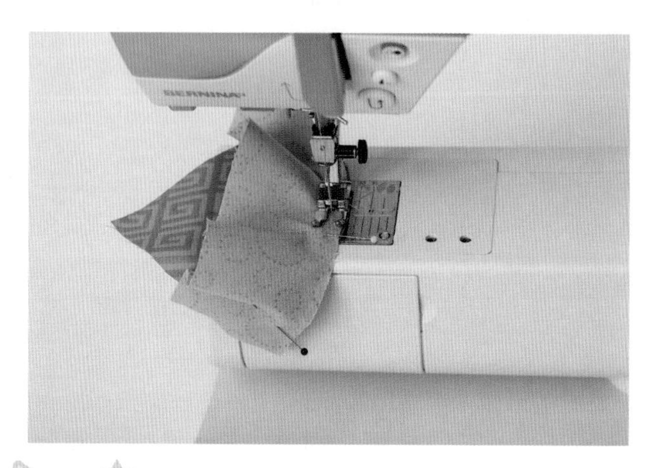

TIP

Stop and Adjust

You may need to stop with the needle down to readjust and realign the pieces many times as you sew together the curves. This is normal. Practice on some scrap pieces first.

There is only one project that uses curved piecing in this book. If you really don't want to sew those curves, you can always appliqué them.

Finishing Touches

The Quilt Sandwich

The quilt sandwich consists of three pieces—a layer of batting sandwiched between a backing and the quilt top. The batting and backing should be at least 4″ larger all around than the quilt top; some longarm quilters prefer 5″.

Batting

Batting is the body of a quilt. Choosing a batting can be the easiest decision to make or the hardest. Many quilters have a favorite they use as a default no matter what, and sometimes there are very limited options available at the local quilt shop. But when it comes to baby quilts there are special factors to consider, such as weight, warmth, and hypoallergenic properties.

Bamboo batting is one of the best for baby quilts. It is naturally antibacterial, super absorbent, lightweight, and warm. It can be paired with wool or polyester loft batting to add "poof" to your quilts, but on its own bamboo is wonderful. A bamboo batting paired with a minky backing is the ultimate absorber and washes very well, too—making this combination perfect for when those little accidents happen. Bamboo has very minimal shrink.

TIP

Bamboo is naturally hypoallergenic, but if a baby or child has severe allergies or asthma, polyester is the way to go. Polyester does not create any dust particles.

Cotton is another great natural option. It comes in different thicknesses, making it perfect for adding a little weight to a quilt without adding too much bulk. It is warm and durable, can be paired with wool or polyester on top for texture, and comes in various blends (including cotton and bamboo).

TIP

Author's Choice

For my quilts, I primarily use Warm & Plush batting by The Warm Company. It is thicker than the typical battings available and quilts really well on both my domestic and TinLizzie18 longarm machines. I also use Quilters Dream Cotton batting, which comes in three different thicknesses and a bamboo option. It quilts up very nicely, and I like the flexibility that comes with the weight and thickness options. My kiddo enjoys weight when he is sleeping, and he sleeps with at least three quilts. I find that both Warm & Plush and Quilters Dream Cotton battings are heavy enough to satisfy him, and he stays just as warm with either.

Backing

The backing for your quilts can be a single fabric, multiple prints, flannel, minky … anything! I tend to stick with minky for baby quilts. Minky comes in a 60″ width and doesn't have to be prewashed. Because it has a bit of stretch, use an adhesive spray to baste together the layers. Wash the finished quilt before gifting to be sure the spray is removed.

Flannels make great backings but should always be prewashed because they *do* shrink—some quite considerably. Flannels are heavier than plain cotton, very warm, and soft after washing. Corduroy is similar to flannel; some fabric companies make lightweight fine-wale cords that are perfect for backing baby quilts. Corduroy is durable, which makes it great for floor quilts and play quilts.

Backings can be pieced or made of wholecloth if the fabric is wide enough. Pieced backings may be made all of one print (which is my preference) or from multiple prints, sometimes incorporating blocks from the front.

For projects that will be finished on a longarm machine, it is best to use horizontal seams on your backing rather than vertical. When a quilt backing is rolled onto the bars of a longarm, vertical seams roll as three layers instead of one, creating a ridge of tight tension in the center and loose floppy fabric at the ends. The distortion isn't as noticeable in small quilts, but horizontal seams are much preferred (and appreciated) by longarm quilters.

Basting

There are many ways to baste a quilt successfully—sprays, safety pins, or running stitches. For most of the projects in this book, a light spray baste or safety pins every 4″–6″ will work well. These quilts are small enough to fit on a long table or the floor. Check your batting brand for basting recommendations—some brands do not recommend the use of spray baste because it can pull the layers of cotton apart if you need to reposition the quilt layers.

TIP Clean the surface you intend to use for basting. No one wants leftover PB and J stuck to the back of a quilt!

Basting a quilt properly does take both space and time, but it is well worth the effort. A properly basted quilt sandwich will remain stable when stitched, and none of the layers will pucker. If you don't have space to baste a bigger quilt on the floor, use a table and baste in sections.

The trick to successful basting is applying and maintaining tension on each layer. This is where painter's tape comes in handy.

HOLD THE LAYERS TAUT WITH TAPE

1. Cut the backing and batting so that each extends 4″ beyond each side of the quilt top.

2. Press the backing well to remove any stubborn creases, and place it wrong side up on the work surface.

3. Tape the top of the backing to the work surface in this order: center, left, and right. For large quilts, add pieces of tape midway between the center and side pieces.

4. From the bottom, pull the backing taut—but not tight—and tape the bottom down in the same order: center, left, and right. Add additional pieces if needed.

5. Tape the sides in the same way as the top and bottom: starting in the center, fixing the corners, and finishing in between. The backing should lie flat and be wrinkle free.

SPRAY, PIN, OR SEW

You're now ready to baste. There are several methods.

Spray Baste

1. Place the batting on top of the secured backing. Tape the bottom in place.

2. Fold the top of the batting back in half to expose the backing. Apply the spray to the backing following the manufacturer's instructions. Lift the batting from the bottom of the quilt and carefully fold it back to the top of the quilt so that there is slight tension on the batting. Lay it back down on the backing so that it sits flat and there are no wrinkles. Tape the top in place, and press the batting down against the backing, starting in the center and working outwards.

3. Repeat for the bottom half.

4. Place the quilt top right side up on the batting, making sure there is about 4″ of batting visible around all the raw edges. Spray baste the quilt top in the same manner as the batting.

5. Attach safety pins about 4″ apart around the perimeter of your quilt top, about 1″ from the raw edge.

Use Safety Pins

1. Tape and layer the batting and quilt top right side up in the same manner as you taped down the backing (see Hold the Layers Taut with Tape, previous page).

2. Place pins through all the layers about 3″ or 4″ apart. Align the pins so that the openings are facing the same direction and every other row is staggered. Use the width of your palm as a guide for how far apart to pin. Start in the center. Pin your way up to the top and then down to the bottom along the midline.

3. Work horizontally from the center of the quilt to the sides and then from the center to each corner. Continue pinning horizontally and vertically across the quilt sandwich until the entire top is pinned.

> **TIP** You may find it helpful to keep your pins open until the entire top is done; that way you can easily readjust as necessary.

Hand Sew

Using a running stitch, or hand basting, is the tried-and-true method for basting a quilt.

1. Sandwich and secure the layers the same way you did with the batting, with the quilt top right side up on top.

2. Sew basting stitches with a long, thin upholstery needle and brightly contrasting thread. Silk thread works very well because it is smooth and easily removed. Place 1″ stitches about 3″ or 4″ apart. Use the width of your palm as a placement guide.

3. Tie a knot in the thread to keep it secured, and keep a long tail so the knot is easy to locate.

4. Start stitching in the center of the quilt. Work in a straight line from the center to the top and then the center to the bottom. Next, work horizontally from the center of the quilt to the sides and then from the center to each corner. Continue stitching horizontally and vertically across the quilt sandwich until the entire top is basted.

> **TIP** Many longarm quilters will baste your quilts with a long running stitch for you.

Quilting

Deciding how to quilt a finished sandwich can be really difficult for any quilter. I am lucky to have a beautiful longarm machine, and still I struggle—custom or pantograph, simple or complex? Too many options!

Sometimes it works to let a quilt speak, to let it "tell" you what it wants. But be practical, too—especially when it comes to quilts for babies and children. Consider how much time you really want to spend. Hours of custom quilting and ruler work on a baby quilt might just render it too fancy for normal use. A simple allover design that lets the quilt design be the focus will hold up great under toddler wear and tear, and it may be a better choice.

Keep It Simple

Simple stitching designs on a baby quilt are more effective because they don't take away from the pieced design.

Another consideration is comfort. The more stitching there is, the stiffer a quilt gets, regardless of batting choice. A very small, dense quilting motif will produce a baby quilt that looks and acts like cardboard. A loose, flowing motif with lots of open spaces will drape wonderfully and feel softer. Most battings only need to be quilted 6″ apart, so don't be afraid to go big.

Binding

The final step is to finish the raw edges of a quilt. The most common method is to use a double-fold binding with mitered corners, but you can also use a single-fold binding. Either can be cut on the grain or on the bias.

Binding can add a striking decorative element while sealing up the raw edges of a quilt and framing the top. I love to play with the bindings and finishing on baby quilts. Curved corners, scallops, and multicolored bindings are all great ways to add small details and big effects to baby quilts.

Photo by Stacey Day

TIP

Leftover binding strips and batting pieces can be given new life in baby quilts. Sew together binding strip scraps to create new and surprising color mixes.

My go-to favorite is a straight-grain double-fold binding. Straight-grain bindings cut fast, look neat, and fold into crisp miters. The binding is sewn after the quilt sandwich has been quilted and trimmed.

STACEY'S FOOLPROOF BINDING

1. Cut enough 2¼″ binding strips to go around the quilt, plus an extra 15″–20″. Sew together all the binding strips on the diagonal, and press the seams open.

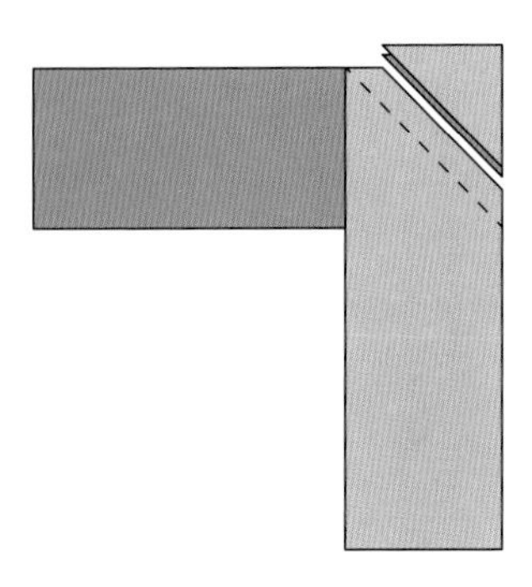

2. Square the quilt by trimming the raw edges of the top, batting, and backing even using a large square ruler. Start in the corner and work around the quilt, leaving enough of the seam allowance to fill the binding. For a 2¼″ double-fold binding, ¼″ is sufficient. Baste around the outside of the quilt to secure the raw edges if needed.

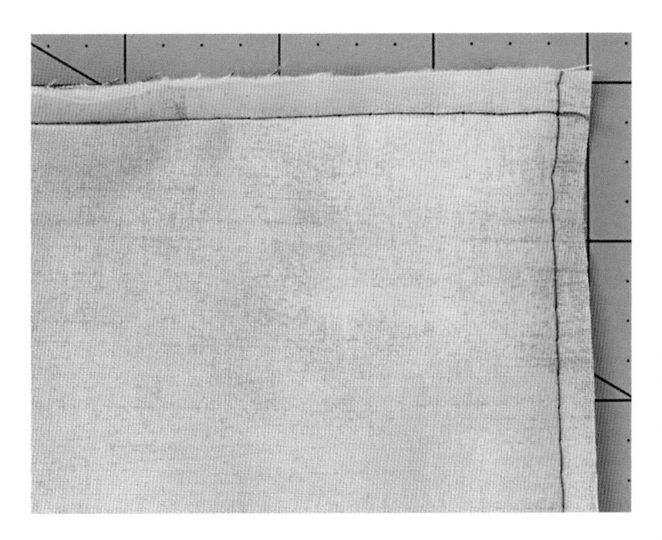

3. Fold the binding in half lengthwise, wrong sides together. Align the raw edges of the binding with the edges of the quilt top, leaving an 8″ tail above the starting point. Start around the middle of a side. Take 2 or 3 backstitches and sew the binding to the quilt, matching the raw edges of the binding and quilt. Stop stitching ¼″ from the edge of the quilt. With the needle in the down position, lift the presser foot and rotate the quilt until the corner is facing you. Stitch off the edge of the quilt at the corner.

4. Turn the quilt and fold the binding back on itself at a 45° angle so the binding is parallel to the raw edge of the quilt. The stitches in the corner will keep the binding lined up and the angle accurate.

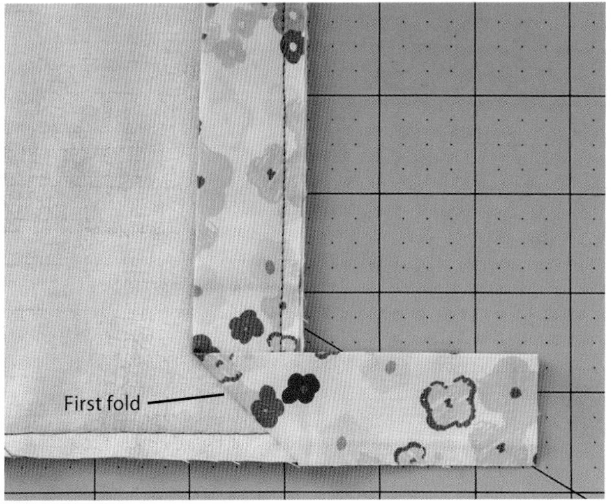

5. Fold the binding back down so there is a new fold parallel with the top corner and the binding is lined up with the edge of the quilt again. Start sewing from the top, backstitching 1 or 2 stitches to secure the corners.

6. Continue sewing around the quilt top, repeating Steps 4 and 5 at each of the corners, until you get about 15″ from the start. Stop and backstitch 2 or 3 stitches.

7. Arrange the quilt so the tails are facing you. Align the left-hand tail with the raw edge of the quilt; open the binding and pin it in place. Open the right-hand tail and place it on top. Pin the ends to the quilt.

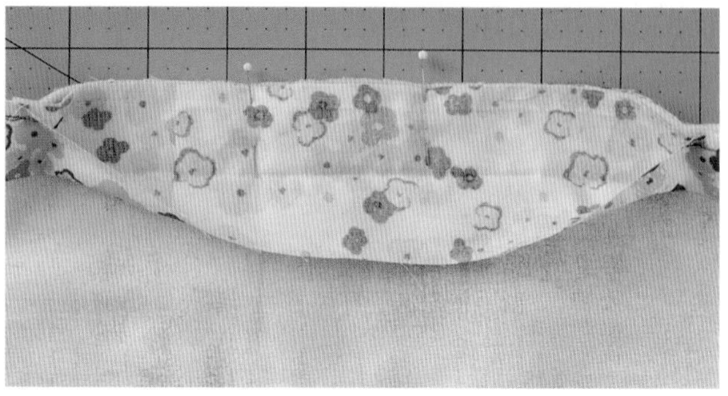

8. Draw a 45° line on the right-hand tail, midway between the end and the stitching. Cut only the right-hand tail on this line.

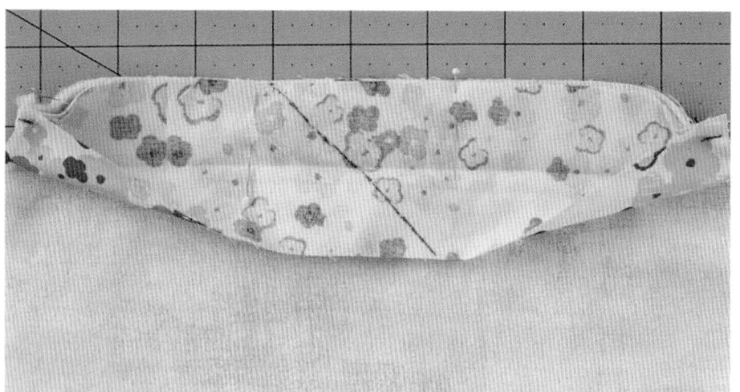

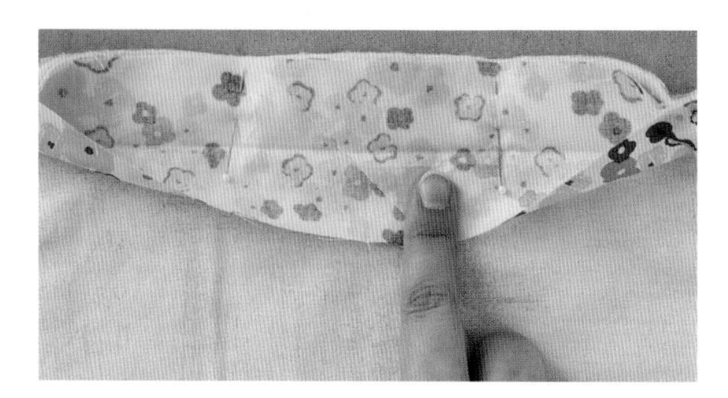

9. Place the tail back down, and trace the cut line on the left tail. Add a ½″ seam allowance to the right side of that line. Cut the left tail on the new line.

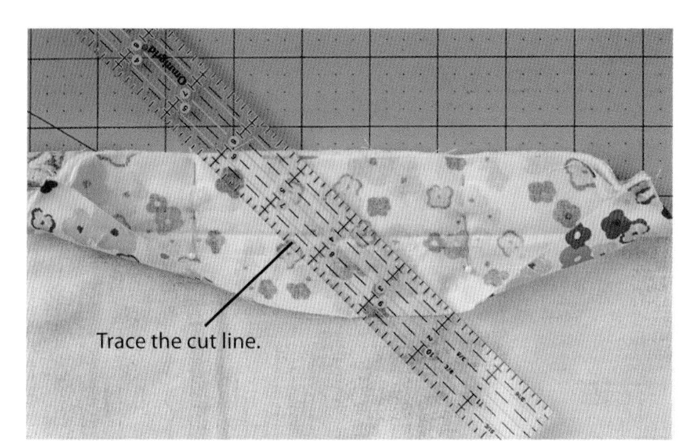

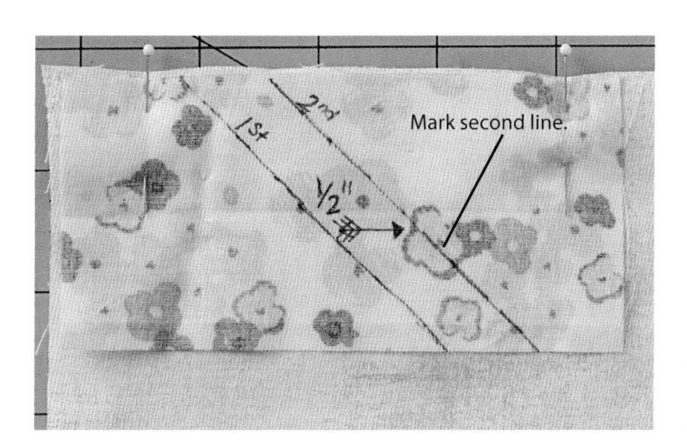

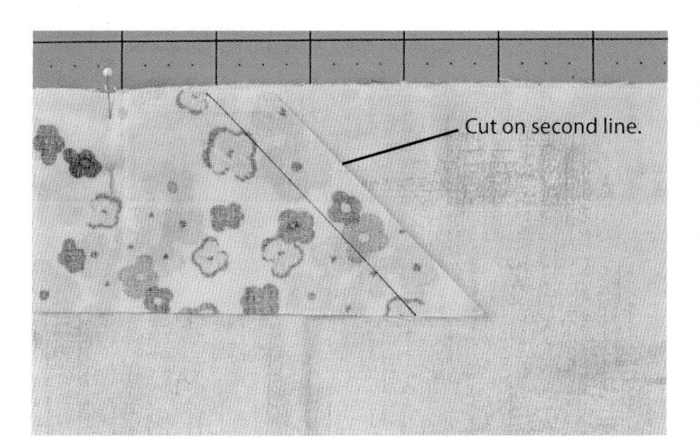

10. Pin the binding right sides together, making sure there are no kinks or twists in the strip and matching the centers and ends. Sew the tails together using a ¼″ seam allowance.

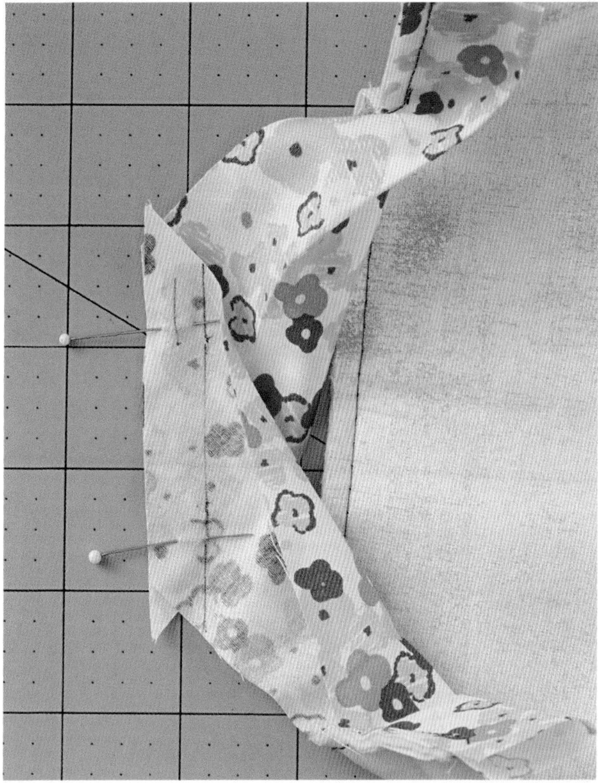

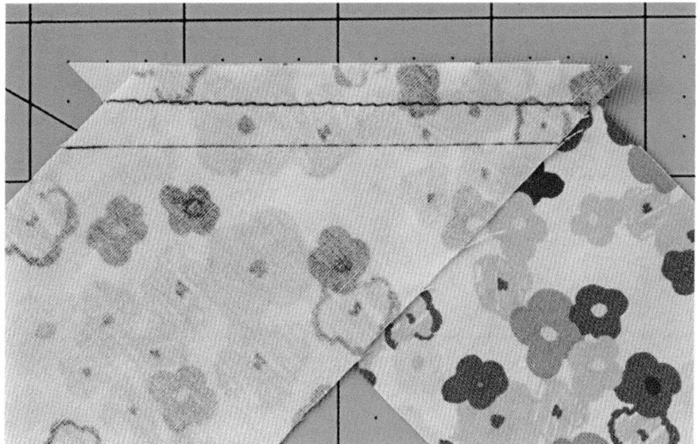

11. Press the seam allowance open. Check to make sure the binding sits flat and smooth on the quilt top. Finish sewing the binding to the quilt.

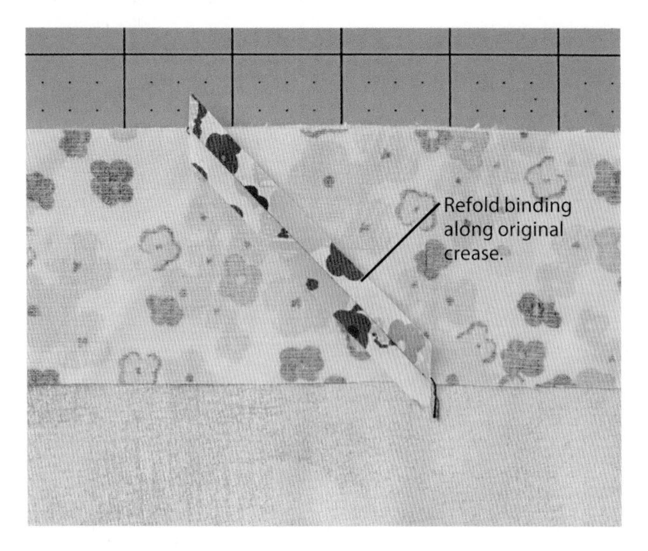

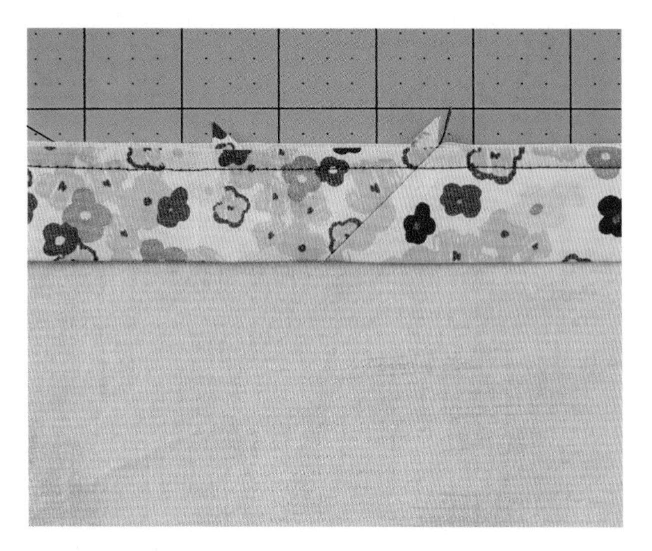

12. Using a steam iron, press the binding flat. Flip the quilt to the back side, wrap the binding over the raw edge, and press, making sure the fold of the binding extends slightly past the stitching. Use clips to hold the binding in place if desired.

13. Machine or hand sew the binding to the back of the quilt.

Little Details

Here are some fun and practical ideas for adding extra details to personalize your projects and set them apart!

CURVED EDGES

Ever been poked in the eye with the corner of a quilt that was being whipped around at top speed by a toddler? I have! So now I often curve the corners of baby quilts. You don't need to make the curves too steep; the base of a large spool of thread is sufficient to blunt a corner. You can use a normal-width binding and either straight-grain or bias binding for such small curves. Straight grain will make the corners curl slightly, and bias will keep the quilt lying flat. A large curve needs to have bias binding in order for the binding to lie flat and smooth.

SCALLOPED EDGES

Scalloped edges require a bias binding, either single or double fold. Scallops will eat up a lot of the raw edges or borders of the quilt top, so you may want to add a 4″ border or extend the existing borders by 2″–4″ so the quilt maintains its finished size. I like an easy scallop where I don't have to miter the inside corners.

1. Calculate the number of scallops that will fit on each side of a quilt by measuring the edges of the top and finding a number that divides equally into each. A large number will make lots of little scallops, and a small number will make big scallops. Let's use 6″ for our example, as it divides equally into a 48″ × 60″ quilt.

2. Mark division lines with a removable-ink marking pen, starting in the corners (solid black lines in the photo below Step 3, next page). Mark the center of each division (black dotted lines): This is where the apex of the curve will be. In the corners, the apex is between the raw edge and the first division line.

3. Find a rounded object, such as a glass or a plate, that will fit between the lines, or hand draw a paper template. It doesn't need to be a perfect fit; you only need a consistent shape for the curves. Trace around the object or template with a removable-ink fabric pen so that the ends of each scallop meet at the division lines.

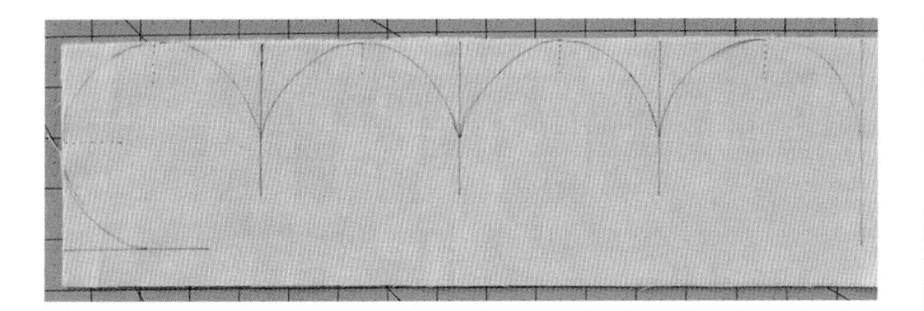

4. Find a smaller rounded object, like a thread spool. Place it at the point where the scallop lines meet so that the edges of the spool are touching the lines on either side. Trace under the spool, joining the scallop lines with a gentle curve.

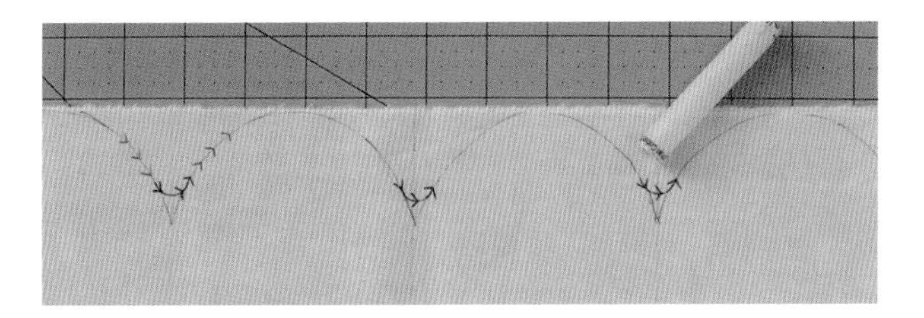

5. Baste ¼″ inside the drawn scallop around the entire perimeter of the quilt top. Cut the scallops out on the drawn line.

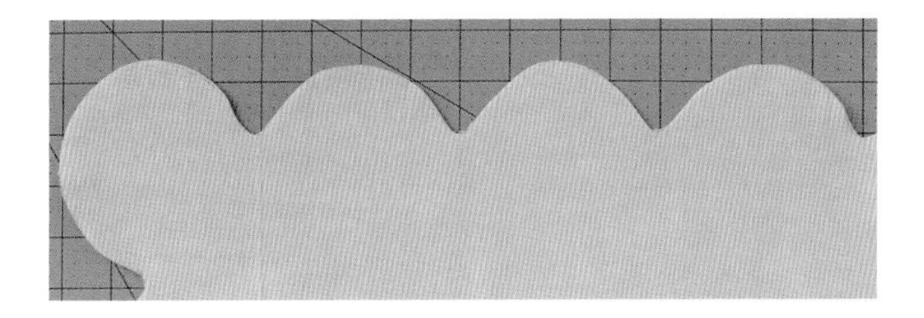

6. Using bias strips, sew the binding to the quilt top by easing the binding around the curved edges. Avoid pulling the binding tight as you sew—you won't have enough "give" in the fold once you turn it to the back. Press the binding out and to the back, easing the curves; then finish by sewing the binding in place by hand.

COLORBOMB BINDINGS

These are super fun and easy to make. Add a splash of color to an otherwise plain binding by inserting a fabric strip of a different color. Cut the binding strip on an angle somewhere (away from the quilt corners), and insert a strip of brightly colored fabric using diagonal seams. Add a single bomb or several to a project. Colorbombs have a particularly big effect when the primary binding fabric matches the background.

Colorbomb on the edge of *Gumdrops* (page 59)

Labels

Labels are a very important part of a baby quilt. Not only do they provide the name of the quiltmaker and the date the quilt was finished, but they can also be used to record birth details such as date, location, and weight. They might feature poems, sayings, well-wishes, bible verses, or anything else that adds meaning and love to a quilt.

Embroidered labels generally last longer than penned ones. For written ones, seek out archival ink because it won't wash away or fade over time. If you place labels in a corner such that two sides extend underneath the binding, they will be extra secure. Finish the edges that aren't under the binding before sewing the binding to the back of the quilt.

APPLIQUÉ PROJECTS

The projects in this section are made of slabs, scraps, or a combination of both. No need to choose one or the other; have fun mixing it up! Note that the yardage listed is provided as a reference—it is the amount required to cut the pieces from a single fabric. Use it as a guideline when making quilts with slabs and scraps. Each appliqué quilt that is suitable for slabs lists the minimum required number and size of slabs in the fabric requirements, so you can be sure you won't run short when cutting out all the pieces.

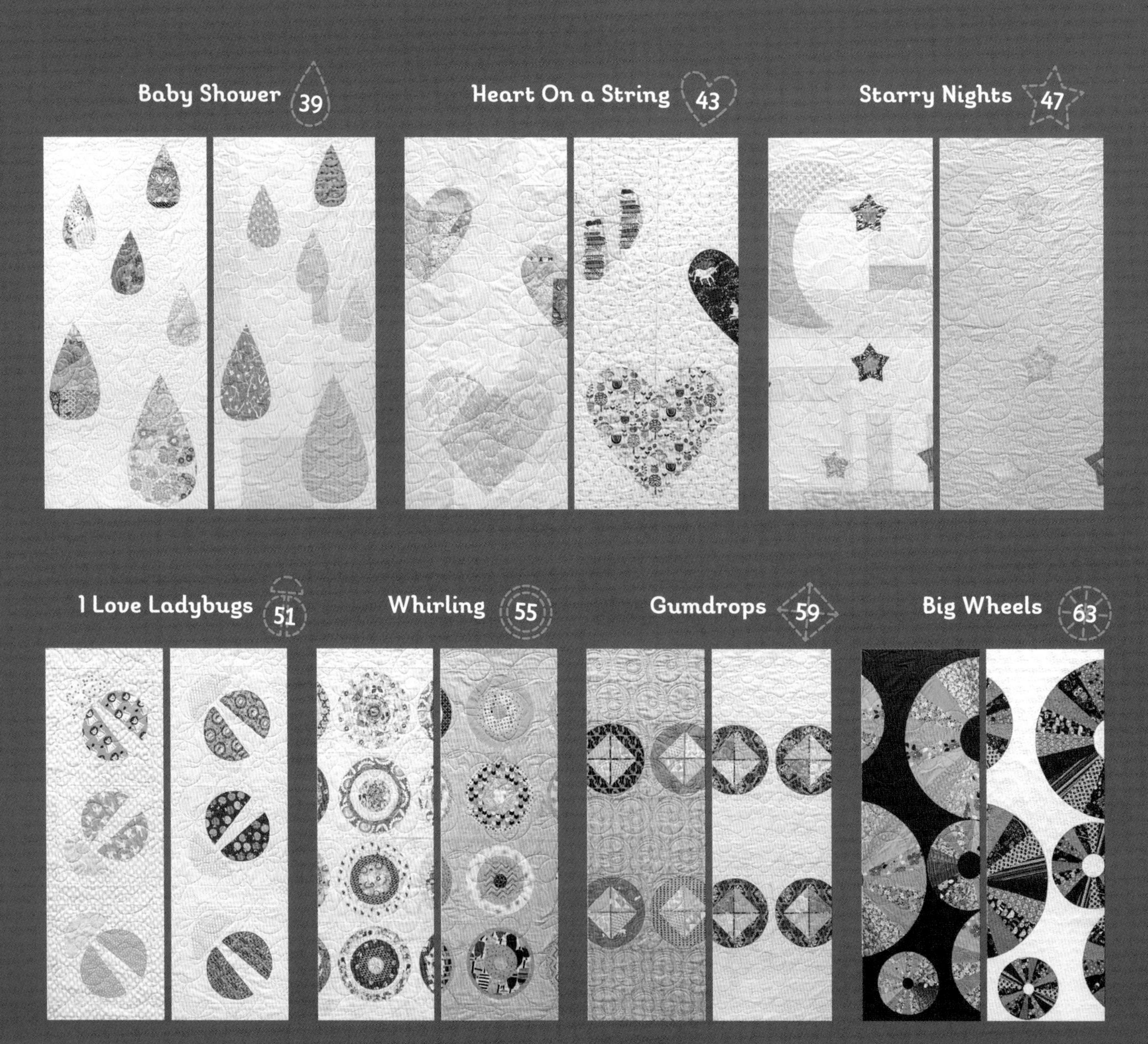

Baby Shower

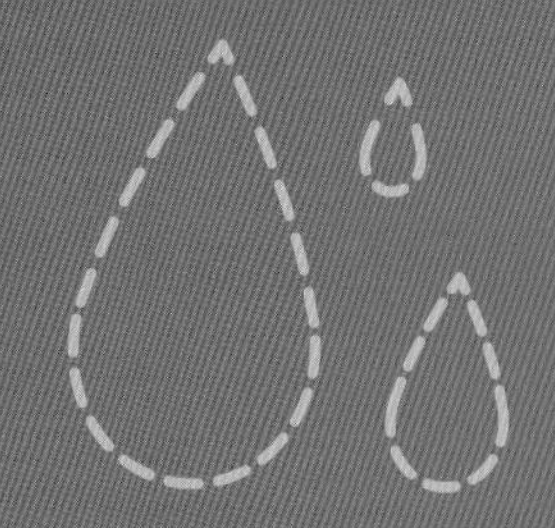

FINISHED QUILT: 48″ × 60″

Pieced by Stacey Day and quilted by Miriam March

Every new baby deserves a quilt! It's a great gift to bring to a meet-the-baby party, where the new arrival is showered with gifts, love, and snuggles while the new (or new-again) mom is showered with love, advice, freezer foods, and helping hands. Pass along some love by giving a quilt featuring carefully hoarded fabrics or favorite scraps.

MATERIALS

Yardage is based on 42″-wide fabric. To use scraps instead of yardage, make slabs in the given dimensions from fabrics in the specified colors. For detailed instructions on this technique, refer to Slabs (page 20).

BACKGROUND: 2¼ yards of off-white *or* 20 slabs 12½″ × 12½″

FABRIC A: 1 fat quarter of medium pink *or* 1 slab 18″ × 22″

FABRIC B: 1 fat quarter of light purple *or* 1 slab 18″ × 22″

FABRIC C: 1 fat quarter of medium purple *or* 1 slab 16½″ × 16½″

FABRIC D: ¼ yard or 1 fat quarter of light pink *or* 1 slab 11″ × 12″

FABRIC E: ¼ yard or 1 fat quarter of yellow *or* 1 slab 13″ × 13″

BINDING: ½ yard

BACKING: 3¼ yards

BATTING: 56″ × 68″

TIP

Raindrop Fun

The raindrops are perfect for fussy cutting from your favorite prints. Have fun combining slabs with solid pieces for a truly unique look.

CUTTING

BACKGROUND (YARDAGE)

- Cut 1 rectangle 40½″ × 60½″.
- Cut 2 rectangles 8½″ × 30½″.

FABRIC A

- Cut 1 of raindrop 4.
- Cut 1 of raindrop 1.

FABRIC B

- Cut 1 of raindrop 4.
- Cut 1 of raindrop 1.

FABRIC C

- Cut 1 of raindrop 3.
- Cut 1 of raindrop 1.

FABRIC D

- Cut 2 of raindrop 1.

FABRIC E

- Cut 1 of raindrop 2.
- Cut 1 of raindrop 1.

BINDING

- Cut 6 strips 2¼″ × 42″.

Making the Quilt

1. Sew together the background pieces, referring to the layout diagram for either full yardage or slabs. Press well.

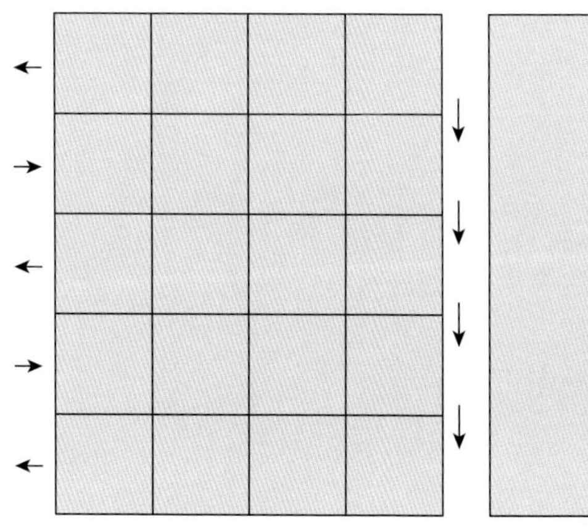

12½″ squares layout

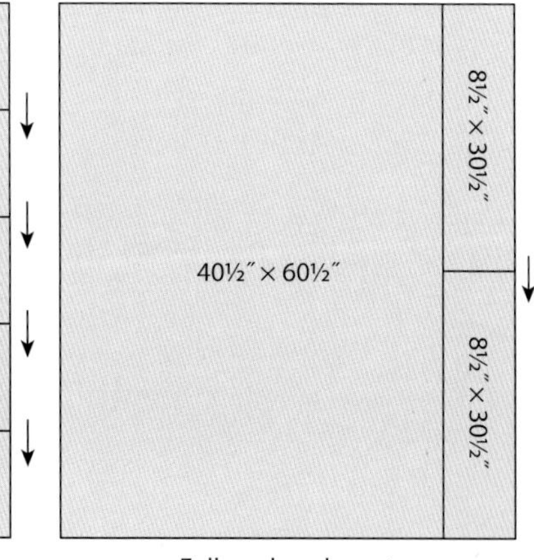

Full yardage layout

Assemble the background using the appropriate layout. Arrows indicate pressing direction.

2. Carefully pin the raindrops in place on the background, following the placement diagram. Make sure the raindrops are smooth and there are no puckers in the background fabric underneath. Spray lightly with temporary adhesive spray to stabilize the raindrops.

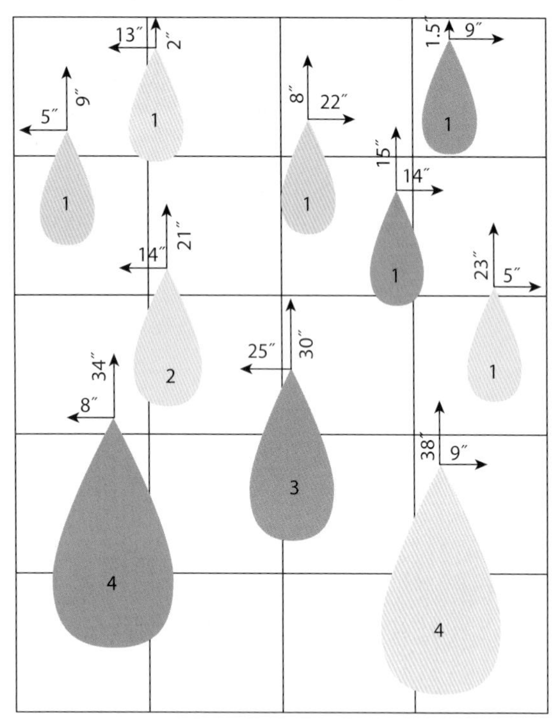

Raindrops placement

3. Sew around each raindrop to secure it to the background piece, using a matching thread and your preferred appliqué stitch. (I used a blanket stitch.)

FINISHING THE QUILT

For detailed instructions on backing, layering, quilting, and binding, refer to Finishing Touches (page 29).

1. Cut and piece the backing fabric so it is 8″ wider and longer than the quilt top. Layer the quilt top with the batting and backing. Baste together the layers.

2. Hand or machine quilt as desired.

3. Square up the quilt sandwich.

4. Prepare and sew the binding to the quilt. Add your label and enjoy!

Cool It Down!

I used some fat quarters I had stashed away from an older collection for this quilt. I wanted to feature the owl, but it was only a small strip, so I turned it into a slab using similar shades of green. To make *Baby Shower* in blues and greens, substitute with these fabrics. Follow the rest of the project instructions as given.

Baby Shower, 48″ × 60″, pieced by Stacey Day and quilted by Miriam March

Background: 2½ yards of off-white

Fabric A: 1 fat quarter of medium green

Fabric B: 1 fat quarter of light turquoise

Fabric C: 1 fat quarter of medium turquoise

Fabric D: ¼ yard or 1 fat quarter of light green

Fabric E: ¼ yard or 1 fat quarter of yellow

Heart on a String

FINISHED QUILT: 48″ × 60″

Pieced by Stacey Day and quilted by Miriam March

The feeling you get when you hold a new baby for the first time is indescribable, whether it's your own child, a grandchild, or a niece or nephew. One look from those bright, new eyes ties strings of love around your heart, and you are forever both lost and found. As they grow, those children will continue to tug on those little heartstrings for better and for worse. Give them a quilt just as special as they are, made from your favorite pieces of fabric and scraps.

MATERIALS

Yardage is based on 42″-wide fabric. To use scraps instead of yardage, make slabs in the given dimensions from fabrics in the specified colors. For detailed instructions on this technique, refer to Slabs (page 20).

BACKGROUND: 2½ yards of ivory *or* 20 slabs 12½″ × 12½″

FABRIC A: 1 fat quarter of light green *or* 1 slab 15″ × 15″

FABRIC B: 1 fat quarter of aqua *or* 1 slab 15″ × 15″

FABRIC C: ⅝ yard of yellow *or* 1 slab 20″ × 20″

BINDING: ½ yard

BACKING: 3¼ yards

BATTING: 56″ × 68″

FUN TIPS

The heartstrings on the quilt can be sewn by machine or by hand. If you are using a machine, try a 28-weight or 30-weight cotton thread paired with a fine metallic thread. Place the thicker thread on the vertical spool holder and the fine thread on the horizontal spool holder, gently twist together the ends, and thread both through the machine at the same time. Increase the stitch length to 3–3.5 mm.

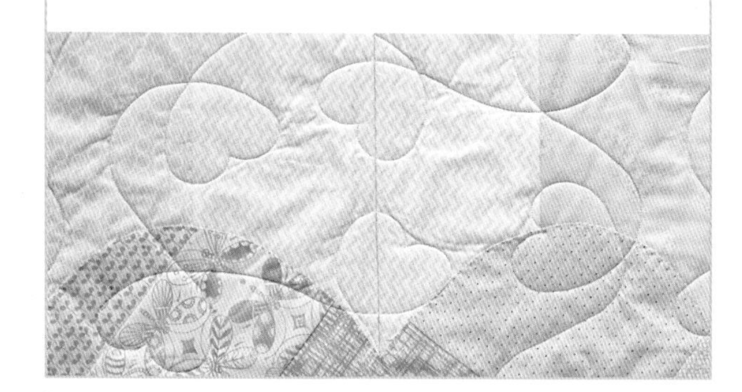

CUTTING

BACKGROUND (YARDAGE)

- Cut 1 rectangle 40½″ × 60½″.
- Cut 2 rectangles 8½″ × 30½″.

FABRIC A

- Cut 1 of heart 1.

FABRIC B

- Cut 1 of heart 1.

FABRIC C

- Cut 1 of heart 2.

BINDING

- Cut 6 strips 2¼″ × 42″.

Making the Quilt

1. Sew together the background pieces, referring to the layout diagram for either full yardage or slabs. Press well.

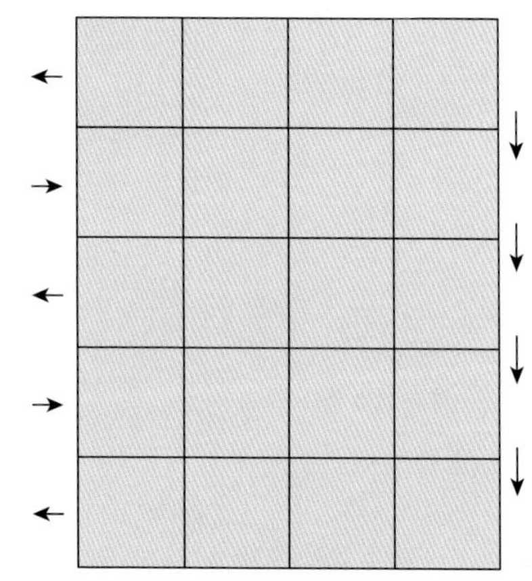

12½″ squares layout

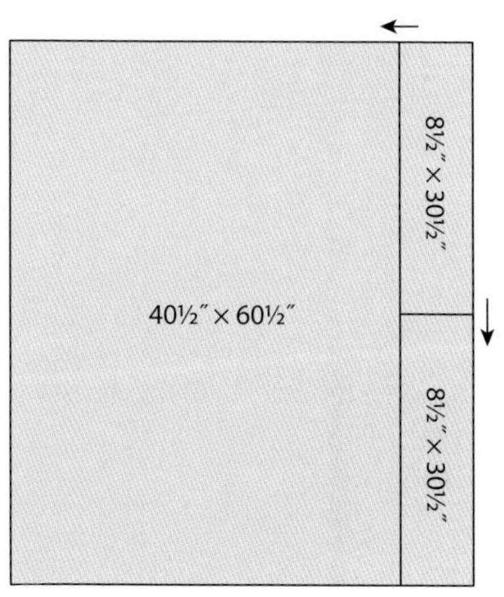

Full yardage layout

Assemble the background using the appropriate layout. Arrows indicate pressing direction.

2. Carefully pin the hearts in place on the background, following the placement diagram. Make sure the hearts are smooth and there are no puckers in the background fabric underneath. Spray lightly with temporary adhesive to stabilize the hearts.

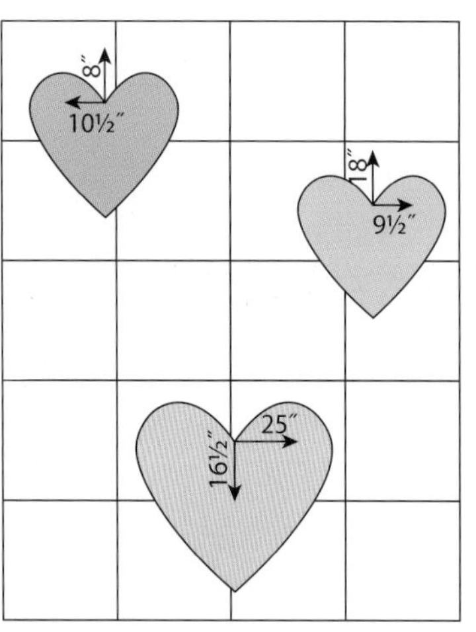

Hearts placement

3. Sew around each heart to secure it to the background piece, using matching thread and your preferred appliqué stitch.

4. Hand or machine sew a straight line from the top of the heart to the top of the quilt using a heavyweight contrasting thread and a longer stitch length.

FINISHING THE QUILT

For detailed instructions on finishing techniques, refer to Finishing Touches (page 29).

1. Cut and piece the backing fabric so it is 8″ wider and longer than the quilt top. Layer the quilt top with the batting and backing. Baste together the layers.

2. Hand or machine quilt as desired.

3. Square up the quilt sandwich.

4. Prepare and sew the binding to the quilt. Add your label and enjoy!

TIP Add a heart-shaped label to the back of the quilt for a special touch!

Warm It Up!

Using unique large-scale prints for each heart and a single-print background gives you the opportunity to fussy cut. I used some of my favorite fat quarters to fussy cut around the princess and the unicorns. To make *Heart on a String* sporting hearts in shades of red and pink, substitute these fabrics. Follow the rest of the project instructions as given.

Heart on a String, 48″ × 60″, pieced by Stacey Day and quilted by Miriam March

Background: 2½ yards of cream

Fabric A: 1 fat quarter of plum

Fabric B: 1 fat quarter of fuchsia

Fabric C: ⅝ yard of light pink

Starry Nights

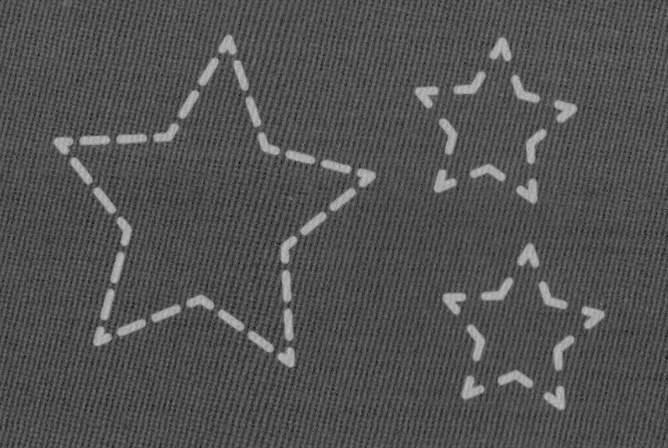

FINISHED QUILT: 50″ × 60″

Pieced by Stacey Day and quilted by Miriam March

There is something magical about a starry night sky that fires the imagination of children young and old. Stars are constant fixtures in an ever-changing world. Looking at the night sky, it's easy to believe that anything is possible. I love that in twenty years, when my son is grown, I can look up at the night sky and gaze at the same stars we watched together from our porch when he was little.

MATERIALS

Yardage is based on 42″-wide fabric. To use scraps instead of yardage, make slabs in the given dimensions from fabrics in the specified colors. For detailed instructions on this technique, refer to Slabs (page 20).

BACKGROUND: 2½ yards of off-white *or* 30 slabs 10½″ × 10½″

FABRIC A: ⅝ yard of yellow *or* 1 slab 20″ × 27″

FABRIC B: ⅜ yard or 1 fat quarter of medium coral *or* 1 slab 11″ × 16″

FABRIC C: ¼ yard or 1 fat quarter of medium fuchsia *or* 1 slab 11″ × 20″

FABRIC D: 1 fat quarter of light pink *or* 1 slab 6″ × 11″

FABRIC E: 1 fat eighth of warm olive *or* 1 slab 8″ × 8″

FABRIC F: 1 fat eighth of lime *or* 1 slab 4″ × 8″

FABRIC G: ⅛ yard or 1 fat eighth of light lime *or* 1 slab 3″ × 6″

BINDING: ½ yard

BACKING: 3⅜ yards

BATTING: 58″ × 68″

FUN TIPS

Both *Starry Nights* quilts are made using a complementary color theme. The inside and outside star colors are opposite each other on the color wheel—this makes the quilts bold and exciting. For a softer look, use colors that are beside each other on the color wheel.

CUTTING

BACKGROUND (YARDAGE)

- Cut 1 rectangle 40½″ × 60½″.
- Cut 2 rectangles 10½″ × 30½″.

FABRIC A

- Cut 1 moon.

FABRIC B

- Cut 3 of star 3.

FABRIC C

- Cut 2 of star 2.

FABRIC D

- Cut 2 of star 1.

FABRIC E

- Cut 3 of star center 3.

FABRIC F

- Cut 2 of star center 2.

FABRIC G

- Cut 2 of star center 1.

BINDING

- Cut 6 strips 2¼″ × 42″.

Making the Quilt

1. Sew together the background pieces, referring to the layout diagram for either full yardage or slabs. Press well.

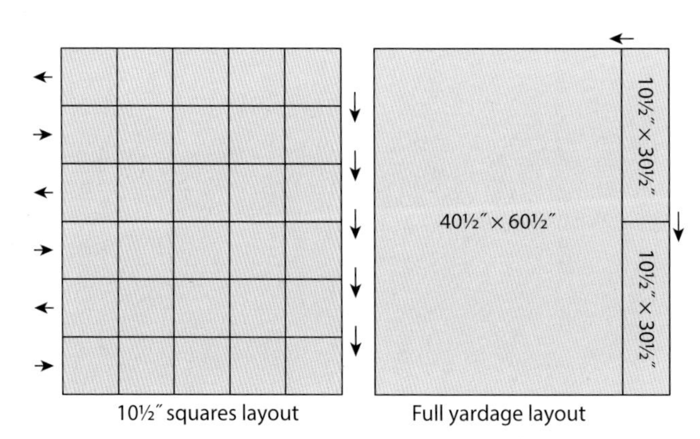

Assemble the background using the appropriate layout. Arrows indicate pressing direction.

2. Carefully pin the matching center star pieces in the center of the large star pieces (star center 1 to star 1 and so on). Sew around the center stars to attach them to the large star pieces.

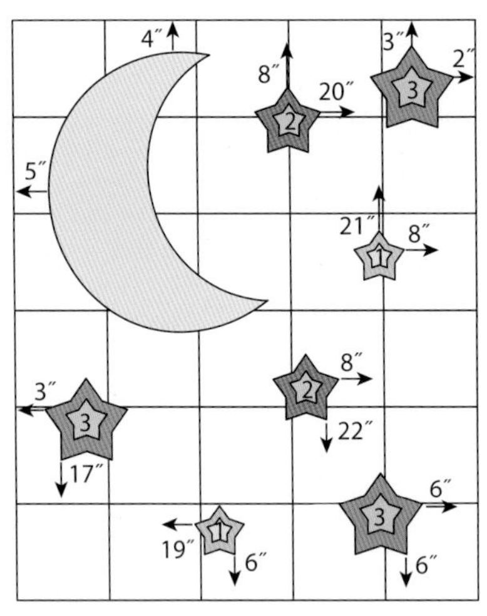

Moon and stars placement

3. Carefully pin the moon and stars on the background, following the placement diagram. Make sure the moon and stars are smooth and there are no puckers in the background fabric underneath. Spray lightly with temporary adhesive to stabilize the moon and stars.

4. Sew around the moon and the large stars to secure them to the background piece, using matching thread and your preferred appliqué stitch.

FINISHING THE QUILT

For detailed instructions on finishing techniques, refer to Finishing Touches (page 29).

1. Cut and piece the backing fabric so it is 8″ wider and longer than the quilt top. Layer the quilt top with the batting and backing. Baste together the layers.

2. Hand or machine quilt as desired.

3. Square up the quilt sandwich.

4. Prepare and sew the binding to the quilt. Add a label and enjoy!

Cool It Down!

Create a harmonious and calm quilt by cutting the stars and moon from single prints. You will have colorful scraps left over, which will be perfect for making slabs for other projects. For a blue-and-yellow version, substitute with these fabrics. Follow the rest of the project instructions as given.

Starry Nights, 50″ × 60″, pieced by Stacey Day and quilted by Miriam March

Background: 2½ yards of light gray

Fabric A: ⅝ yard of lemon yellow

Fabric B: ⅜ yard or 1 fat quarter of dark aqua

Fabric C: ¼ yard or 1 fat quarter of medium aqua

Fabric D: 1 fat quarter of light blue

Fabric E: 1 fat eighth of deep yellow-orange

Fabric F: 1 fat eighth of medium yellow-orange

Fabric G: ⅛ yard or 1 fat eighth of light yellow-orange

I Love Ladybugs

FINISHED QUILT: 48″ × 60″

Pieced by Stacey Day and quilted by Miriam March

When my son was young and still learning about the world, he had a love for and a phobia of bugs. I thought that ladybugs might be a good way to ease him into insects, so we visited the local Honeybee Center where they have a room dedicated to different bugs. He was enthralled by the ladybugs behind glass, but when he turned around and saw the ladybug puppet I had on my hand, he got so scared we almost had to leave! *I Love Ladybugs* will let little ones get close to bugs without fear.

MATERIALS

Yardage is based on 42″-wide fabric. To use scraps instead of yardage, make slabs in the given dimensions from fabrics in the specified colors. For detailed instructions on this technique, refer to Slabs (page 20).

BACKGROUND: 2½ yards of cream

FABRIC A: 1 fat quarter of light blue *or* 1 slab 18″ × 22″

FABRIC B: 1 fat quarter of minty green *or* 1 slab 18″ × 22″

BINDING: ½ yard

BACKING: 3¼ yards

BATTING: 56″ × 68″

FUN TIPS

You can cut the required number of pieces from the slab for each fabric, so you only have to make one per color! If you want to use large-size scraps in place of yardage or make different slabs for each piece, they must be at least 4″ × 7½″. You can also use a selection of bright, busy prints in place of the slabs.

CUTTING

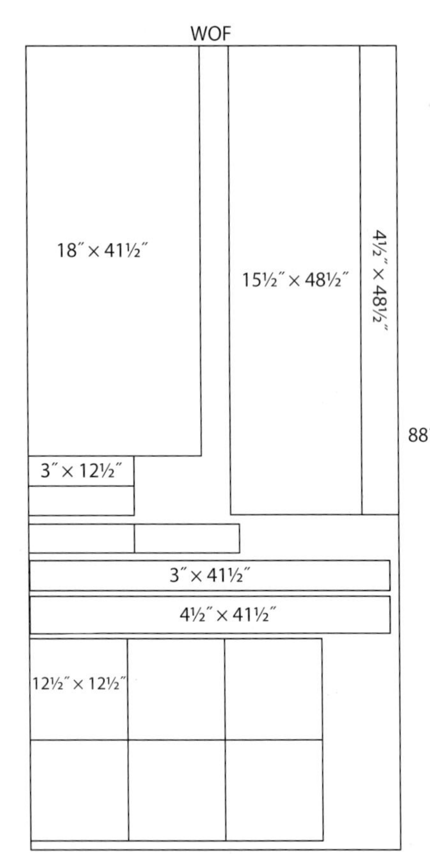

Background fabric cutting

BACKGROUND

- Cut 1 strip 18″ × 41½″.
- Cut 1 strip 4½″ × 41½″.
- Cut 1 strip 15½″ × 48½″.
- Cut 1 strip 4½″ × 48½″.
- Cut 4 strips 3″ × 12½″.
- Cut 1 strip 3″ × 41½″.
- Cut 6 squares 12½″ × 12½″.

FABRIC A

- Cut 6 of half-circle 1.

FABRIC B

- Cut 12 of half-circle 2.

BINDING

- Cut 6 strips 2¼″ × 42″.

Making the Quilt

1. Fold the 12½″ background squares on the diagonal and finger-press to mark the centers. Pin a fabric A half-circle and 2 fabric B half-circles to the background squares, as shown in the block assembly diagram.

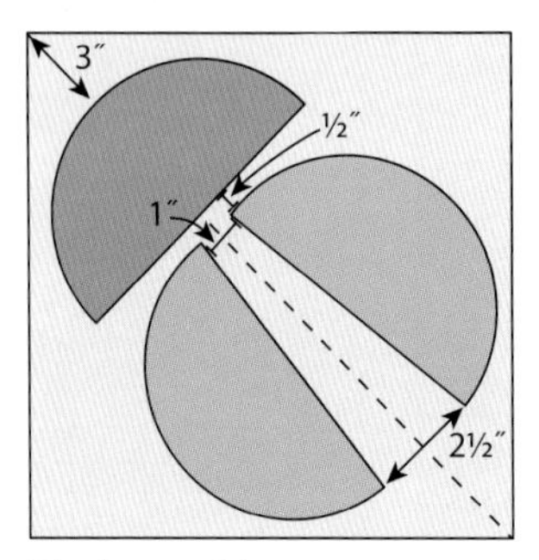

Block assembly

2. Using matching thread and your preferred appliqué stitch, sew around the half-circles to secure them to the background squares.

3. Sew 3 Ladybug blocks into a column with a 3″ × 12½″ rectangle between them. Repeat to make a second column. Sew the columns together with a 3″ × 41½″ strip between them. Press the seams toward the Ladybug blocks.

4. Make the quilt top. Sew the 4½″ × 41½″ and 18″ × 41½″ background pieces to the sides. Sew the 15½″ × 48½″ and 4½″ × 48½″ background pieces to the top and bottom. Press the seams toward the Ladybug blocks.

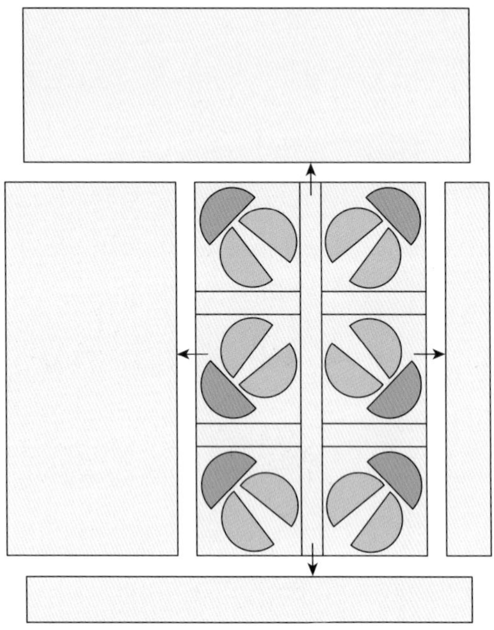

Quilt assembly

FINISHING THE QUILT

For detailed instructions on finishing techniques, refer to Finishing Touches (page 29).

1. Cut and piece the backing fabric so it is 8″ wider and longer than the quilt top. Layer the quilt top with the batting and backing. Baste together the layers.

2. Hand or machine quilt as desired.

3. Square up the quilt sandwich.

4. Prepare and sew the binding to the quilt. Add your label and enjoy!

Warm It Up!

I really wanted to use a particular print for the background but fell short. I found a similar-tone ivory print and blended the background fabrics. To make an *I Love Ladybugs* quilt in shades of pink and yellow, substitute with these fabrics. Follow the rest of the project instructions as given.

I Love Ladybugs, 48″ × 60″, pieced by Stacey Day and quilted by Miriam March

Background: 2½ yards of ivory

Fabric A: 1 fat quarter of yellow

Fabric B: 1 fat quarter of pink

Whirling

FINISHED QUILT: 45" × 57"

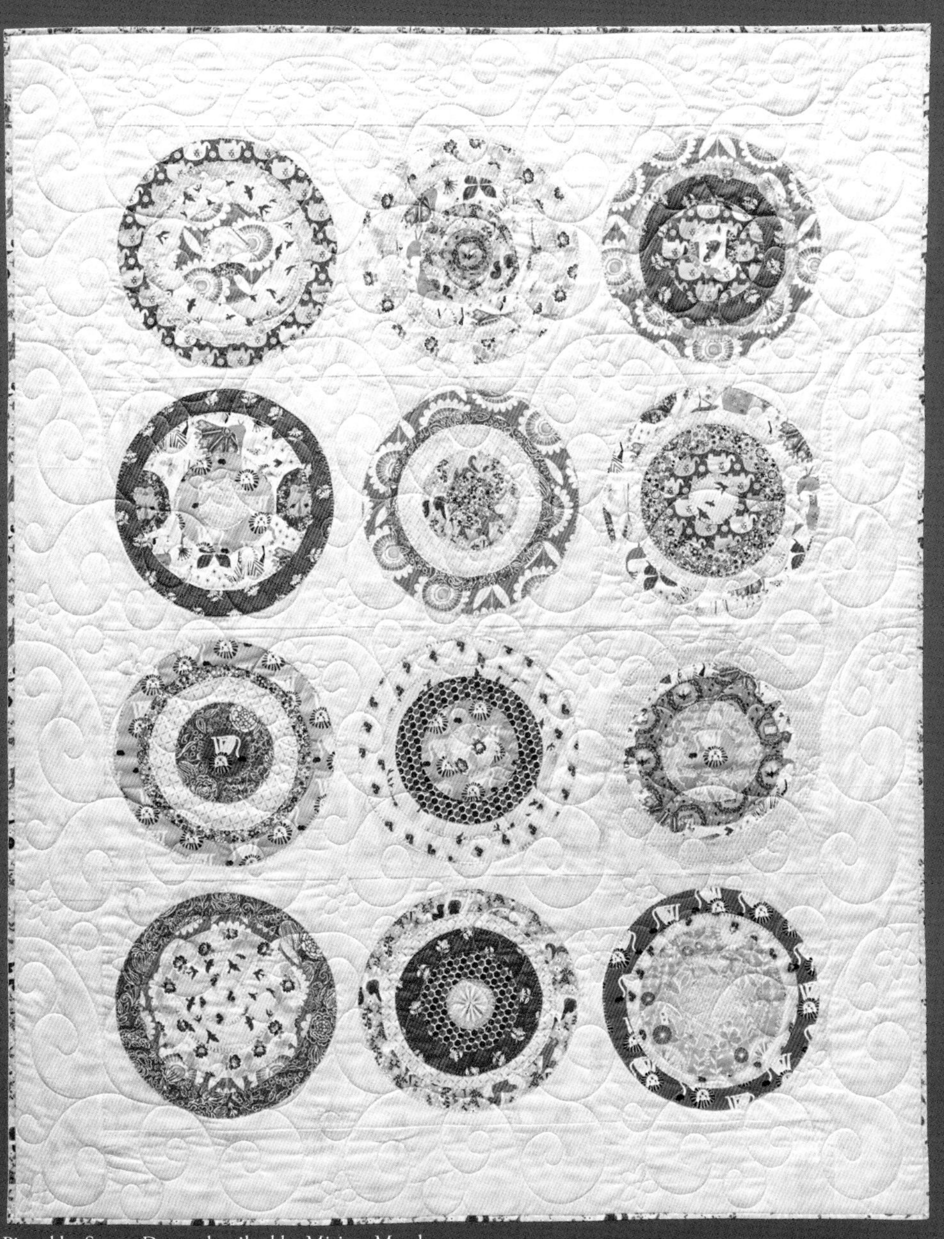

Pieced by Stacey Day and quilted by Miriam March

Whirling is a super-quick, easy-to-make quilt that is perfect for sparking the imagination of little ones. Backed in a flannel or light corduroy, it makes an amazing floor quilt and provides hours of entertainment. Children love playing games, so include some fun suggestions in a card. Beanbag toss, frog hopping from circle to circle, and of course the classic I spy will get them started. It won't be long before they are making up their own fun games!

MATERIALS

Yardage is based on 42″-wide fabric.

BACKGROUND: 2½ yards of cream

FABRIC A: ¾ yard of light coral

FABRIC B: ½ yard of medium purple

FABRIC C: ¾ yard of light purple

FABRIC D: ¾ yard of medium coral

FABRIC E: ½ yard of yellow

FABRIC F: ⅝ yard of white

BINDING: ½ yard

BACKING: 3½ yards

BATTING: 53″ × 65″

CUTTING

Arches are cut on the fold to make full circles.

BACKGROUND

- Cut 2 strips 5″ × 57½″ along the length of fabric.
- Cut 2 strips 5″ × 36½″ along the length of fabric.
- Cut 12 squares 12½″ × 12½″.

FABRIC A

- Cut 3 center circles.
- Cut 1 of arch 1.
- Cut 3 of arch 2.
- Cut 3 of arch 3.
- Cut 1 of arch 4.

FABRIC B

- Cut 1 center circle.
- Cut 1 of arch 1.
- Cut 4 of arch 2.
- Cut 1 of arch 3.
- Cut 1 of arch 4.

FABRIC C

- Cut 2 center circles.
- Cut 7 of arch 1.
- Cut 1 of arch 3.
- Cut 3 of arch 4.

FABRIC D

- Cut 1 center circle.
- Cut 2 of arch 1.
- Cut 2 of arch 3.
- Cut 4 of arch 4.

FABRIC E

- Cut 3 center circles.
- Cut 1 of arch 2.
- Cut 1 of arch 3.
- Cut 2 of arch 4.

FABRIC F

- Cut 2 center circles.
- Cut 1 of arch 1.
- Cut 4 of arch 2.
- Cut 4 of arch 3.
- Cut 1 of arch 4.

BINDING

- Cut 6 strips 2¼″ × 42″.

FUN TIP

Choose prints in similar colors to make the rings. Once they are layered, it creates the illusion of broader rings.

Making the Quilt

1. Finger-press the fabric A circles and rings in half. Fold them in half again in the other direction. Repeat for the circles and rings of fabrics B, C, D, E and F and the background squares.

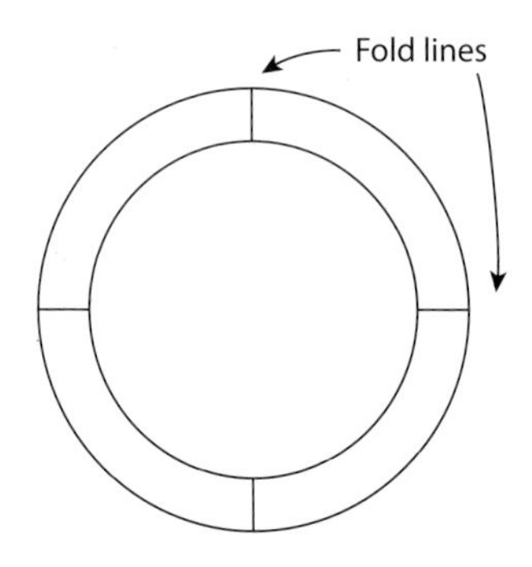

2. Arrange different-color rings from largest to smallest on a 12½″ background square, matching the finger-pressed center points. Arrange the center circles in a similar fashion. The pieces will overlap by ¼″. Pin the circles and rings to the background, or use a temporary spray adhesive to secure each ring.

HORTON HATCHES THE EGG

Layer the same color in different prints to create the look of wider rings.

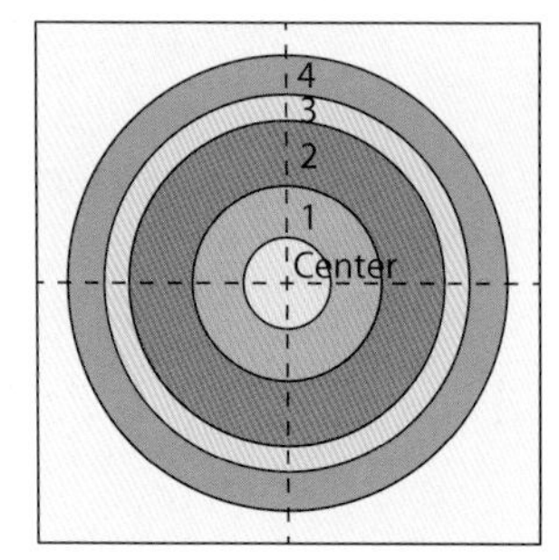

Layer rings from largest to smallest.

3. Using matching thread and your preferred appliqué stitch, sew around each ring and the center circle through all layers to secure them to the background squares.

4. Arrange the finished Ring blocks into 4 rows of 3 blocks each. When you are happy with the layout, sew the blocks together into rows, pressing the seams in alternating directions. Then sew together the rows.

5. Sew the 5″ × 36½″ strips to the top and bottom of the quilt top, matching the ends and centers. Press out toward the strips.

6. Sew the 5″ × 57½″strips to the sides of the quilt top, matching the ends and centers. Press the seams out toward the strips.

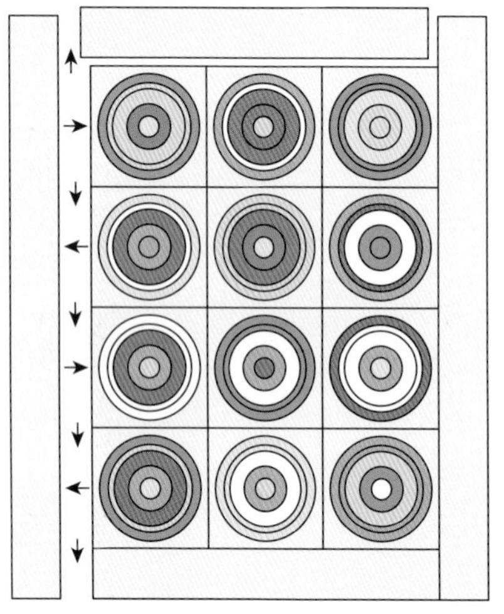
Quilt assembly

FINISHING THE QUILT

For detailed instructions on finishing techniques, refer to Finishing Touches (page 29).

1. Cut and piece the backing fabric so it is 8″ wider and longer than the quilt top. Layer the quilt top with the batting and backing. Baste together the layers.

2. Hand or machine quilt as desired.

3. Square up the quilt sandwich.

4. Prepare and sew the binding to the quilt. Add your label and enjoy!

Cool It Down!

To make a *Whirling* quilt with rings in shades of blue, yellow, and green, substitute with these fabrics. Follow the rest of the project instructions as given.

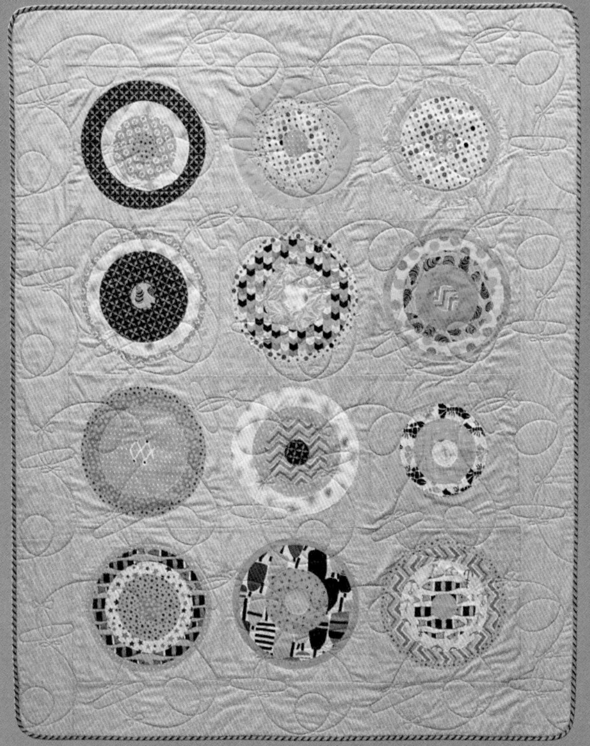
Whirling, 45″ × 57″, pieced by Matt Wheeler and quilted by Miriam March

Background: 2½ yards of silver

Fabric A: ¾ yard of medium green

Fabric B: ¾ yard of light green

Fabric C: ¾ yard of light turquoise

Fabric D: ¾ yard of medium blue

Fabric E: ½ yard of yellow

Fabric F: ¼ yard of white

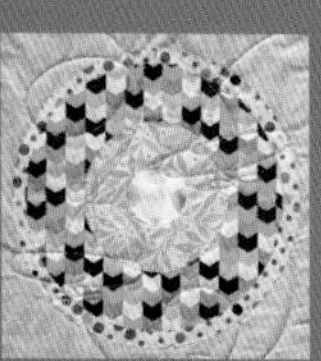
While the pattern directions are for the scrappy version, Matt Wheeler used the layout diagram to determine which rings he could turn into single-print circles. Cut full circles of your chosen prints, layer them, and appliqué the same as normal. You won't need to cut as many full circles as you do rings.

Gumdrops

FINISHED QUILT: 48" × 60"

Pieced by Stacey Day and quilted by Miriam March

Gumdrops deliberately includes soft and hard edges, and the contrasting shapes and how they play together fascinates me. I chose a fun layout and contrasting colors to emphasize the sharpness of the triangles against the smoothness of the round curves. Kids love gumdrop candies, but I always found they look softer than they are. Of course, that never stopped me from enjoying them!

MATERIALS

Yardage is based on 42"-wide fabric.

BACKGROUND: 2½ yards of gray

FABRIC A: ¼ yard or 1 fat quarter of pale yellow

FABRIC B: ¼ yard or 1 fat quarter of light yellow

FABRIC C: ¼ yard or 1 fat quarter of medium yellow

FABRIC D: ¼ yard or 1 fat quarter of dark yellow

FABRIC E: 1⅛ yards of teal

BINDING: ½ yard

BACKING: 3¼ yards

BATTING: 56″ × 68″

FUN TIPS

I used an assortment of large teal scraps, but any of the *Gumdrops* shapes can also be cut from slabs. The circle requires an 11¼″ × 11¼″ slab, and you can cut two accent triangles from a single 4¾″ × 4¾″ slab. If you notice that the background colors are showing through the yellow triangles, cut and fuse a lightweight layer of white interfacing to the back of the triangles.

Fusible interfacing prevents the dark print from showing through the light triangles.

CUTTING

BACKGROUND

- Cut 3 strips 12½″ × 48½″ lengthwise on the fabric.
- Cut 8 squares 12½″ × 12½″.

FABRIC A

- Cut 4 squares 4¾″ × 4¾″; subcut on the diagonal to make 8 half-square triangles.

FABRIC B

- Cut 4 squares 4¾″ × 4¾″; subcut on the diagonal to make 8 half-square triangles.

FABRIC C

- Cut 4 squares 4¾″ × 4¾″; subcut on the diagonal to make 8 half-square triangles.

FABRIC D

- Cut 4 squares 4¾″ × 4¾″; subcut on the diagonal to make 8 half-square triangles.

FABRIC E

- Cut 8 gumdrop circles.

BINDING

- Cut 6 strips 2¼″ × 42″.

Making the Quilt

1. Fold the fabric E circles in half and then in half again. Finger-press to mark the centers of the circles.

2. Fold the 12½″ background squares in half and then in half again to mark the centers. Pin the fabric E circles on the background squares, matching the centers.

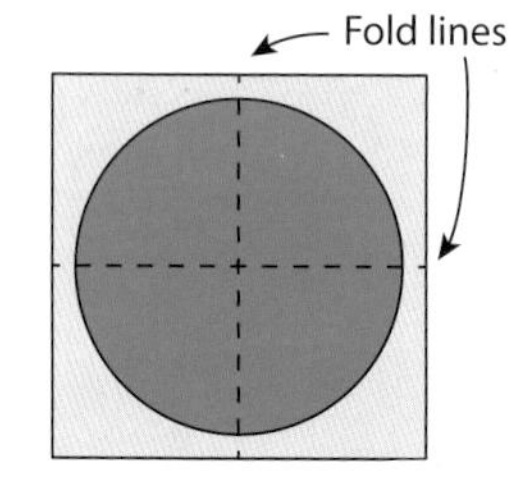

3. Sew around each circle to secure it to the background piece, using a matching thread and your preferred appliqué stitch. (I used a blanket stitch.)

4. Pin a fabric A, B, C, and D half-square triangle to each circle as shown, arranging them ⅛″ from the center folds. Sew around the triangles in the same manner as the circles to secure them to the piece.

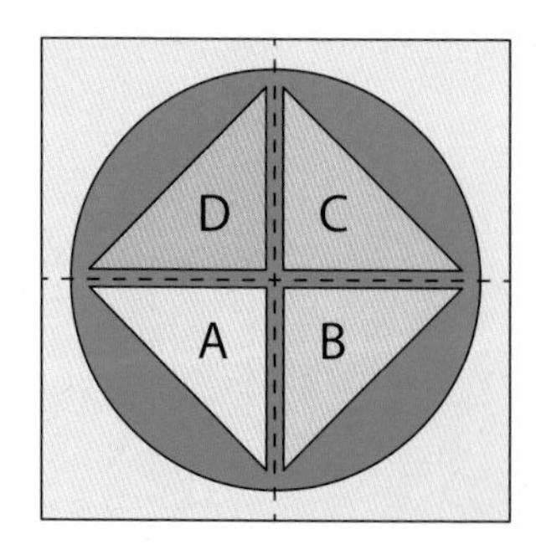

5. Sew the Gumdrop blocks together into 2 rows of 4 blocks each. Press the seams to one side.

6. Sew together the rows with the background strips as shown, matching the ends and centers.

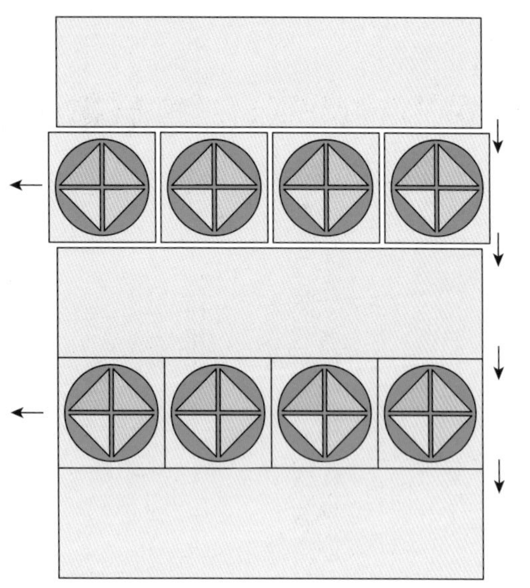

Quilt assembly

TIP To make a colorbomb binding as shown, sew together 2¼″ × 4½″ fabric A, B, and C strips using a diagonal seam. Repeat to make 2 color-block sections. Set aside. Sew together the plain binding strips using diagonal seams, press the seams open, and cut the strips into 2 equal sections. Insert a colorbomb strip between the cuts, and attach a colorbomb to one open end using a diagonal seam. Press the seams open; bind as usual. For more information, see Colorbomb Bindings (page 37).

FINISHING THE QUILT

For detailed instructions on finishing techniques, refer to Finishing Touches (page 29).

1. Cut and piece the backing fabric so it is 8″ wider and longer than the quilt top. Layer the quilt top with the batting and backing. Baste together the layers.

2. Hand or machine quilt as desired.

3. Square up the quilt sandwich.

4. Prepare and sew the binding to the quilt. Add your label and enjoy!

Warm It Up!

I used a single busy print for the circles of this pink-and-yellow quilt. The triangles blend into the block, further softening the quilt's look. To make a warm-hued *Gumdrops,* substitute with these fabrics. Follow the rest of the project instructions as given.

Gumdrops, 48″ × 60″, pieced by Stacey Day and quilted by Miriam March

Background: 2½ yards of off-white

Fabric A: ¼ yard or 1 fat quarter of pale yellow

Fabric B: ¼ yard or 1 fat quarter of light yellow

Fabric C: ¼ yard or 1 fat quarter of medium yellow

Fabric D: ¼ yard or 1 fat quarter of dark yellow

Fabric E: 1⅛ yards of fuchsia

Big Wheels

FINISHED QUILT: 60″ × 72″

Pieced by Stacey Day and quilted by Miriam March

When we are making quilts for ourselves or for others, time can quickly slip away from us. Before you know it, the "baby" is having a first (or maybe even second!) birthday. At that point, you may decide on a bigger quilt and more age-appropriate fabrics. This layout is great for showcasing a single collection or using different fabrics for each wheel wedge to make a modified I spy quilt. *Big Wheels* is slab friendly—just make a slab big enough to cover the pattern piece you are replacing.

MATERIALS

Yardage is based on 42″-wide fabric. To replace the background with slabs, make 30 squares 12½″ × 12½″ and arrange them in a 5 × 6 grid.

BACKGROUND: 3⅝ yards of navy blue

FABRIC A: 4 fat quarters of red

FABRIC B: 4 fat quarters of orange

FABRIC C: 4 fat quarters of yellow

FABRIC D: 4 fat quarters of green

FABRIC E: 4 fat quarters of blue

BINDING: ⅝ yard

BACKING: 3⅞ yards

BATTING: 68″ × 80″

CUTTING

BACKGROUND

- Cut 2 rectangles 36½″ × 60½″.

FABRICS A, B, C, D, AND E

- Cut 1 of wedge 1, 2, 3, 4, 5, and 6 from *each* fat quarter.

BINDING

- Cut 7 strips 2¼″ × 42″.

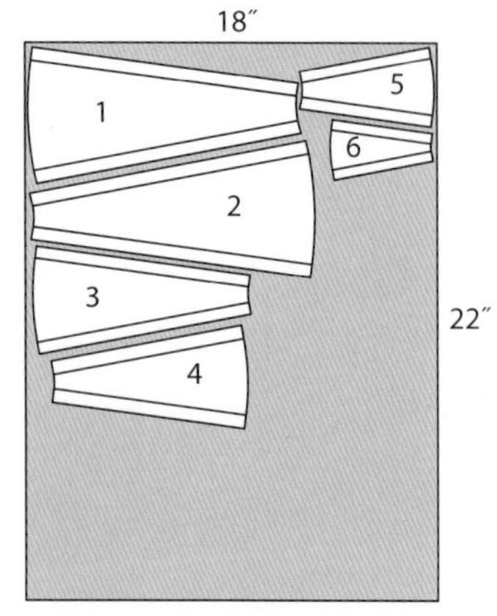

Wedge cutting. Cut a set of 6 wedges from *each* print.

CUTTING TIP

To help keep things in order, stack the fat quarters of the same color on top of each other in order, and cut the templates from them at the same time. Stack up to six prints at a time (any more and the cutting becomes less accurate).

Making the Quilt

1. Separate the wedges into pattern groups: pattern 1 with 1, pattern 2 with 2, and so on for each fabric. Stack the wedges in each group in the order you will sew.

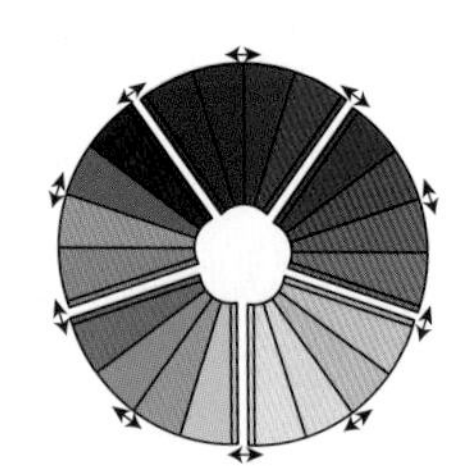

2. Sew together the wedges in pairs. Press the seams open, arrange the wedges in order, and sew together the pairs. Continue pressing open the seams and sewing together the wedge groups into full circles.

3. Check that the wheel sits flat. You may need to adjust the seams slightly in order to achieve this. Repeat Steps 1 and 2 for the remaining sets of wedges to make 6 full wheels.

4. Press the 2 background pieces. Sew them together to make a large piece measuring 60½″ × 72½″. Press the background well to remove all the wrinkles.

5. Pin each wheel to the background piece, as shown. Appliqué the wheels to the quilt using a blanket stitch and coordinating thread.

3¾″ 1¾″ 2½″ 1¾″ 12¾″ 1″ 1¼″ 19¼″ 13″ ¾″ 23¾″ 1¼″

Wheel placement

FINISHING THE QUILT

For detailed instructions on finishing techniques, refer to Finishing Touches (page 29).

1. Cut and piece the backing fabric so it is 8″ wider and longer than the quilt top. Layer the quilt top with the batting and backing. Baste together the layers.

2. Hand or machine quilt as desired.

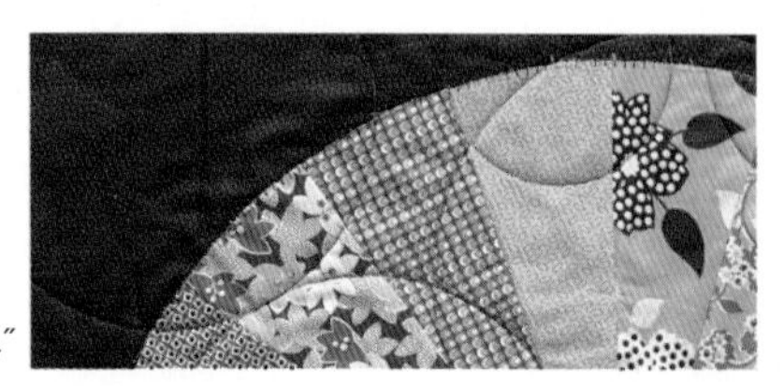

Big Wheels looks great when quilted with a variegated rainbow thread.

3. Square up the quilt sandwich.

4. Prepare and sew the binding to the quilt. Add your label and enjoy!

Cool It Down!

This version of *Big Wheels* was made from a single collection that only had ten prints, so each piece was cut twice. We used a full yard of each print in order to fussy cut each wedge. If you don't want to fussy cut, you will only need ten fat quarters. Cut two of each pattern piece from each fat quarter. Then follow the project directions and arrange the wheels as you wish.

Big Wheels, 60″ × 72″, pieced by Amy Dame and quilted by Joan Nicholson

PIECED PROJECTS

The quilts in this next section are well suited for scrap piecing. For a majority of the quilts, I used ¼-yard cuts of similar hues to build up to the required yardage. The backgrounds can be cut from a single background fabric or from multiple similar background fabrics. Some of the quilt projects can also incorporate slabs. Slab sizes for those quilts will be included in the tips. If you need a refresher, refer to Slabs (page 20). Have fun shaping these projects to your tastes!

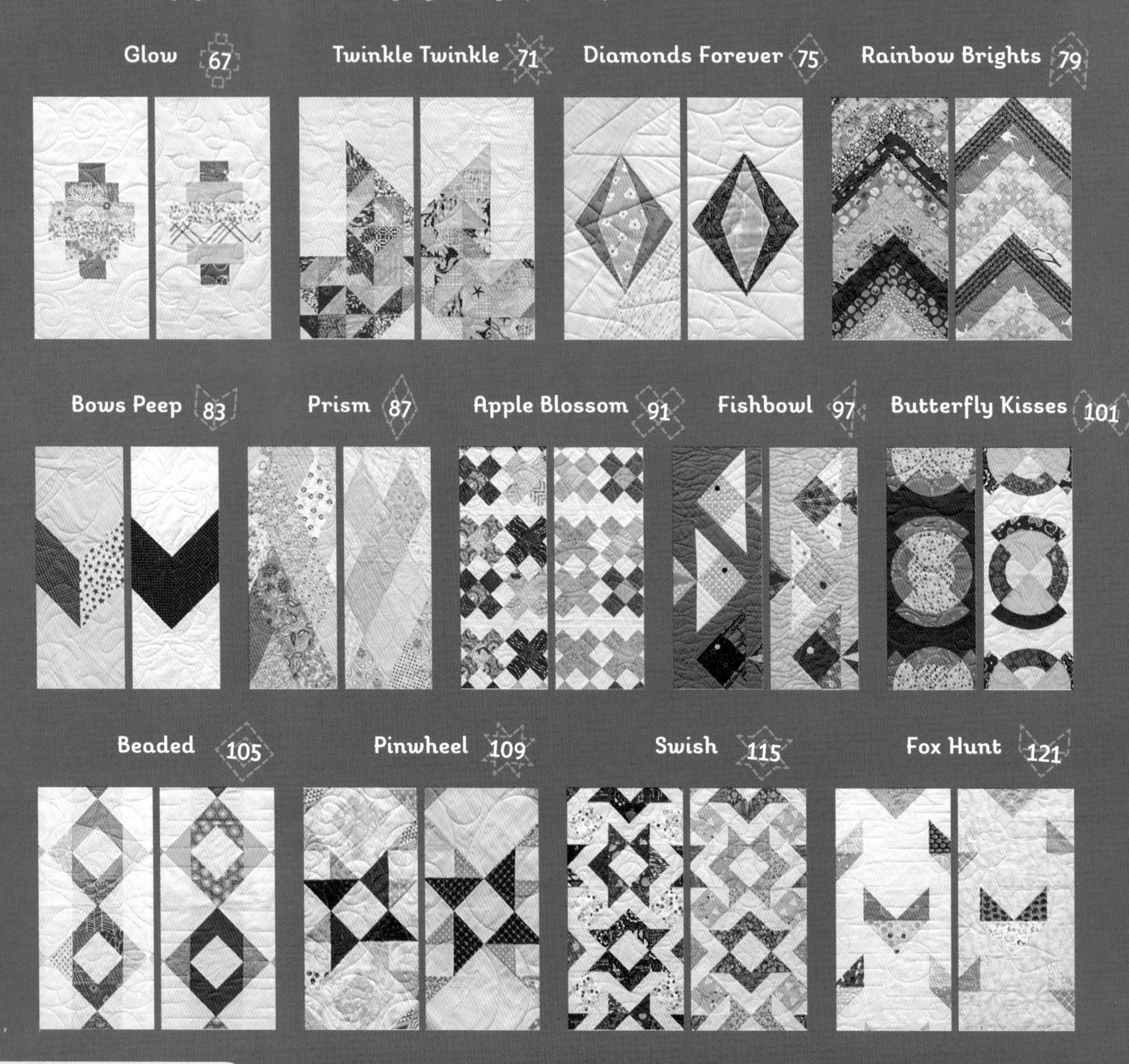

Glow

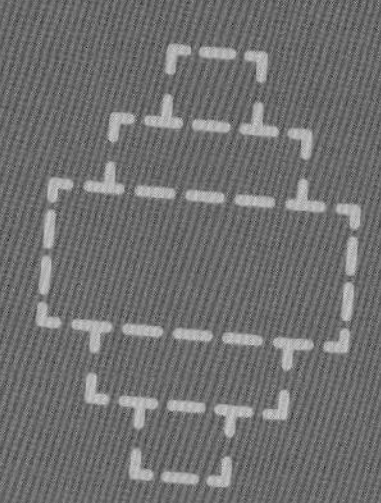

FINISHED QUILT: $57^3/_4$" × $65^1/_4$"

Pieced by Paul Krampitz and quilted by Miriam March

Glow was inspired by the gentle radiance of a night-light. Cradling my newborn in soft and gentle light, with the scent of summer lingering in the air, I was content and peaceful. My mind left to wander the paths of an imaginary garden lit by paper lanterns. Choose a variety of fabrics with subtle contrast to create the illusion of a soft glow. This design is great for using up small strips of fabric and leftover squares.

MATERIALS

Yardage is based on 42″-wide fabric.

BACKGROUND: 3⅓ yards of ivory

FABRIC A: ¼ yard of deep coral

FABRIC B: ⅓ yard of medium coral

FABRIC C: ½ yard of light coral

BINDING: ⅝ yard

BACKING: 3⅝ yards

BATTING: 65″ × 73″

FUN TIPS

Glow looks fantastic in a monochromatic range but would also be wonderful in a rainbow of colors. Use contrast to your advantage with a rainbow. For a glowing, gradient effect, use deeper colors on the outside of the blocks and transition to lighter colors on the inside.

CUTTING

BACKGROUND

- Cut 6 rectangles 11″ × 22¼″.
- Cut 6 squares 11″ × 11″.
- Cut 2 rectangles 5″ × 40½″.
- Cut 2 rectangles 5″ × 14½″.
- Cut 28 rectangles 2¼″ × 4¾″.
- Cut 28 rectangles 2¼″ × 3⅛″.
- Cut 2 rectangles 2″ × 20″.
- Cut 2 rectangles 2″ × 12½″.
- Cut 28 rectangles 1⅝″ × 2¼″.

FABRIC A

- Cut 14 rectangles 2¼″ × 2½″.
- Cut 36 squares 2″ × 2″.

FABRIC B

- Cut 14 rectangles 2¼″ × 5¾″.
- Cut 40 squares 2″ × 2″.

FABRIC C

- Cut 14 rectangles 2¼″ × 8¾″.
- Cut 40 squares 2″ × 2″.

BINDING

- Cut 7 strips 2¼″ × 42″.

Making the Quilt

1. Sew the 2¼″ × 4¾″ background rectangles to either end of the 2¼″ × 2½″ fabric A rectangles. Press the seams toward fabric A and set aside.

2. Sew the 2¼″ × 3⅛″ background rectangles to either end of the 2¼″ × 5¾″ fabric B rectangles. Press the seams toward fabric B and set aside.

3. Sew the 1⅝″ × 2¼″ background rectangles to either end of the 2¼″ × 8¾″ fabric C rectangles. Press the seams toward fabric C and set aside.

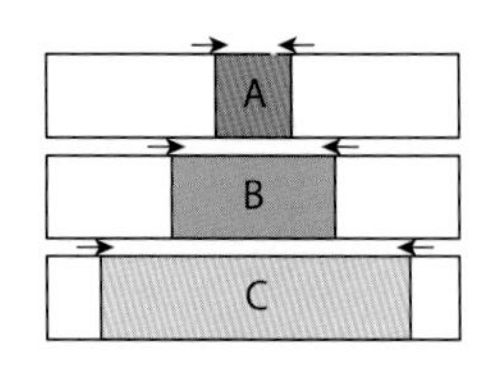

4. Sew together the fabric A, B, and C pieces in order, matching the ends and centers. Press all the seams toward fabric C to make 14 half-blocks 5¾″ × 11″.

5. Sew together the half-blocks as shown. Press the seams to one side. Trim to 11″ × 11″ if necessary.

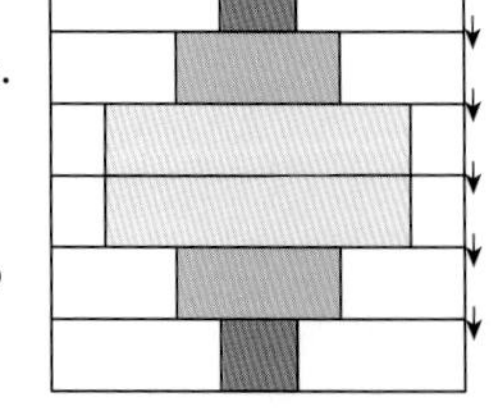

6. Sew the 2″ fabric A squares into 4 rows of 5 squares and 4 rows of 4 squares. Sew the fabric B and C squares into 10 rows of 5 squares to make 8 border strips of each fabric.

7. Sew together the 5″ × 40½″ and 5″ × 14½″ background rectangles to make 2 rectangles 5″ × 54½″.

8. Sew together the finished blocks, background squares, and background rectangles into rows, as shown in the quilt assembly diagram. Press the seams in opposite directions and sew together the rows.

9. Sew the 5″ × 54½″ rectangles to the top and bottom of the quilt. Referring to the quilt assembly diagram, sew together the border strips and the 2″ × 12½″ and 2″ × 20″ background strips into vertical and horizontal border pieces. Sew the horizontal pieces to the quilt top; then add the vertical pieces. Press the seams toward the center.

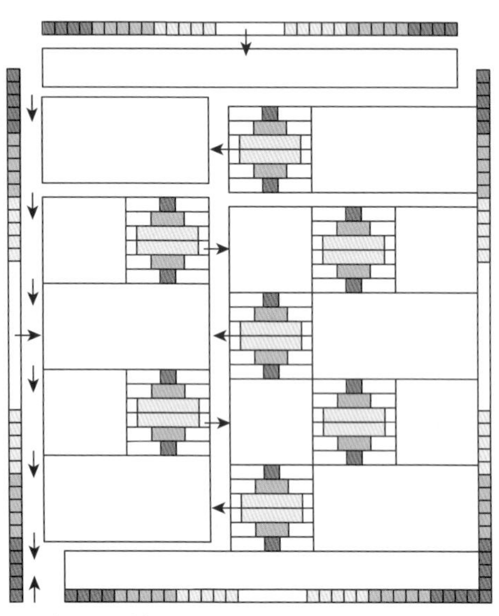

Quilt assembly

FINISHING THE QUILT

For detailed instructions on finishing techniques, refer to Finishing Touches (page 29).

1. Cut and piece the backing fabric so it is 8″ wider and longer than the quilt top. Layer the quilt top with the batting and backing. Baste together the layers.

2. Hand or machine quilt as desired.

3. Square up the quilt sandwich.

4. Prepare and sew the binding to the quilt. Add your label and enjoy!

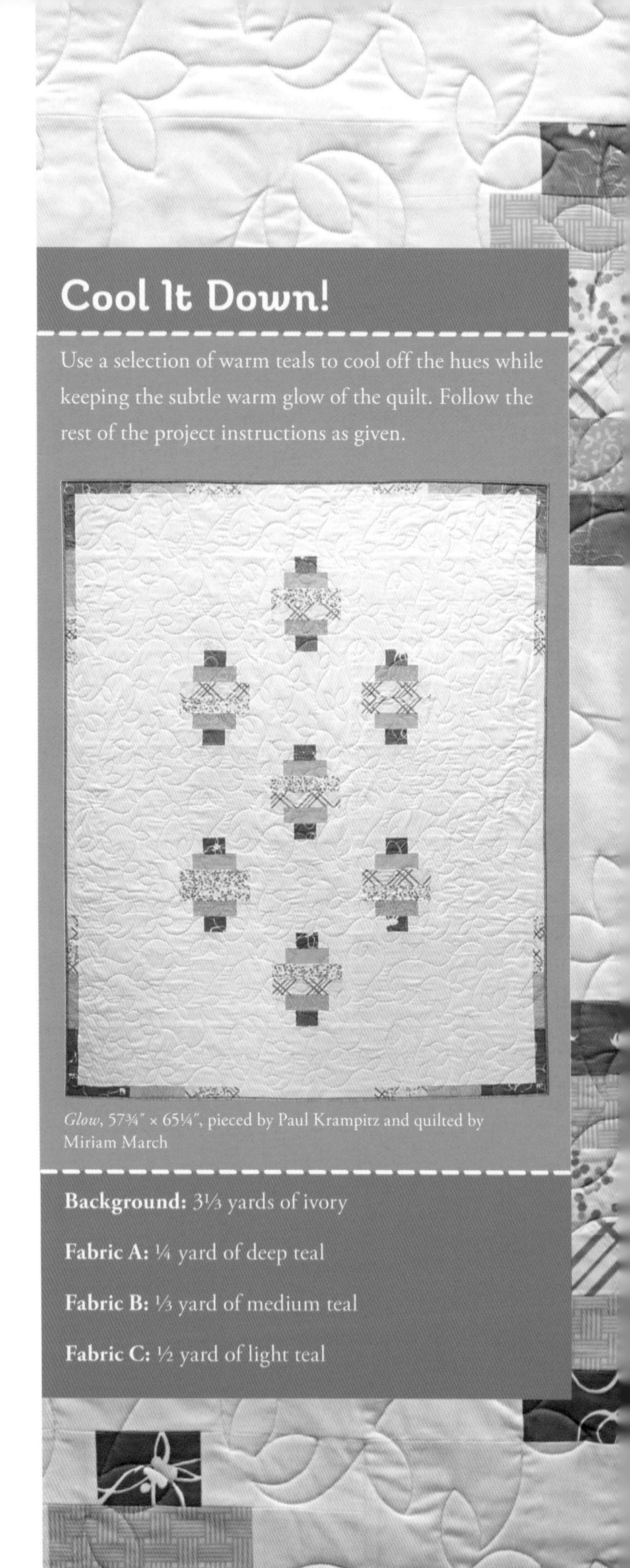

Cool It Down!

Use a selection of warm teals to cool off the hues while keeping the subtle warm glow of the quilt. Follow the rest of the project instructions as given.

Glow, 57¾″ × 65¼″, pieced by Paul Krampitz and quilted by Miriam March

Background: 3⅓ yards of ivory

Fabric A: ¼ yard of deep teal

Fabric B: ⅓ yard of medium teal

Fabric C: ½ yard of light teal

Twinkle Twinkle

FINISHED QUILT: 48″ × 60″

Pieced by Paul Krampitz and quilted by Miriam March

Stars have a special place in my heart. I have always used star analogies to refer to my eldest son. "Twinkle, Twinkle, Little Star" was the first song he learned to sing. I watched my first meteor shower with him in my lap, and my first show quilt was a star that I dedicated to him. Now I have a pair of little stars. Shining brightly, my boys are the guiding lights in my life.

MATERIALS

Yardage is based on 42″-wide fabric.

BACKGROUND: 2½ yards of off-white

FABRIC A: ⅜ yard of medium coral

FABRIC B: ⅜ yard of medium fuchsia

FABRIC C: ⅜ yard of light coral

FABRIC D: ⅜ yard of medium yellow

FABRIC E: ⅜ yard of light yellow

BINDING: ½ yard

BACKING: 3¼ yards

BATTING: 56″ × 68″

TIP *Twinkle Twinkle* is perfect for scraps. If you have scrap pieces you really want to incorporate but they aren't large enough for the squares that get cut down into triangles, you can cut single triangles from rectangles or longer strips. For the smaller triangles, cut the strip 1¾″ wide and at least 3½″ long. Turn a square grid ruler 45° so that the corner is touching the top of the strip, and cut on either side to make a triangle. Repeat down the strip. For the larger triangles, use a strip 2¾″ wide and at least 5¾″ long.

CUTTING

BACKGROUND

- Cut 2 rectangles 12½″ × 36½″.
- Cut 4 squares 12½″ × 12½″.
- Cut 4 squares 4¾″ × 4¾″.
- Cut 16 squares 3½″ × 3½″.
- Cut 3 squares 12⅞″ × 12⅞″; subcut on the diagonal to make 6 half-square triangles.
- Cut 4 squares 7½″ × 7½″; subcut on both diagonals to make 16 quarter-square triangles.

FABRIC A

- Cut 10 squares 3⅞″ × 3⅞″; subcut on the diagonal to make 20 half-square triangles.
- Cut 20 squares 2⅜″ × 2⅜″; subcut on the diagonal to make 40 half-square triangles.

FABRIC B

- Cut 10 squares 3⅞″ × 3⅞″; subcut on the diagonal to make 20 half-square triangles.
- Cut 19 squares 2⅜″ × 2⅜″; subcut on the diagonal to make 38 half-square triangles.

FABRIC C

- Cut 10 squares 3⅞″ × 3⅞″; subcut on the diagonal to make 20 half-square triangles.
- Cut 19 squares 2⅜″ × 2⅜″; subcut on the diagonal to make 38 half-square triangles.

FABRIC D

- Cut 10 squares 3⅞″ × 3⅞″; subcut on the diagonal to make 20 half-square triangles.
- Cut 19 squares 2⅜″ × 2⅜″; subcut on the diagonal to make 38 half-square triangles.

FABRIC E

- Cut 10 squares 3⅞″ × 3⅞″; subcut on the diagonal to make 20 half-square triangles.
- Cut 19 squares 2⅜″ × 2⅜″; subcut on the diagonal to make 38 half-square triangles.

BINDING

- Cut 6 strips 2¼″ × 42″.

Cool It Down!

Yellow is the star player in both versions of *Twinkle Twinkle*. It gives the quilt its glow no matter the color scheme. To make a *Twinkle Twinkle* quilt with shades of blue and green, substitute with these fabrics. Follow the rest of the project instructions as given.

Twinkle Twinkle, 48" × 60", pieced by Paul Krampitz and quilted by Miriam March

Background: 2½ yards of off-white

Fabric A: ⅜ yard of medium green

Fabric B: ⅜ yard of medium turquoise

Fabric C: ⅜ yard of light turquoise

Fabric D: ⅜ yard of medium yellow

Fabric E: ⅜ yard of light yellow

Making the Quilt

1. Mix the 2⅜″ fabric A, B, C, D, and E half-square triangles together into a large pile.

2. Grab 2 triangles at random from the pile; sew them together on the diagonal to make a half-square triangle square. Press and trim to 2″ × 2″. Repeat randomly pairing triangles to make 48 half-square triangle squares.

3. Grab 2 triangles at random from the pile. Sew them to adjacent sides of a half-square triangle square made in Step 2 to make a pieced half-square triangle. Press. Repeat to make 48 pieced triangles.

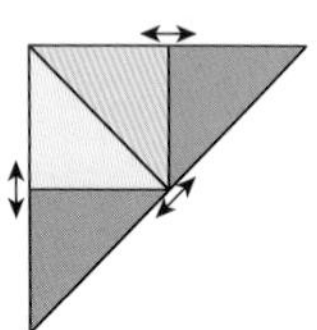

Pieced half-square triangle

4. Sew a pair of pieced triangles to opposite sides of a 4¾″ background square. Press. Sew another pair of pieced half-square triangles to the remaining sides, as shown. Press again, and trim to 6½″ × 6½″ to make unit A. Make 4.

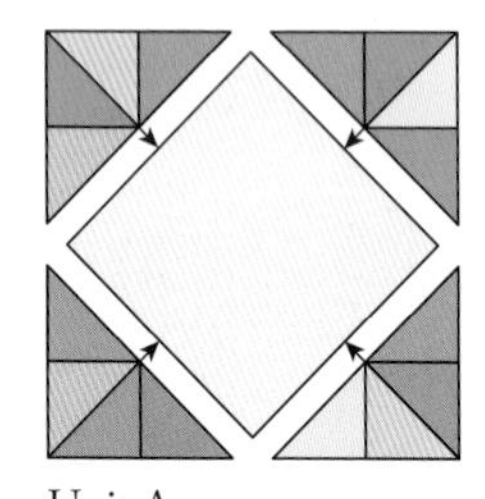

Unit A

5. Sew a pieced half-square triangle to a short side of a 7½″ background quarter-square triangle. Press. Sew another pieced half-square triangle to the other side. Press and trim to 3½″ × 12½″ to make unit B. Make 16.

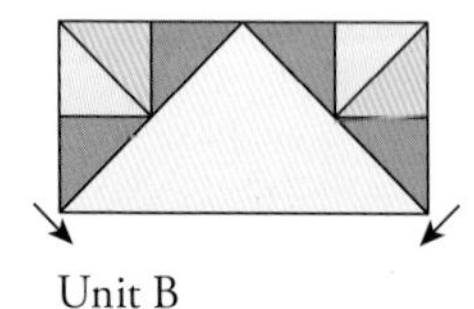

Unit B

6. Sew together 1 unit A, 4 units B, and 4 background 3½″ squares to make 1 A block. Press and trim the block to 12½″ × 12½″. Make 4.

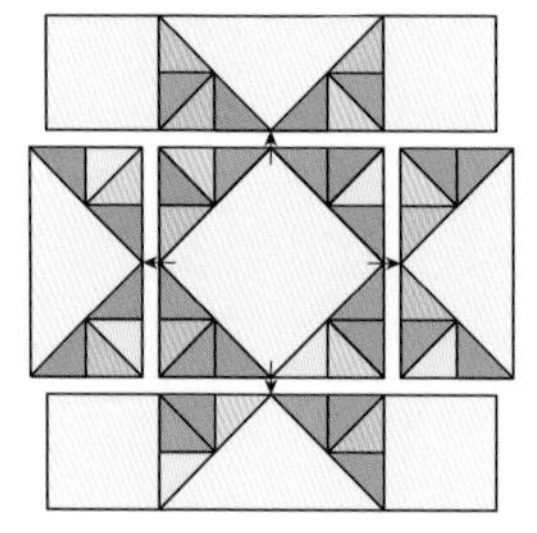

A block

7. Repeat Steps 1 and 2 using the 3⅞″ fabric A, B, C, D, and E triangles to make 36 large pieced half-square triangle squares. Press and trim to 3½″ × 3½″.

8. Sew together 6 of these triangle squares, along with 4 of the remaining triangles, to form a large pieced triangle.

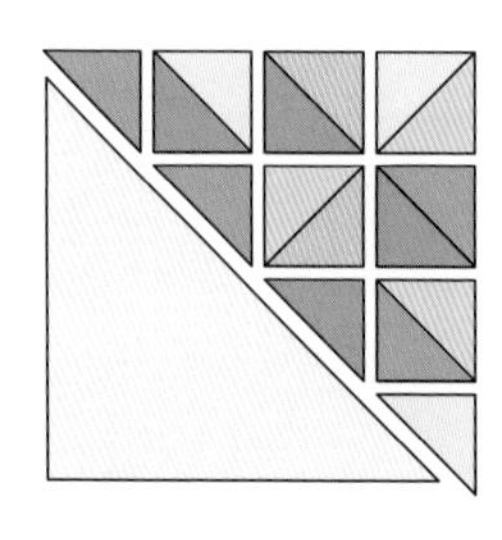

9. Sew together a 12⅞″ background half-square triangle and the large pieced triangle, as shown. Press and trim to 12½″ × 12½″ to make 1 B block. Repeat to make 6 B blocks.

B block

10. Referring to the quilt assembly diagram, sew together the 12½″ × 36½″ and 12½″ × 12½″ background pieces into 2 rows 12½″ × 48½″. Sew together the row of A block stars. Sew together the 2 rows of B block pieced triangles with the remaining 12½″ background squares, as shown. Press the seams in alternating directions.

11. Sew all 5 rows together.

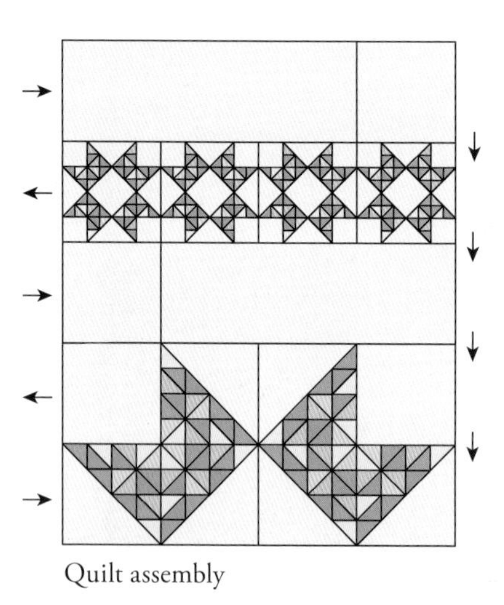

Quilt assembly

FINISHING THE QUILT

For detailed instructions on finishing techniques, refer to Finishing Touches (page 29).

1. Cut and piece the backing fabric so it is 8″ wider and longer than the quilt top. Layer the quilt top with the batting and backing. Baste together the layers.

2. Hand or machine quilt as desired.

3. Square up the quilt sandwich.

4. Prepare and sew the binding to the quilt. Add your label and enjoy!

Diamonds Forever

FINISHED QUILT: 44" × 56"

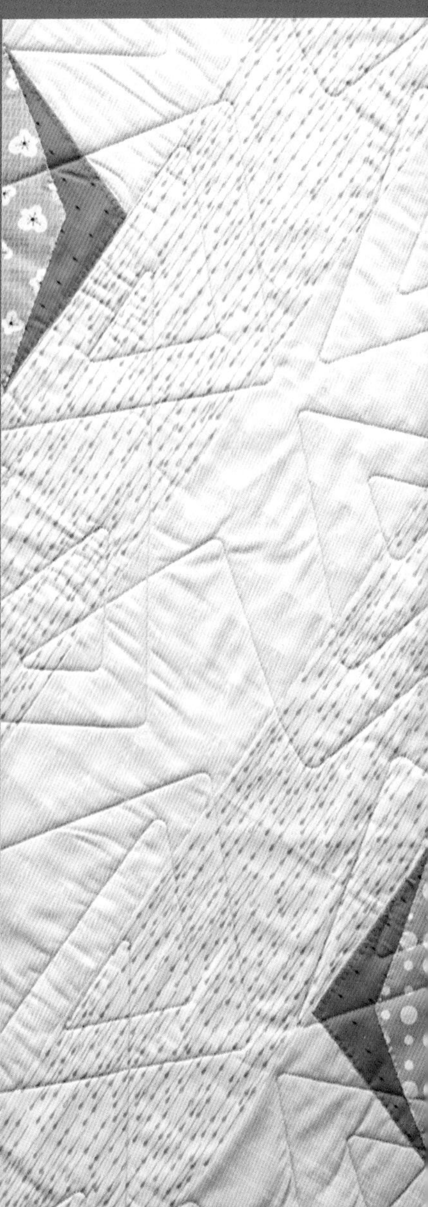

Pieced by Stacey Day and quilted by Miriam March

Tradition calls for giving diamonds to represent that love lasts forever. Since babies don't wear jewelry, show them everlasting love with fabric diamonds instead. *Diamonds Forever* combines piecing and appliqué techniques. Cut the background rectangles from one fabric or several—or build them from slabs.

MATERIALS

Yardage is based on 42″-wide fabric.

BACKGROUND: 3⅜ yards of gray

FABRIC A: ½ yard of medium teal

FABRIC B: ⅜ yard of lime green

BINDING: ½ yard

BACKING: 3 yards

BATTING: 52″ × 64″

CUTTING

BACKGROUND

- Cut 1 rectangle 4⅞″ × 56½″.
- Cut 1 rectangle 4⅞″ × 52¼″.
- Cut 1 rectangle 4⅞″ × 47½″.
- Cut 1 rectangle 4⅞″ × 47″.
- Cut 1 rectangle 4⅞″ × 38¼″.
- Cut 1 rectangle 4⅞″ × 34″.
- Cut 1 rectangle 4⅞″ × 29¼″.
- Cut 5 rectangles 4⅞″ × 25″.
- Cut 9 rectangles 4⅞″ × 20½″.
- Cut 2 rectangles 4⅞″ × 16″.
- Cut 5 rectangles 4⅞″ × 11″.

FABRIC A

- Cut 1 diamond A.
- Cut 6 diamonds B.

FABRIC B

- Cut 1 diamond accent A.
- Cut 6 diamond accents B.

BINDING

- Cut 7 strips 2¼″ × width of fabric.

TIP

Cut first the background strips that are longer than 42″ from the length of your fabric. Then cut the remaining strips from the remaining width of the fabric.

Making the Quilt

1. Center the diamond accent A piece right side up on the diamond A piece and pin in place. Repeat with the diamond accent B and diamond B pieces. Appliqué them together using a blanket stitch and matching thread. *Note:* Diamond A has a seam allowance, but the remaining pieces do not. The large diamond is pieced into the quilt and the smaller diamonds are appliquéd after the top is constructed.

2. Sew an 11″ background strip to one side of diamond A, as shown. Trim the ends at the same angle as the diamond.

3. Add a 16″ strip to the right-hand side of the diamond, Log Cabin style. Continue adding background strips to the diamond and trimming the ends until the background is complete. Pay close attention to the quilt assembly diagram, which shows the order that strips are added. The strip lengths are as follows.

Strip number	Strip length
1	11″
2	16″
3	16″
4	20½″
5	20½″
6	11″
7	20½″
8	25″
9	25″
10	20½″
11	34″
12	25″
13	20½″
14	47½″

Strip number	Strip length
15	25″
16	20½″
17	52¼″
18	25″
19	56½″
20	20½″
21	11″
22	20½″
23	11″
24	47″
25	38¼″
26	29¼″
27	20½″
28	11″

4. Pin the diamond B pieces to the quilt top as shown. Appliqué them to the top using a blanket stitch and matching thread.

5. Trim the quilt top to 44½″ × 56½″.

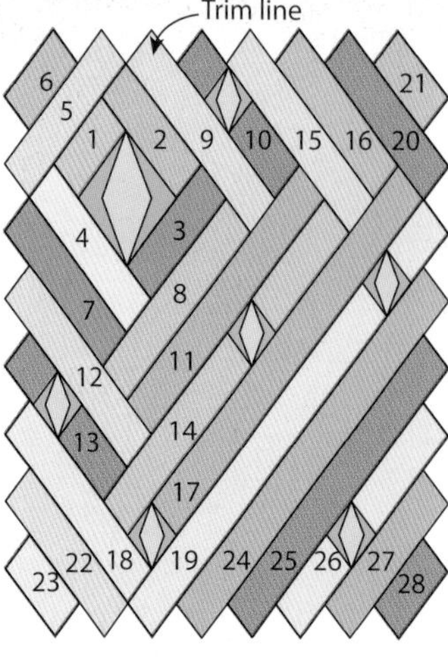

Quilt assembly

TIP

Bias Beware

The edges of the quilt top are all on the bias. Here are some techniques to help prevent the edges of the quilt from stretching out of shape:

- Quilt the top first; then trim the quilt to size.
- Make sure the quilt is well basted before quilting.
- Quilt along the diagonal lines, which are on the straight of grain.

FINISHING THE QUILT

For detailed instructions on finishing techniques, refer to Finishing Touches (page 29).

1. Cut and piece the backing fabric so it is 8″ wider and longer than the quilt top. Layer the quilt top with the batting and backing. Baste together the layers.

2. Hand or machine quilt as desired.

3. Square up the quilt sandwich.

4. Prepare and sew the binding to the quilt. Add your label and enjoy!

TIP

If you do use a wholecloth background, try taking your longest grid ruler and drawing lines on the top in removable fabric marker where the pieced strips would have been. Quilt along those lines to create the illusion of seams without the need to cut up and sew together strips of the same fabric.

Warm It Up!

For this version, I used some of my favorite designer prints for the diamonds. To make the diamonds in subtle pinks and rich-hued purples, substitute with these fabrics. Follow the rest of the project instructions as given.

Diamonds Forever, 44″ × 56″, pieced by Stacey Day and quilted by Miriam March

Background: 3 yards of shimmer silver

Fabric A: ½ yard of medium purple

Fabric B: ⅜ yard of light pink

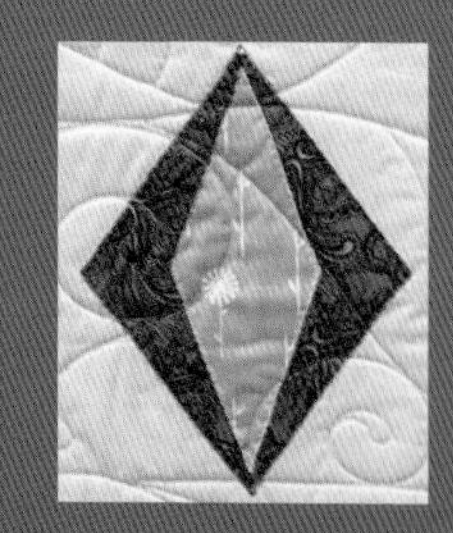

I had a very large cut of the gorgeous shimmer silver dot that I really wanted to use for the background, but I was loathe to cut it all up just to sew it back together diagonally. So instead I made a plain square background 44″ × 56″ and appliquéd each diamond in the same place it would have been on a pieced background. If you choose to appliqué the large diamond, remove the ¼″ seam allowance all around it.

Rainbow Brights

FINISHED QUILT: 50″ × 61″

Pieced by Stacey Day and quilted by Miriam March

One of my earliest memories is going to the video store with my mom and picking out a movie from the kids section. I always picked *Rainbow Brite*. It was my favorite movie of all time. (I can still hum the theme song!) My favorite part was when the heroine returned all the colors to Rainbowland. This quilt is a nod to that part of my childhood. You never know which memories will stick with you, but I hope that this quilt will be remembered by your special little person.

MATERIALS

Yardage is based on 42″-wide fabric.

BACKGROUND: 1¼ yards of medium blue

FABRIC A: ⅔ yard of deep blue

FABRIC B: ½ yard of green

FABRIC C: ½ yard of yellow

FABRIC D: ½ yard of orange

FABRIC E: ⅝ yard of red

BINDING: ½ yard

BACKING: 3¼ yards

BATTING: 58″ × 69″

TIPS

Rainbow Brights is perfect for using up 2½″ precut strips. For a completely different look, use different shades of each color and make a gradient instead of repeating the colors. You can also piece small scraps together into long slab strips.

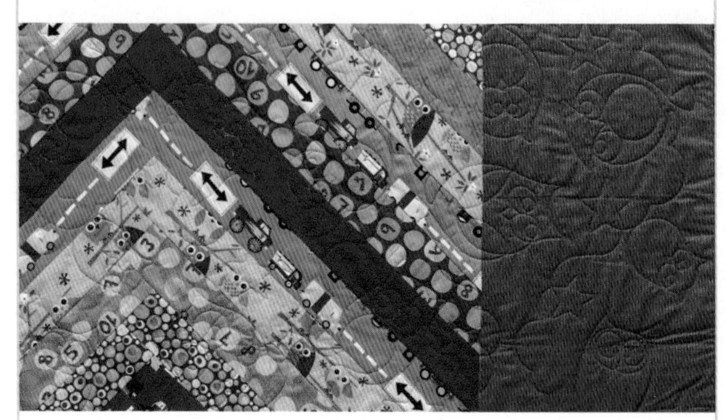

Whimsical quilting that matches the prints makes this quilt complete.

CUTTING

BACKGROUND

- Cut 2 strips 11″ × 40½″.
- Cut 2 strips 11″ × 20½″.
- Cut 2 strips 2″ × 29¼″.

FABRIC A

- Cut 3 strips 2½″ × 23″.
- Cut 5 strips 2½″ × 21″.
- Cut 1 square 4⅞″ × 4⅞″; subcut on the diagonal to make 2 half-square triangles. Put 1 in your scrap bin for another project.

FABRIC B

- Cut 3 strips 2½″ × 23″.
- Cut 3 strips 2½″ × 21″.
- Cut 2 strips 2½″ × 17″.
- Cut 1 strip 2½″ × 9″.
- Cut 1 strip 2½″ × 7″.

FABRIC C

- Cut 3 strips 2½″ × 23″.
- Cut 3 strips 2½″ × 21″.
- Cut 3 strips 2½″ × 13″.
- Cut 1 strip 2½″ × 11″.

FABRIC D

- Cut 3 strips 2½″ × 23″.
- Cut 3 strips 2½″ × 21″.
- Cut 1 strip 2½″ × 17″.
- Cut 1 strip 2½″ × 15″.
- Cut 2 strips 2½″ × 9″.

FABRIC E

- Cut 3 strips 2½″ × 23″.
- Cut 4 strips 2½″ × 21″.
- Cut 1 strip 2½″ × 19″.
- Cut 2 strips 2½″ × 5″.

BINDING

- Cut 6 strips 2¼″ × 42″.

Warm It Up!

Desaturating the colors makes the quilt appear softer and more feminine while still achieving a rainbow. To make the quilt in varied hues of coral, yellow, mint, aqua, and violet, substitute with these fabrics. Follow the rest of the project instructions as given.

Rainbow Brights, 50″ × 61″, pieced by Stacey Day and quilted by Miriam March

Background: 1¼ yards of light lavender

Fabric A: ⅔ yard of light coral

Fabric B: ½ yard of light yellow-orange

Fabric C: ½ yard of light green

Fabric D: ½ yard of light blue

Fabric E: ⅝ yard of light violet

Making the Quilt

1. Fold the 2½″ × 5″ fabric E strips in half and finger-press to mark the center. Repeat with the 2½″ × 9″ fabric D strips, 2 fabric C 2½″ × 13″ strips, 2½″ × 17″ fabric B strips, and 2 fabric A 2½″ × 21″ strips.

2. Sew together the strips into 2 corner units as shown, matching the centers. Press the seams toward the fabric B strips and set aside. Make 2.

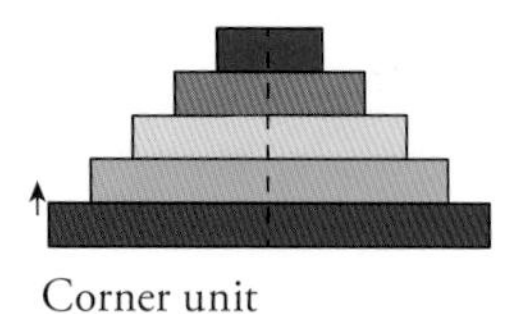
Corner unit

3. Sew the 2½″ × 7″ fabric B strip to the right side of the fabric A half-square triangle, as shown. Press the seam toward fabric B. Sew the 2½″ × 9″ fabric B strip to the opposite side. Press the seam toward fabric B.

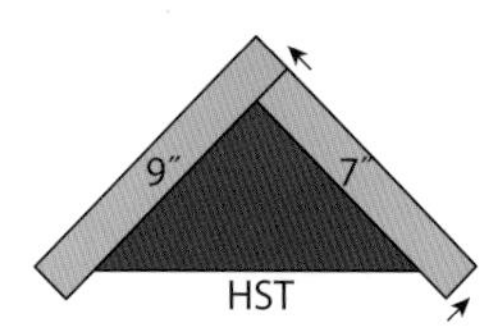

Press seams toward half-square triangle.

4. Continue sewing the strips in order, following the diagram and pressing the seams away from the initial triangle each time, to complete the rainbow stripe.

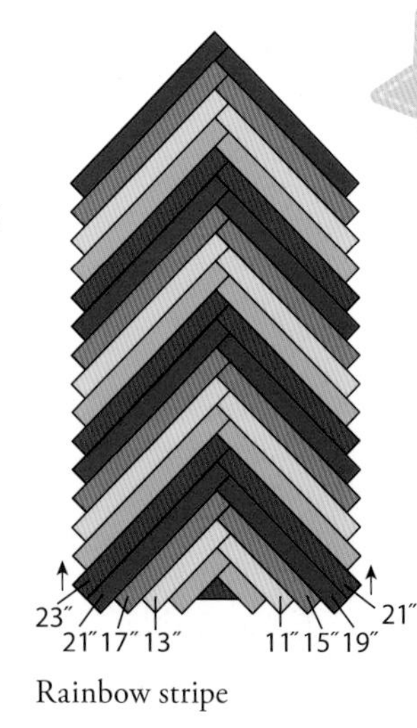

Rainbow stripe

5. Sew 1 corner unit to the top of the rainbow stripe, making sure that the corner unit extends past the top of the rainbow stripe by ¼″. Repeat with the other corner unit.

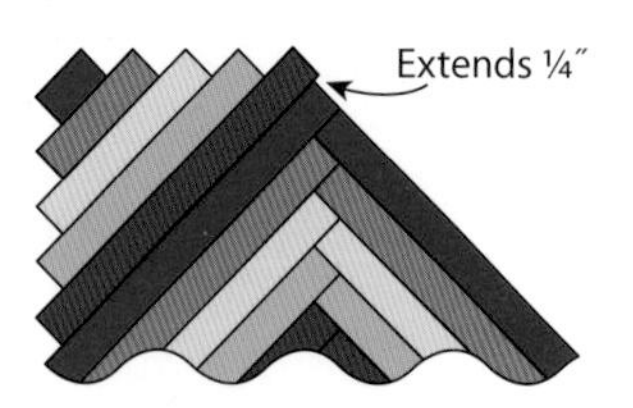

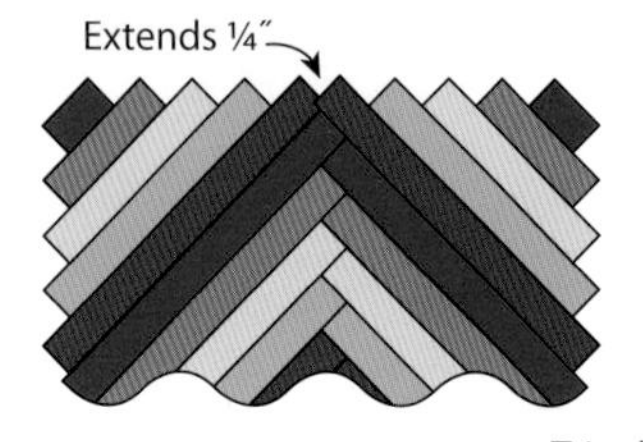

6. Trim the rainbow-stripe panel to 29¼″ × 58½″.

> **TIP** The edges of this quilt are on the bias and are prone to stretching. Place the quilt top against your machine's feed dogs when attaching the border strips. As you sew, the feed dogs will help ease the quilt top to match the border strips and help to minimize stretching.

7. Sew the 2″ × 29¼″ background strips to the top and bottom, matching the ends and centers.

8. Sew the 11″ × 40½″ background strips to the 11″ × 20½″ background fabric strips to make 2 side borders 11″ × 60½″. Sew the side borders to the rainbow stripe, matching the ends and centers.

Quilt assembly

FINISHING THE QUILT

For detailed instructions on finishing techniques, refer to Finishing Touches (page 29).

1. Cut and piece the backing fabric so it is 8″ wider and longer than the quilt top. Layer the quilt top with the batting and backing. Baste together the layers.

2. Hand or machine quilt as desired.

3. Square up the quilt sandwich.

4. Prepare and sew the binding to the quilt. Add your label and enjoy!

Bows Peep

FINISHED QUILT: 55″ × 73½″

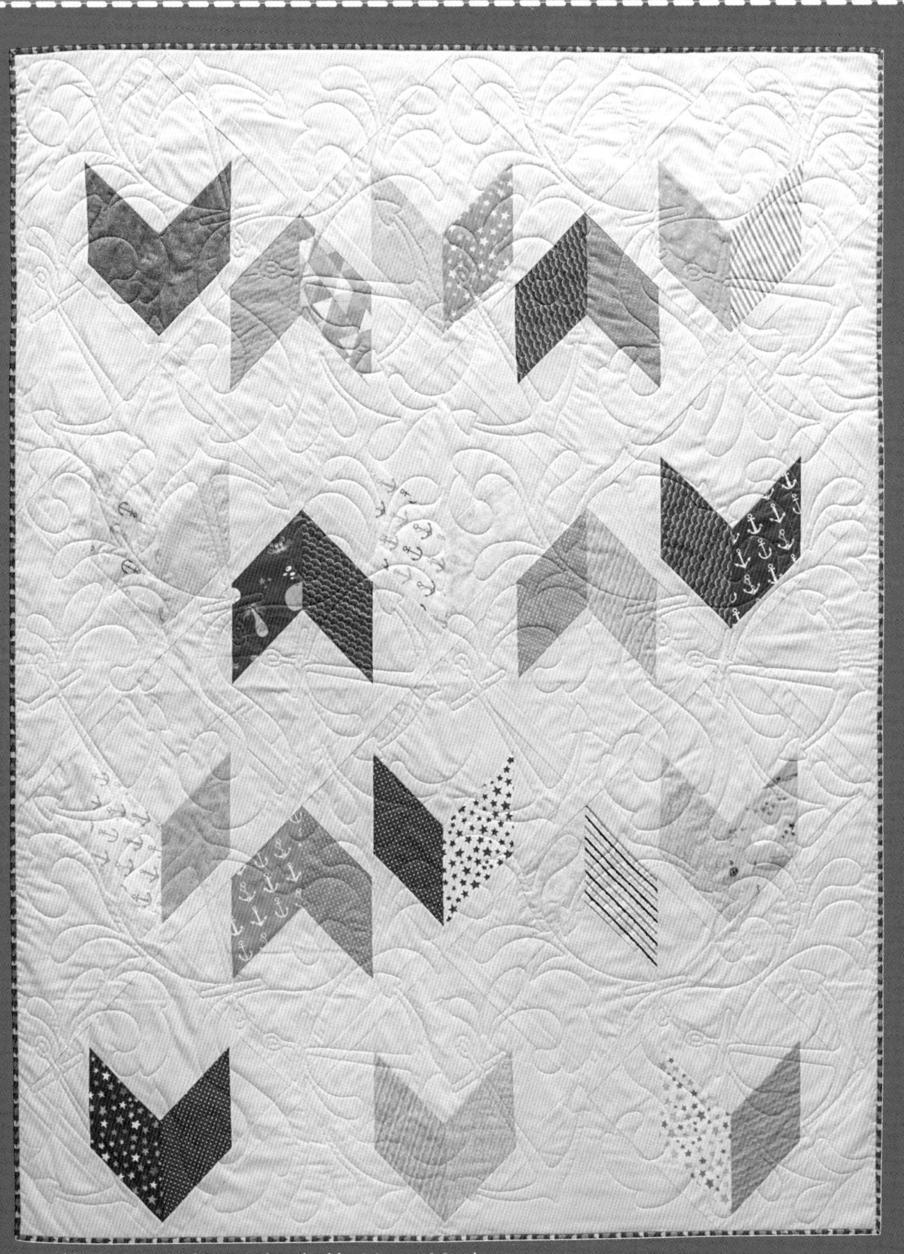

Pieced by Kristen Andrews and quilted by Miriam March

When we were kids, my mother used to read to us every day. Our favorite books were the Berenstain Bears books. We had the entire library, and every night we would argue over who got to pick that night's story. My mother saved all those books, and now I read the same ones to my own children. The diamonds of *Bows Peep* were inspired by the bow in Sister Bear's hair. In the Bear family portrait, the bow just peeps over the top of her head.

MATERIALS

Yardage is based on 42″-wide fabric.

BACKGROUND: 4 yards of off-white

FABRIC A: ⅔ yard of turquoise

FABRIC B: ⅔ yard of aqua

FABRIC C: ⅔ yard of green

BINDING: ⅝ yard

BACKING: 3⅝ yards

BATTING: 63″ × 82″

TIP This project is perfect for using up the larger scraps in your stash or utilizing leftover 10″ precut squares. You can make a diamond template by drawing a 5½″ × 15″ rectangle on a piece of cardboard or freezer paper and then drawing the diagonal lines following the measurements in the pattern to form the diamond. You can also cut pieced diamonds from a 5½″ × 15″ slab.

CUTTING

BACKGROUND

- Cut 3 squares 18¼″ × 18¼″; subcut on both diagonals to make 12 quarter-square triangles. Put 2 in your scrap bin for another project.
- Cut 2 squares 9½″ × 9½″; subcut on the diagonal to make 4 half-square triangles.
- Cut 18 squares 7½″ × 7½″.
- Cut 18 squares 5⅞″ × 5⅞″; subcut on the diagonal to make 36 half-square triangles.
- Cut 6 strips 1½″ × 42″.
- Cut 2 strips 1½″ × 27″.
- Cut 2 strips 1½″ × 15½″.
- Cut 24 strips 1½″ × 12½″.

FABRIC A

- Cut 3 strips 5½″ × 42″.

FABRIC B

- Cut 3 strips 5½″ × 42″.

FABRIC C

- Cut 3 strips 5½″ × 42″.

BINDING

- Cut 7 strips 2¼″ × 42″.

Making the Quilt

1. Place the 5½″ × 42″ fabric A strips right side up on a cutting surface, one on top of the other. Line up the 45° line of an acrylic ruler with the bottom of the strips, and trim the end of the strips on an angle.

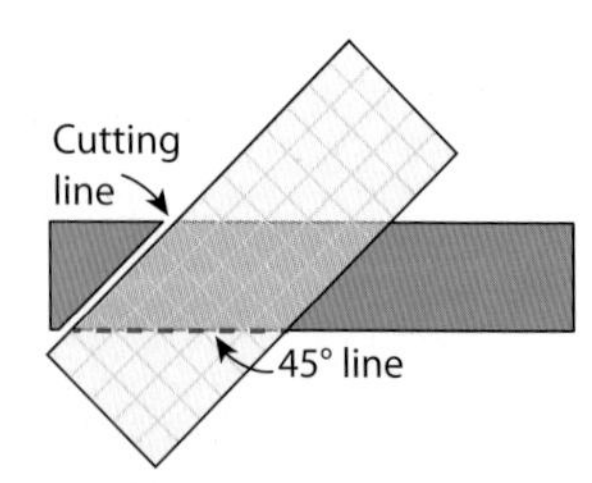

2. Line up the 5½″ line of the ruler with the cut angle of the fabric strips and the 45° line with the top of the fabric strips. Cut out 3 diamonds at a time, as shown. Cut 12 diamonds total from fabric A. Repeat with fabrics B and C.

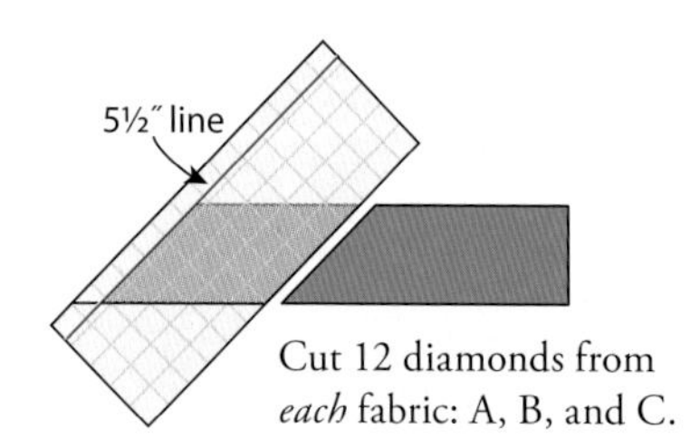

Cut 12 diamonds from *each* fabric: A, B, and C.

3. Mark the seam allowances in each corner of the 7½″ background squares. Repeat for the fabric A, B, and C diamonds.

4. Pin a fabric A diamond unit to one side of a 7½″ background square, matching the seam allowances and marks.

5. Sew together the pieces from mark to mark, backstitching at the ends. Stop exactly on the marked seam al-

Warm It Up!

To make a *Bows Peep* quilt that sports bows in shades of fuchsia and yellow, substitute with these fabrics. Follow the rest of the project instructions as given.

Bows Peep, 55" × 73½", pieced by Stacey Day and quilted by Miriam March

Background: 4 yards of cream

Fabric A: ⅔ yard of dark fuchsia

Fabric B: ⅔ yard of light fuchsia

Fabric C: ⅔ yard of yellow

lowance; do not sew all the way to the end of the fabric. Press the seams toward the diamond.

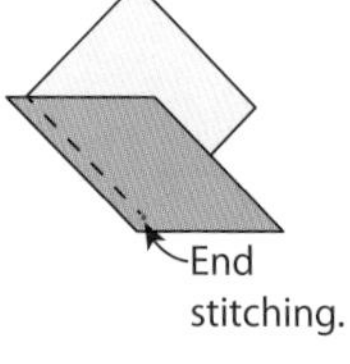

6. Pin a second fabric A diamond unit to the adjacent side of the square, matching the marked seam allowances as before. Sew in the same manner, being careful not to catch the seam allowances of the previous diamond unit in the stitching. Press the seams toward the diamond unit.

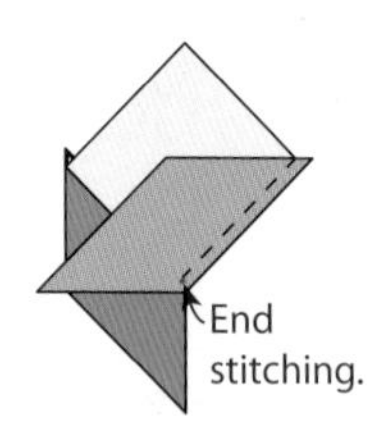

7. Fold the piece so that the fabric A diamonds are right sides together, matching the seam allowances. Pin them together at the bottom of the diamonds.

Start
stitching.

8. Sew together the diamonds from mark to mark, backstitching at each end and being careful not to catch the previous seam allowances in the stitching. Press the seam to one side.

9. Sew a pair of background half-square triangles to either side of the diamond units. Press toward the diamonds to make a Bow block.

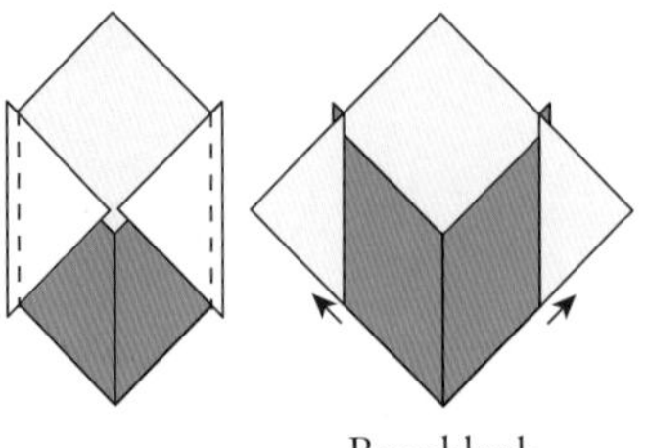

Bow block

10. Repeat Steps 4–9 using the remaining fabric A, B, and C diamonds to make 6 A blocks, 6 B blocks, and 6 C blocks. Trim and square all the blocks to 12½″ × 12½″. Set aside for now.

11. Sew the 1½″ × 27″ background strips to a pair of 1½″ × 42″ background strips to make 2 sashing 1½″ × 68″ strips. Sew together 2 background 1½″ × 42″ strips and trim to make a 1½″ × 82″ sashing strip.

12. Using the quilt assembly diagram as a guide, sew together the finished blocks, background half-square triangles, background quarter-square triangles, and 1½″ × 12½″ background rectangles into diagonal rows, pressing toward the sashing rectangles.

13. Sew together the diagonal rows and the long sashing strips, matching the center of the sashing strip with the center of each diagonal row and lining up the seam allowances of the blocks in each row. Press the seams toward the sashing strips, and trim the quilt top to 56½″ × 74½″.

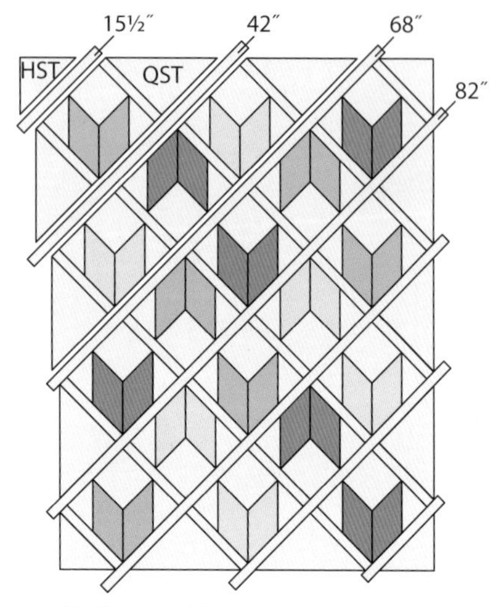

Quilt assembly

FINISHING THE QUILT

For detailed instructions on finishing techniques, refer to Finishing Touches (page 29).

1. Cut and piece the backing fabric so it is 8″ wider and longer than the quilt top. Layer the quilt top with the batting and backing. Baste together the layers.

2. Hand or machine quilt as desired.

3. Square up the quilt sandwich.

4. Prepare and sew the binding to the quilt. Add your label and enjoy!

Prism

FINISHED QUILT: 50″ × 62″

Pieced by Paul Krampitz and quilted by Miriam March

Diamonds are such a versatile shape; I love to play with the different angles and effects you can create by combining them. *Prism* is the result of one such experiment. The color placement was inspired by a geode my son showed me on one of our adventure days. The clear crystals inside were radiant and sparkling, and they matched the beaming smile on his face. The success of this quilt is due in large part to the background of multiple prints in similar hues. They add a subtle texture and depth that brings the quilt to life.

MATERIALS

Yardage is based on 42″-wide fabric.

BACKGROUND: 2¼ yards of cream

FABRIC A: ½ yard of medium pink

FABRIC B: ¼ yard of light pink

FABRIC C: ½ yard of light green

FABRIC D: ¼ yard of coral

FABRIC E: ½ yard of light purple

FABRIC F: ½ yard of purple

BINDING: ½ yard

BACKING: 3⅓ yards

BATTING: 58″ × 70″

TIPS

The diamond pieces are great candidates to cut from slabs. Or you could piece the diamonds as a four-patch, which creates a very effective transition between the colors and the background. To do this, make additional copies of the pattern. Divide it into quarters with a pencil, add seam allowances to the inside cut edges, and cut out the new smaller diamond.

CUTTING

BACKGROUND

- Cut 38 prisms A.
- Cut 9 prisms B.
- Cut 7 prisms C.
- Cut 3 prisms D.

FABRIC A

- Cut 4 prisms A.
- Cut 2 prisms B.
- Cut 1 prism D.

FABRIC B

- Cut 5 prisms A.

FABRIC C

- Cut 5 prisms A.
- Cut 1 prism B.
- Cut 1 prism C.

FABRIC D

- Cut 3 prisms A.
- Cut 1 prism B.

FABRIC E

- Cut 7 prisms A.
- Cut 1 prism B.

FABRIC F

- Cut 6 prisms A.

BINDING

- Cut 6 strips 2¼″ × 42″.

Making the Quilt

1. Following the quilt assembly diagram, sew together the prism A pieces into diagonal rows. Start and end each row with either a prism B, C, or D piece according to the diagram. Label each diagonal row as shown. Press the seams open.

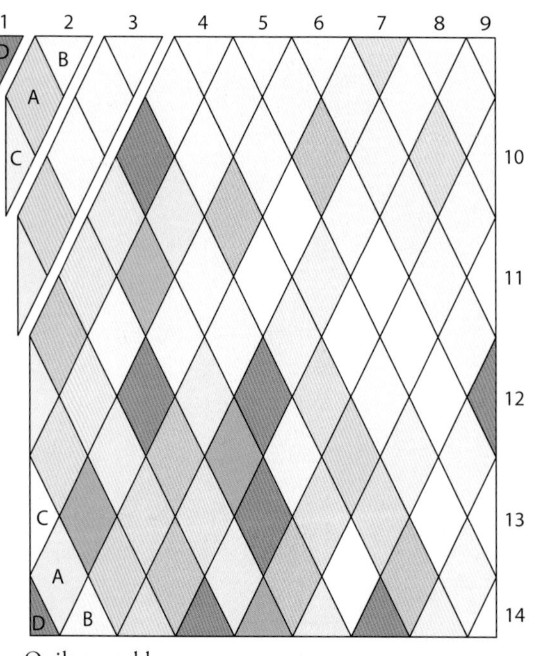

Quilt assembly

2. Sew together the diagonal rows, matching the seam allowances carefully. Press the seams open.

FINISHING THE QUILT

For detailed instructions on finishing techniques, refer to Finishing Touches (page 29).

1. Cut and piece the backing fabric so it is 8″ wider and longer than the quilt top. Layer the quilt top with the batting and backing. Baste together the layers.

2. Hand or machine quilt as desired.

3. Square up the quilt sandwich.

4. Prepare and sew the binding to the quilt. Add your label and enjoy!

Cool It Down!

To make a *Prism* quilt that scintillates in shades of blue and green, substitute with these fabrics. Follow the rest of the project instructions as given.

Prism, 50″ × 62″, pieced by Paul Krampitz and quilted by Miriam March

Background: 2¼ yards of off-white

Fabric A: ½ yard of medium green

Fabric B: ¼ yard of light blue

Fabric C: ½ yard of light yellow

Fabric D: ¼ yard of yellow-orange

Fabric E: ½ yard of light green

Fabric F: ½ yard of aqua

Apple Blossom

FINISHED QUILT: 52" × 64¾"

Pieced by Arita Rai and quilted by Miriam March

We are lucky enough to have family that live among orchards in British Columbia, where the scent of apples fills the air. Every year we visit their house and sit on the deck, taking in the beauty. Those orchards fill many family memories, from my husband's childhood to our wedding and our son's first bite of a sweet apple.

MATERIALS

Yardage is based on 42″-wide fabric.

BACKGROUND: 2½ yards of off-white

FABRIC A: ⅝ yard of dark pink

FABRIC B: ⅝ yard of medium pink

FABRIC C: ⅝ yard of light purple

FABRIC D: ⅝ yard of light pink

FABRIC E: ¼ yard of light green

BINDING: ½ yard

BACKING: 3½ yards

BATTING: 60″ × 73″

FUN TIP

Long strips of fabric make this quilt a breeze to piece. It's a great design for using up extra 2½″ precut strips or leftover fabric ends in the scrap bin. Small prints can be fussy cut and inserted into the strips.

CUTTING

BACKGROUND

- Cut 60 squares 4″ × 4″; subcut on both diagonals to make 240 quarter-square triangles.
- Cut 5 strips 2½″ × 42″.
- Cut 5 strips 2½″ × 11″.
- Cut 40 squares 2¼″ × 2¼″; subcut on the diagonal to make 80 half-square triangles.
- Cut 8 strips 1½″ × 42″.
- Cut 2 rectangles 1½″ × 24″.
- Cut 15 rectangles 1½″ × 11¾″.
- Cut 6 rectangles 1½″ × 9¼″.

FABRIC A

- Cut 3 strips 2½″ × 42″.
- Cut 3 rectangles 2½″ × 11″.
- Cut 20 squares 2½″ × 2½″.

FABRIC B

- Cut 4 strips 2½″ × 42″.
- Cut 4 rectangles 2½″ × 11″.
- Cut 20 squares 2½″ × 2½″.

FABRIC C

- Cut 5 strips 2½″ × 42″.
- Cut 5 rectangles 2½″ × 11″.

FABRIC D

- Cut 5 strips 2½″ × 42″.
- Cut 5 rectangles 2½″ × 11″.

FABRIC E

- Cut 1 strip 2½″ × 42″.
- Cut 1 rectangle 2½″ × 11″.

BINDING

- Cut 6 strips 2¼″ × 42″.

Making the Quilt

1. Sew 2 background quarter-square triangles to the opposite sides of a 2½″ fabric A square. Press the seams toward fabric A. Sew a background half-square triangle to one of the remaining sides. Press the seam toward fabric A, and set aside as unit A. Make 20.

Unit A

2. Repeat Step 1 with the 2½″ fabric B squares, and set aside as unit G. Make 20.

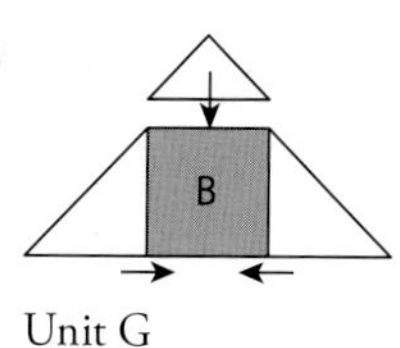

Unit G

3. Sew 2 fabric A 2½″ × 42″ strips to either side of a fabric B 2½″ × 42″ strip on the long edges. Press the seams toward fabric A to make a strip set. Repeat using the 2½″ × 11″ fabric A and B strips to make a small strip set.

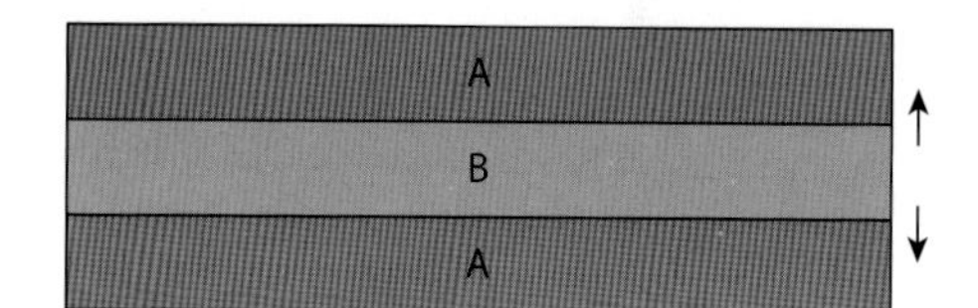

4. Subcut both strip sets from Step 3 into 20 strips 2½″ wide. Sew a background quarter-square triangle to the ends of the strips, as shown. Press the seams toward fabric A, and set aside as unit B. Make 20.

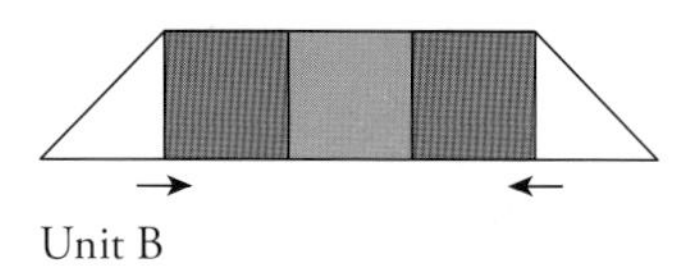

Unit B

5. Using the strips that measure 2½″ × 42″, sew together another strip set in the following order: fabric C, background, fabric A, background, and fabric D. Press the seams toward fabrics A, C, and D. Repeat the pattern using the 2½″ × 11″ rectangles, sewing them together in the same order.

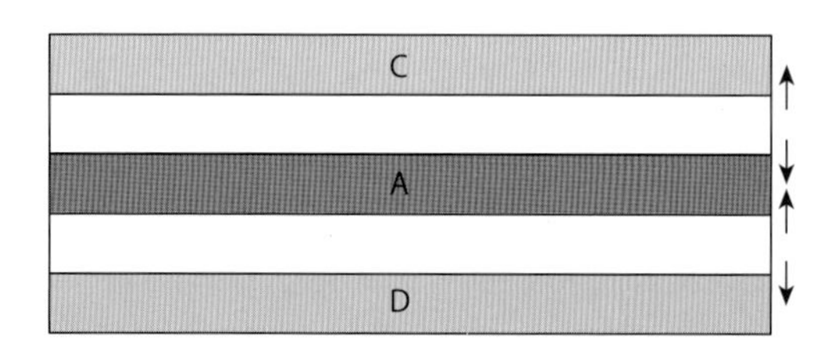

6. Subcut both strip sets from Step 5 into 20 pieces 2½″ wide. Sew a background quarter-square triangle to the ends of the strips, as shown. Press the seams toward the darker fabric, and set aside as unit C. Make 20.

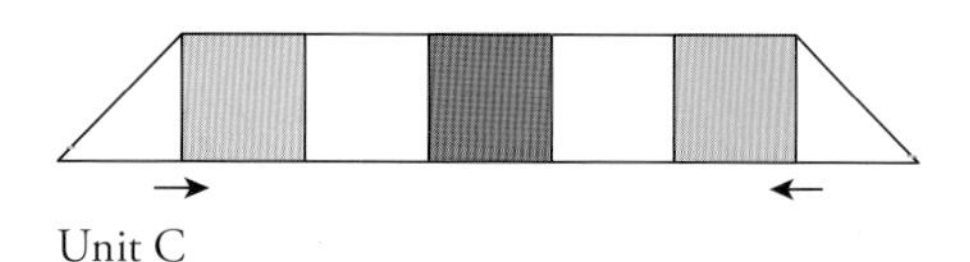

Unit C

7. Using the strips that measure 2½″ × 42″, sew together another strip set in the following order: fabric C, fabric D, fabric C, background, fabric D, fabric E, and fabric D. Press the seams as shown. Repeat the pattern using the 2½″ × 11″ rectangles, sewing them together in the same order.

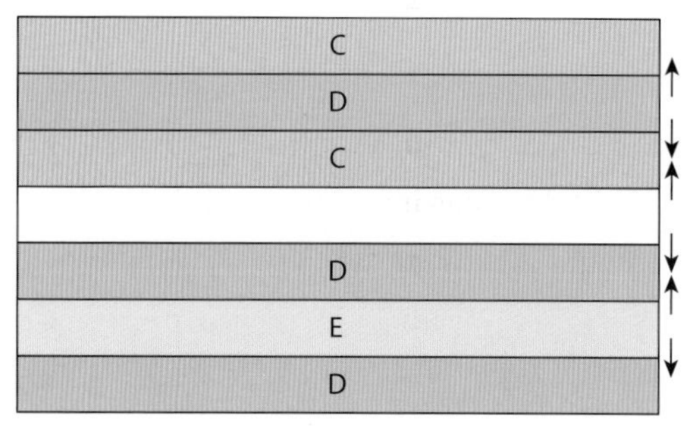

Strip set. Press in the direction of the arrows.

8. Subcut both strip sets from Step 7 into 20 pieces 2½″ wide. Sew a background half-square triangle to the ends of the strips, as shown. Press the seams toward the darker fabric, and set aside as unit D. Make 20.

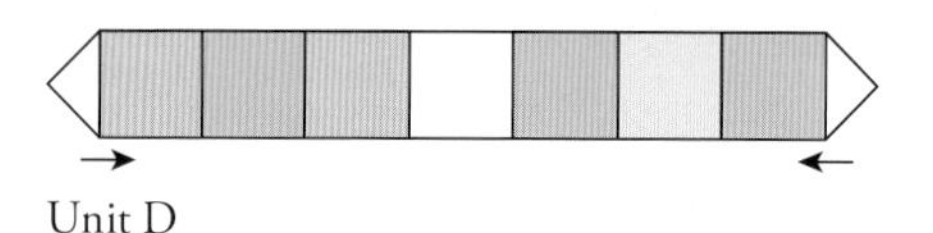

Unit D

9. Using the strips that measure 2½″ × 42″, sew together another strip set in the following order: fabric C, background, fabric B, background, and fabric D. Repeat using the 2½″ × 11″ rectangles, sewing them together in the same order. Press the seams away from the background fabric.

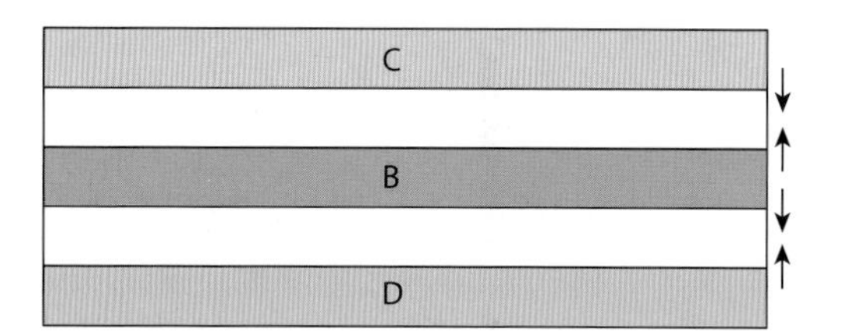

10. Subcut both strip sets from Step 9 into 20 pieces 2½″ wide. Sew a background quarter-square triangle to the ends of the strips, as shown. Press the seams toward the darker fabric, and set aside as unit E. Make 20.

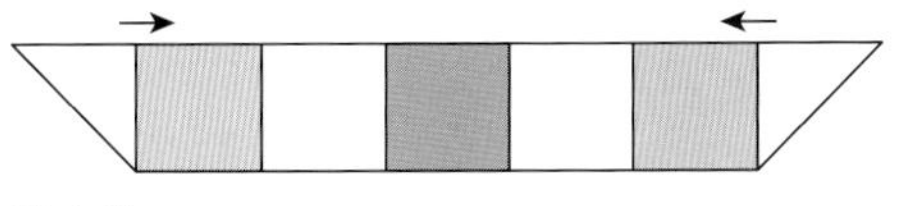

Unit E

11. Using the strips that measure 2½″ × 42″, sew together another strip set in the following order: fabric B, fabric C, and fabric B. Repeat the pattern using the 2½″ × 11″ rectangles, sewing them together in the same order. Press the seams toward fabric B.

B
C
B

12. Subcut both strip sets from Step 11 into 20 pieces 2½″ wide. Sew a background quarter-square triangle to the ends of the strips, as shown. Press the seams toward the darker fabric, and set aside as unit F. Make 20.

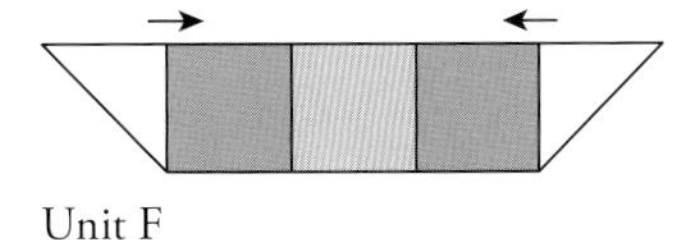

Unit F

13. Sew together units A–G in alphabetical order, as shown, to make the finished block. Match the seam allowances carefully and press them all in one direction. Trim and square the blocks to 11¾″ × 11¾″.

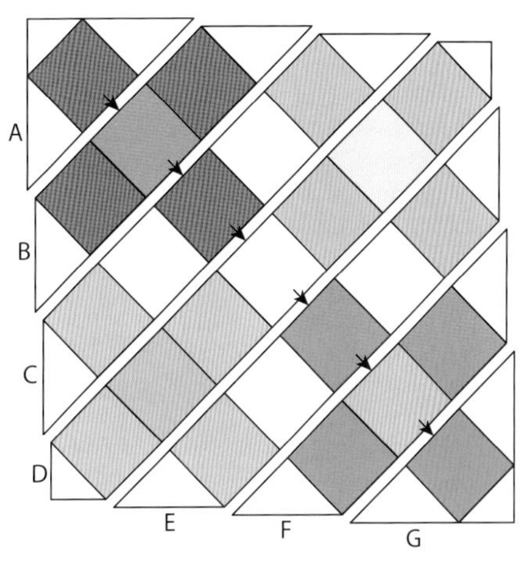

Finished block. Make 20. Sew together diagonal rows in order, and press seams as indicated by arrows.

14. Sew a 1½″ × 9¼″ background rectangle to one end of a 1½″ × 42″ background strip. Repeat to make 6 horizontal 50½″ sashing strips.

15. Take the 2 remaining 1½″ × 42″ background strips and sew a 1½″ × 24″ background strip to the end to make 2 vertical 65¼″ sashing strips.

16. Using the quilt assembly diagram as a guide, sew the blocks together into 5 rows of 4 blocks each, with a 1½″ × 11¾″ sashing strip in between each block. Pay attention to the orientation of the blocks in each row.

17. Sew together the rows with a 1½" × 50½" horizontal sashing strip in between each row, matching the ends and centers. Add a 1½" × 50½" horizontal sashing strip to the top and bottom of the quilt. Sew the 1½" × 65¼" vertical sashes to the sides of the quilt, matching the ends and centers, to finish the quilt top.

Quilt assembly

FINISHING THE QUILT

For detailed instructions on finishing techniques, refer to Finishing Touches (page 29).

1. Cut and piece the backing fabric so it is 8" wider and longer than the quilt top. Layer the quilt top with the batting and backing. Baste together the layers.

2. Hand or machine quilt as desired.

3. Square up the quilt sandwich.

4. Prepare and sew the binding to the quilt. Add your label and enjoy!

Cool It Down!

To make an *Apple Blossom* quilt that sports squares in shades of blue and teal, substitute with these fabrics. Follow the rest of the project instructions as given.

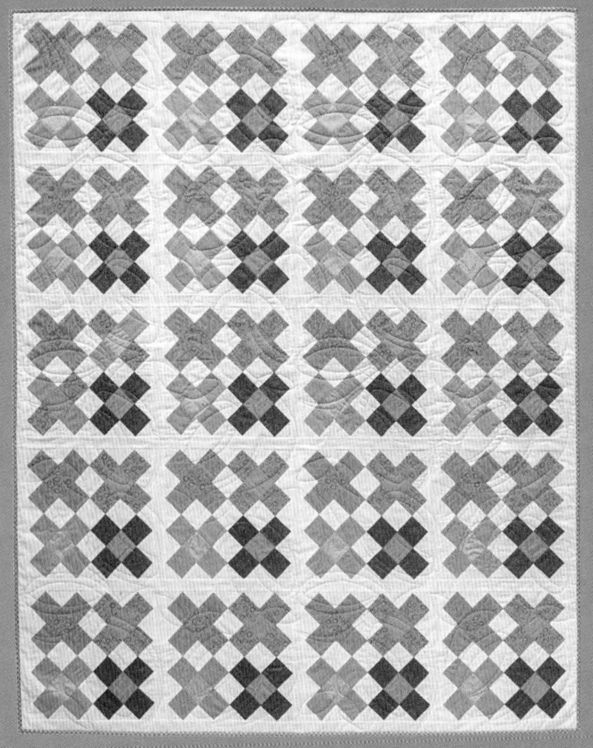

Apple Blossom, 52" × 64¾", pieced by Jade Prosser and quilted by Miriam March

Background: 2½ yards of off-white

Fabric A: ⅝ yard of dark blue

Fabric B: ⅝ yard of medium teal

Fabric C: ⅝ yard of light teal

Fabric D: ⅝ yard of light blue

Fabric E: ¼ yard of light green

Fishbowl

FINISHED QUILT: 38″ × 51″

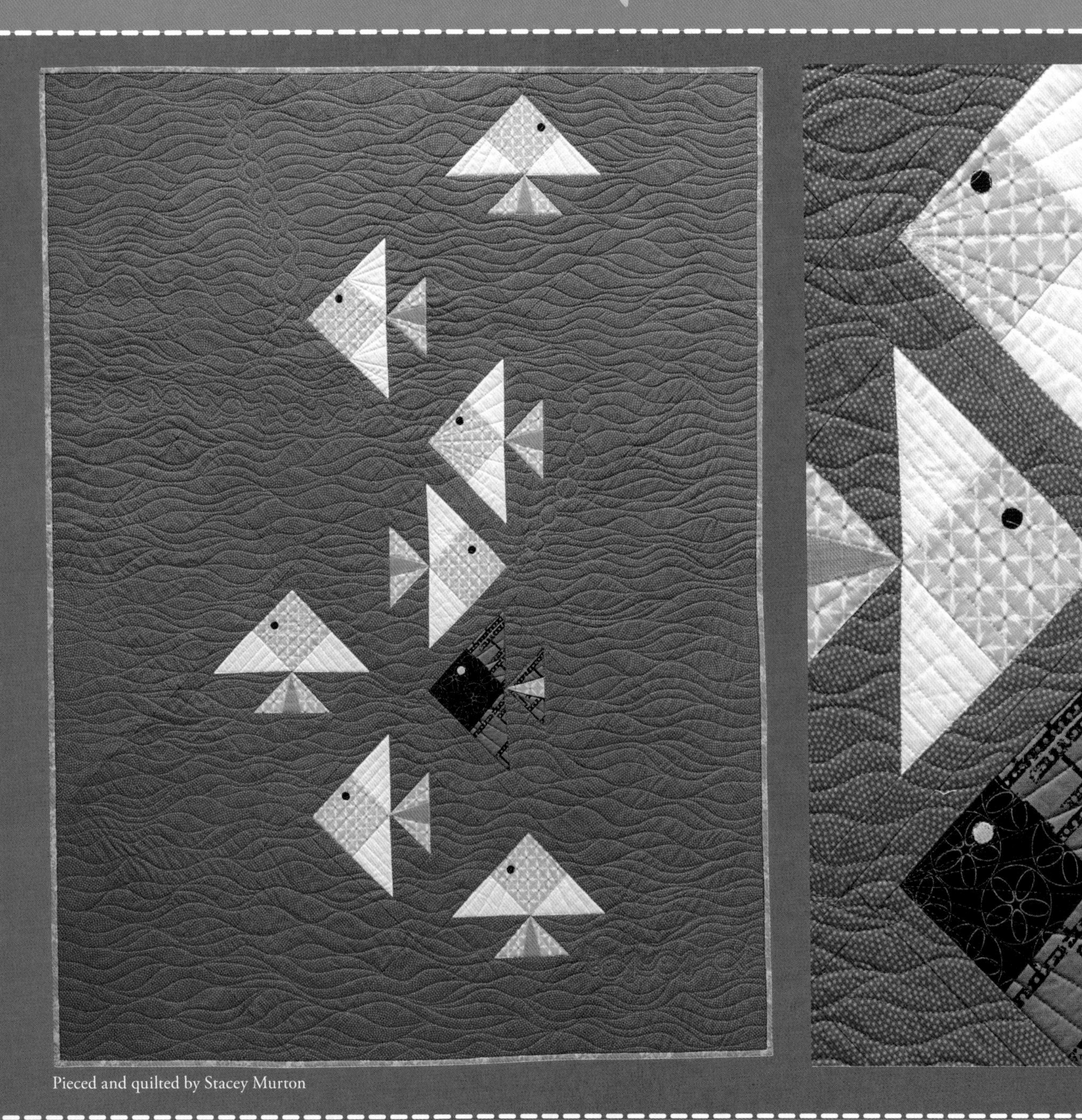

Pieced and quilted by Stacey Murton

When I was a child, I had some goldfish that thought they were birds. Every day when I returned home with my family, we would find a fish on the floor. We'd plop it back into the fishbowl and cover it again. Eventually the bowl of goldfish evolved into an elaborate tank of exotic freshwater fish, but I will always remember my goldies that thought they could fly.

MATERIALS

Yardage is based on 42″-wide fabric.

BACKGROUND: 1⅞ yards of medium blue

FABRIC A: ¼ yard of orange

FABRIC B: ⅛ yard of pale yellow

FABRIC C: ⅛ yard of light orange

FABRIC D: ⅛ yard of black

FABRIC E: ⅛ yard of light gray

BINDING: ½ yard

BACKING: 3 yards

BATTING: 46″ × 59″

TIP Batiks make a great background for *Fishbowl* because they have a watery look. You may substitute felt for the eyes, but if the quilt is for a baby or toddler, avoid beads, buttons, or other small objects that could be swallowed. If you want to upgrade from bowl to tank, add additional diagonal rows by making more fish and cutting more background squares and quarter-square triangles.

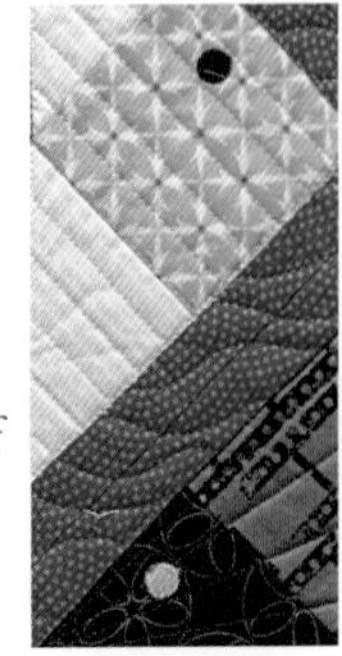

Fabric or felt make great eyes.

CUTTING

BACKGROUND

- Cut 2 squares 14″ × 14″; subcut on both diagonals to make 8 quarter-square triangles. Put 2 in your scrap bin for another project.
- Cut 2 squares 14″ × 14″; subcut on the diagonal to make 4 half-square triangles.
- Cut 9 squares 9½″ × 9½″.
- Cut 12 squares 3⅞″ × 3⅞″; subcut on the diagonal to make 24 half-square triangles.
- Cut 8 rectangles 2¾″ × 8¾″.
- Cut 8 rectangles 2¾″ × 6½″.
- Cut 8 rectangles 1¼″ × 9½″.
- Cut 8 rectangles 1¼″ × 8¾″.

FABRIC A

- Cut 4 squares, 3⅞″ × 3⅞″; subcut on the diagonal to make 8 half-square triangles. Discard 1.
- Cut 7 squares 3½″ × 3½″
- Cut 1 fin detail.

FABRIC B

- Cut 7 squares 3⅞″ × 3⅞″; subcut on the diagonal to make 14 half-square triangles.
- Cut 1 fish eye.

FABRIC C

- Cut 7 fin detail.

FABRIC D

- Cut 1 square 3½″ × 3½″.
- Cut 7 fish eyes.

FABRIC E

- Cut 2 squares 3⅞″ × 3⅞″; subcut on the diagonal to make 4 half-square triangles. Discard 1.

BINDING

- Cut 6 strips 2¼″ × 42″.

Making the Quilt

1. Sew together each fabric A half-square triangle with a background half-square triangle to make a half-square triangle square. Repeat with fabrics B and E. Trim each to 3½″ × 3½″. You will have 7 fabric A units, 14 fabric B units, and 3 fabric E units.

2. Sew together a 3½″ fabric A square, 2 fabric B half-square triangle squares, and a fabric A half-square triangle square as shown to make a fish unit. Trim to 6½″ × 6½″. Repeat to make 7 fish units.

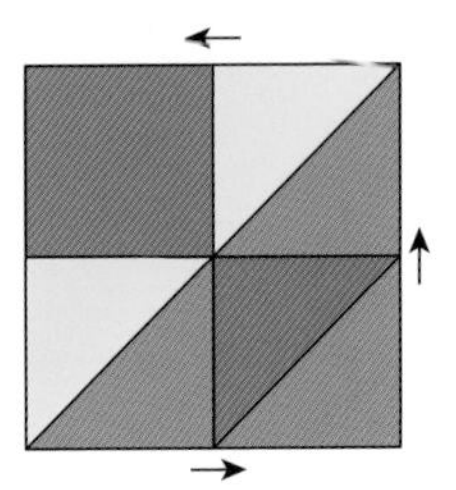

Fish unit

Warm It Up!

I used an assortment of warm, bright pinks for this version of *Fishbowl*. The result is a scrappier quilt with less contrast than the cool version. To make tropical fish in hues of pink and yellow, substitute with these fabrics. Follow the rest of the project instructions as given.

Fishbowl, 38″ × 51″, pieced by Stacey Day and quilted by Stacey Murton

Background: 1⅞ yards of light blue

Fabric A: ¼ yard of light pink

Fabric B: ⅛ yard of pale yellow

Fabric C: ⅛ yard of medium pink

Fabric D: ⅛ yard of plum

Fabric E: ⅛ yard of medium coral

3. Sew the 3½″ fabric D square and the fabric E half-square triangle squares together to make 1 contrast fish unit. Trim to 6½″ × 6½″.

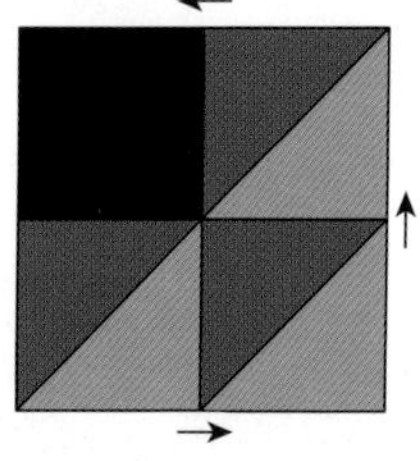

Contrast fish unit

4. Sew a 2¾″ × 6½″ background rectangle to the bottom of each fish unit, as shown. Press the seam toward the rectangle. Sew a 2¾″ × 8¾″ background rectangle to the right side of each fish unit. Press toward the new rectangle.

5. Sew a 1¼″ × 8¾″ background rectangle to the left side of each fish unit, as shown. Press the seam toward the rectangle. Sew a 1¼″ × 9½″ background rectangle to the top of each fish unit. Press the seam toward the rectangle to make 7 yellow Fish blocks and 1 black Contrast Fish block.

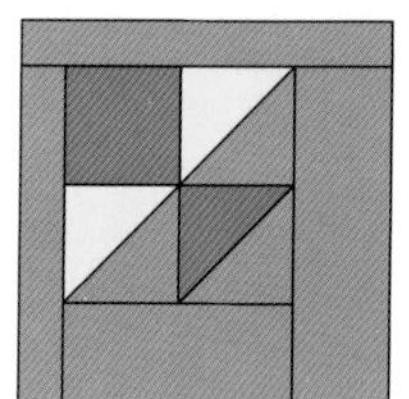

Fish block

Contrast Fish block

6. Pin the fabric B fish eye on the "head" of the contrast fish. Pin the fabric A fin detail on the center of the "tail." Appliqué both to the Contrast Fish block. Repeat with the Fish blocks, using fabric D fish eyes and fabric C fin detail pieces. Note the placement of the fish eyes on the fish: Make 4 blocks with the fish looking left and 3 blocks with the fish looking right.

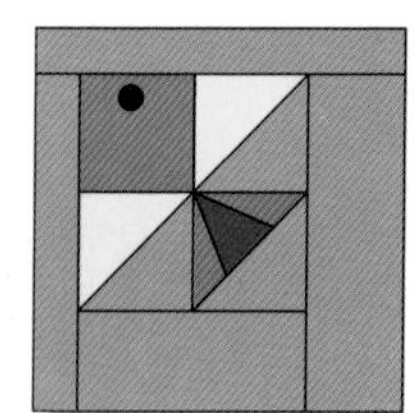

Left-facing Fish block. Make 4.

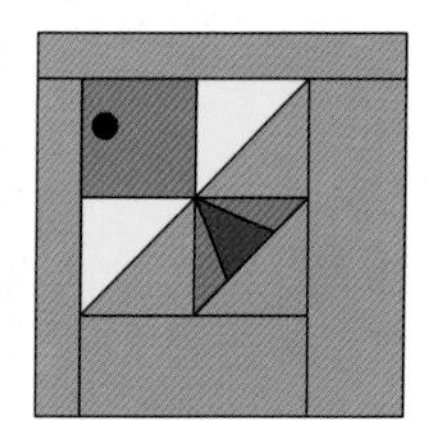

Right-facing Fish block. Make 3.

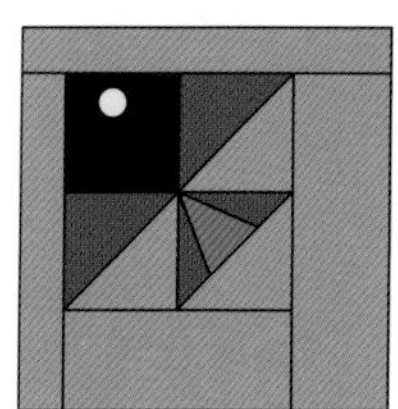

Contrast Fish block. Make 1.

7. Sew together the Fish blocks, Contrast Fish block, 9½″ background squares, and the background quarter-square triangles (QST) into diagonal rows, as shown. Press the seams in alternating directions. Sew together the diagonal rows in order, matching the seam allowances carefully. Press the seams toward the bottom.

8. Sew the long edge of a half-square triangle (HST) to each corner of the quilt top. Press the seams toward the triangles.

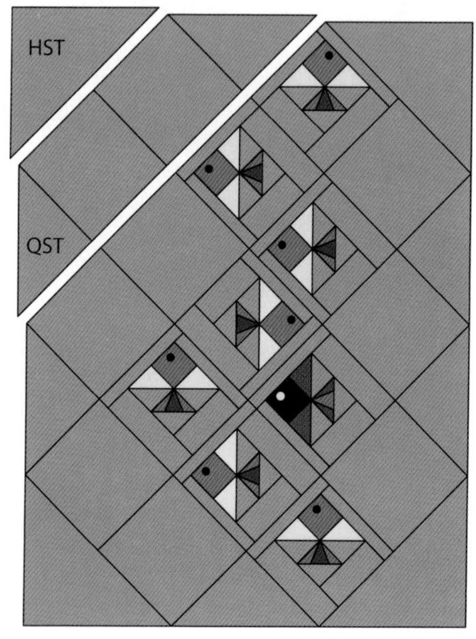

Quilt assembly

FINISHING THE QUILT

For detailed instructions on finishing techniques, refer to Finishing Touches (page 29).

1. Cut and piece the backing fabric so it is 8″ wider and longer than the quilt top. Layer the quilt top with the batting and backing. Baste together the layers.

2. Hand or machine quilt as desired.

3. Square up the quilt sandwich.

4. Prepare and sew the binding to the quilt. Add your label and enjoy!

Butterfly Kisses

FINISHED QUILT: 48″ × 60″

Pieced by Stacey Day and quilted by Miriam March

With both of my children, a surefire way to get giggles was to give them butterfly kisses all over their tummies. A soft brush of eyelashes was irresistibly ticklish, and their bubbly laughter and bright smiles always made my day. I captured those memories in the bright, bold colors and the suggestion of a blinking eye.

MATERIALS

Yardage is based on 42″-wide fabric.

BACKGROUND: 3 yards of medium blue

FABRIC A: ⅝ yard of orange

FABRIC B: ½ yard of yellow

FABRIC C: ¾ yard of dark green

FABRIC D: 1⅛ yards of lime green

BINDING: ½ yard

BACKING: 3¼ yards

BATTING: 56″ × 68″

TIPS

Treat the fabric with a light spray starch before cutting to help keep the pieces from stretching as you sew. To cut the pattern pieces from slabs, make the slabs slightly bigger than the templates and mark the centers with a removable-ink marking pen, since the slabs may not hold a finger-pressed crease. Follow the pressing directions exactly to nest the seams.

CUTTING

BACKGROUND

- Cut 40 of butterfly 1.
- Cut 40 of butterfly 2.

FABRIC A

- Cut 40 of butterfly 3.

FABRIC B

- Cut 40 of butterfly 4.

FABRIC C

- Cut 40 of butterfly 5.

FABRIC D

- Cut 40 of butterfly 6.

BINDING

- Cut 6 strips 2¼″ × 42″.

Making the Quilt

1. Fold every piece cut from butterfly patterns 1, 2, 3, 4, 5, and 6 in half. Finger-press to mark the centers. While the piece is folded, clip the concave (inside) curve of the background, fabric A, and fabric C butterfly pieces about ⅛″ into the seam allowance.

2. Pin together the fabric B and A pieces with right sides facing. Match the ends and center notches; then sew them together along the curve. Press the seam toward fabric A. Pin the pattern 1 background piece to the top, matching the ends and centers. Sew them together, and press the seam toward fabric A to make unit A. Make 40.

Unit A

3. Repeat Step 2 using fabric C and D pieces and the pattern 2 background piece to make unit B. Press the seams toward fabric C. Make 40.

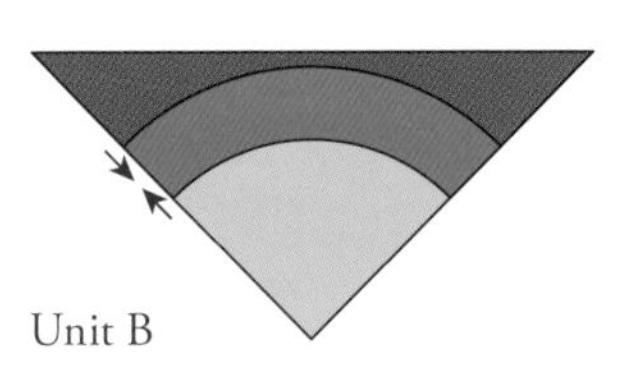

Unit B

4. Sew together pairs of units A and B, as shown, to make a Kiss block. Press the seams toward the units A, and trim to 12½″ × 12½″.

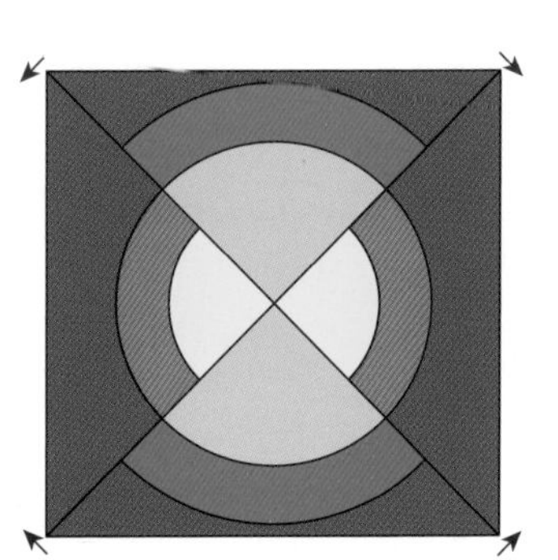

Kiss block

NOISY FARM
NOISY DINOSAURS

5. Sew the Kiss blocks into 5 rows of 4 blocks each, referring to the quilt assembly diagram for the orientation of each block. Press the seams in alternating directions for each row. Rows 1, 3, and 5 will have the even-numbered blocks rotated, and rows 2 and 4 will have the odd-numbered blocks rotated.

6. Sew together the rows, matching the seam allowances carefully.

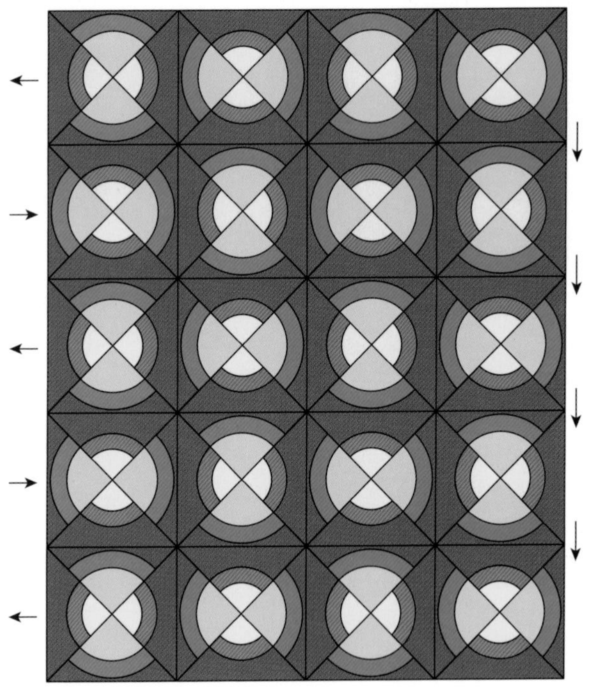

Quilt assembly

FINISHING THE QUILT

For detailed instructions on finishing techniques, refer to Finishing Touches (page 29).

1. Cut and piece the backing fabric so it is 8″ wider and longer than the quilt top. Layer the quilt top with the batting and backing. Baste together the layers.

2. Hand or machine quilt as desired.

3. Square up the quilt sandwich.

4. Prepare and sew the binding to the quilt. Add your label and enjoy!

Warm It Up!

I used an assortment of my favorite prints for the warm version of this quilt. The background is lighter to make the quilt softer overall. To make a *Butterfly Kisses* quilt in shades of pink and purple, substitute with these fabrics. Follow the rest of the project instructions as given.

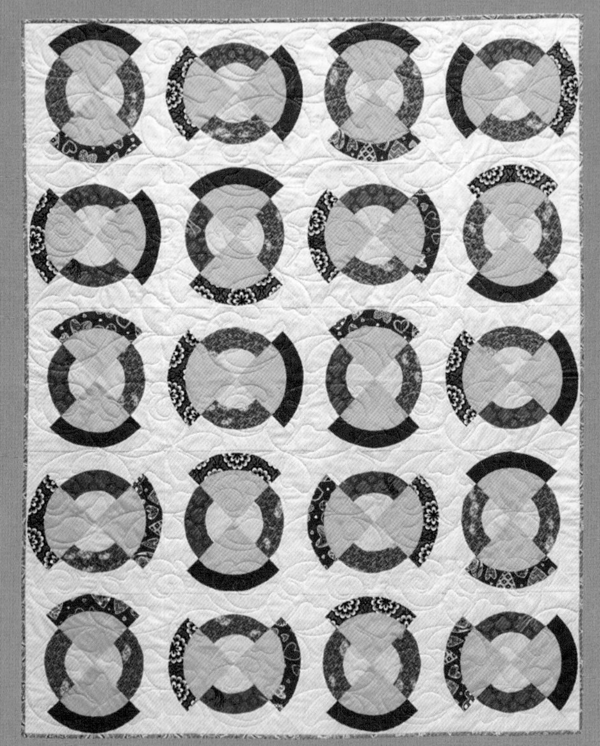

Butterfly Kisses, 48″ × 60″, pieced by Paul Krampitz and quilted by Miriam March

Background: 3 yards of light pink

Fabric A: ⅝ yard of medium pink

Fabric B: ½ yard of light yellow

Fabric C: ¾ yard of purple

Fabric D: 1⅛ yards of gold

Beaded

FINISHED QUILT: 60″ × 72″

Pieced by Paul Krampitz and quilted by Miriam March

Beaded arts and crafts were always a favorite of mine as a kid, and now my kids love them as well. There is something about running one's fingers through a container of beads that is both soothing and fun. My oldest likes to glue large plastic beads to anything he can find, but babies and beads certainly do not mix—so save this quilt for older kids.

MATERIALS

Yardage is based on 42″-wide fabric.

BACKGROUND A: 1⅞ yards of light cream

BACKGROUND B: 1¼ yards of dark cream

FABRIC A: ½ yard of light pink

FABRIC B: ¾ yard of medium pink

FABRIC C: ½ yard of light green

FABRIC D: ¾ yard of medium green

BINDING: ⅝ yard

BACKING: 3⅞ yards

BATTING: 68″ × 80″

TIP

Beaded is perfect for auditioning different complementary-color pairs. Purple and yellow, aqua and coral, or even a completely monochromatic quilt in various shades of gray will work—as long as there is enough contrast between the light and dark hues.

CUTTING

BACKGROUND A

- Cut 60 squares 3⅞″ × 3⅞″; subcut on the diagonal to make 120 half-square triangles.
- Cut 120 squares 3½″ × 3½″.

BACKGROUND B

- Cut 30 squares 4¾″ × 4¾″.
- Cut 60 squares 3⅞″ × 3⅞″; subcut on the diagonal to make 120 half-square triangles.

FABRIC A

- Cut 8 squares 7¼″ × 7¼″; subcut on both diagonals to make 32 quarter-square triangles. Discard 2.

FABRIC B

- Cut 8 squares 7¼″ × 7¼″; subcut on both diagonals to make 32 quarter-square triangles. Discard 2.
- Cut 30 squares 3⅞″ × 3⅞″; subcut on the diagonal to make 60 half-square triangles.

FABRIC C

- Cut 8 squares 7¼″ × 7¼″; subcut on both diagonals to make 32 quarter-square triangles. Discard 2.

FABRIC D

- Cut 8 squares 7¼″ × 7¼″; subcut on both diagonals to make 32 quarter-square triangles. Discard 2.
- Cut 30 squares 3⅞″ × 3⅞″; subcut on the diagonal to make 60 half-square triangles.

BINDING

- Cut 7 strips 2¼″ × 42″.

Making the Quilt

1. Sew a pair of 3⅞″ fabric B half-square triangles to either side of a 4¾″ background B square. Press the seams toward the triangles. Sew a second pair of fabric B half-square triangles to the remaining sides. Press the seams toward the triangles, and trim the block to 6½″ × 6½″ to make unit A. Make 15.

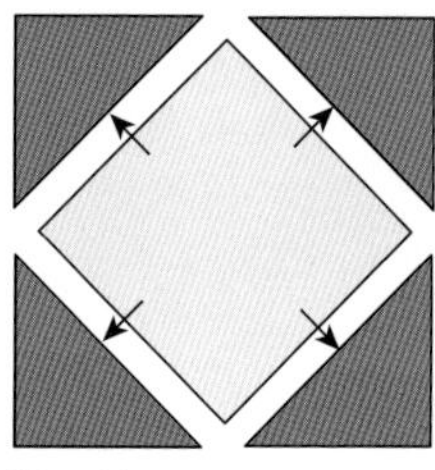

Unit A

2. Repeat Step 1 using the 3⅞″ fabric D half-square triangles and the remaining 4¾″ background B squares to make unit B. Make 15.

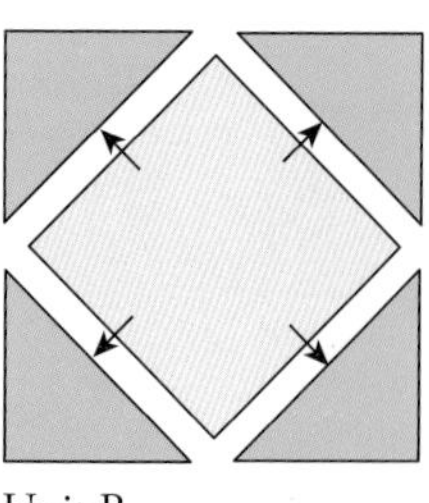

Unit B

Cool It Down!

Blue and orange are powerful complementary colors. I used hues that were lower in contrast between the light and dark and about the same intensity between the blue and orange to keep the quilt from becoming overwhelming. It still has visual impact, but it isn't jarring. To make a *Beaded* quilt in shades of blue and orange, substitute with these fabrics. Follow the rest of the project instructions as given.

Beaded, 60" × 72", pieced by Paul Krampitz and quilted by Miriam March

Background A: 1⅞ yards of light tan

Background B: 1¼ yards of medium tan

Fabric A: ½ yard of light blue

Fabric B: ¾ yard of medium blue

Fabric C: ½ yard of light orange

Fabric D: ¾ yard of medium orange

3. Sew a pair of 3⅞″ background B half-square triangles to either side of a 7¼″ fabric B quarter-square triangle. Press the seams toward fabric B, and trim to 3½″ × 6½″ to make unit C. Make 30.

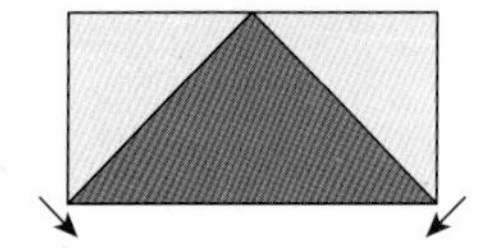

Unit C

4. Repeat Step 3 using the same background triangles and a 7¼″ fabric D quarter-square triangle to make unit D. Make 30.

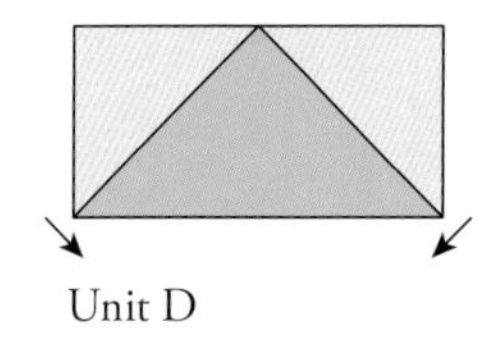

Unit D

5. Sew a pair of 3⅞″ background A half-square triangles to either side of a 7¼″ fabric A quarter-square triangle. Press the seams toward fabric A, and trim to 3½″ × 6½″ to make unit E. Make 30.

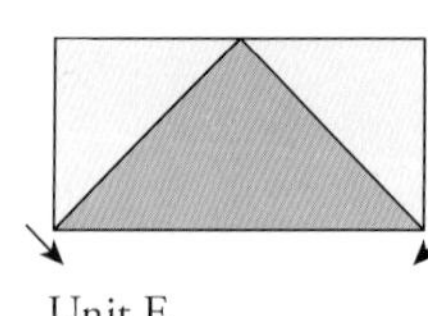

Unit E

6. Repeat Step 5 using the same background triangles and a 7¼″ fabric C quarter-square triangle to make unit F. Make 30.

Unit F

7. Sew together units A, C, and E with 4 background A 3½″ squares to make 1 A block. Make 15.

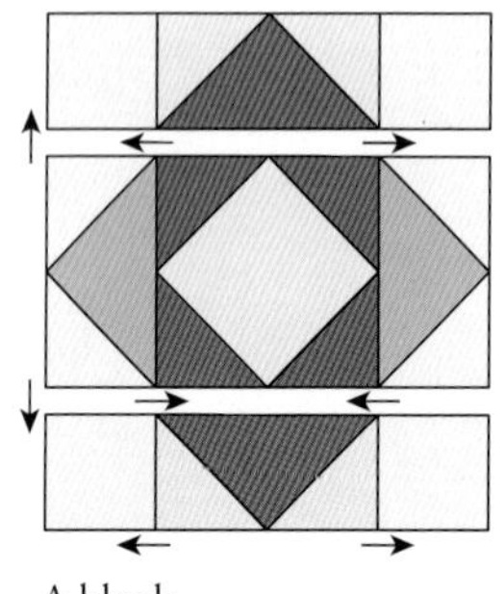

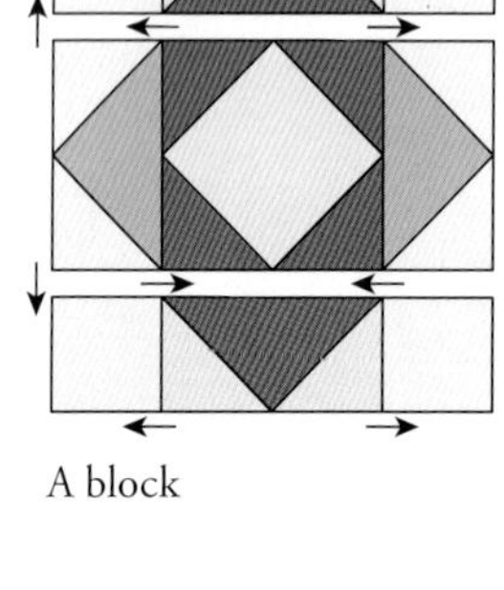

A block

8. Sew together units B, D, and F with 4 background A 3½″ squares to make 1 B block. Make 15.

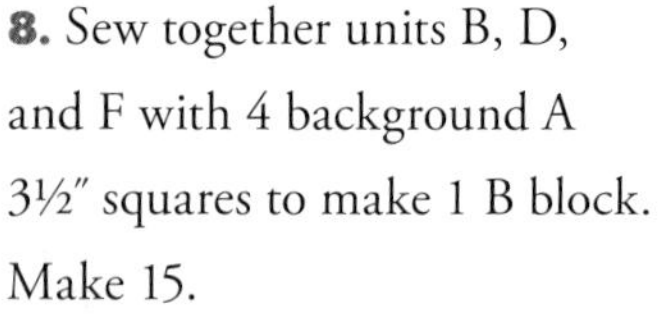

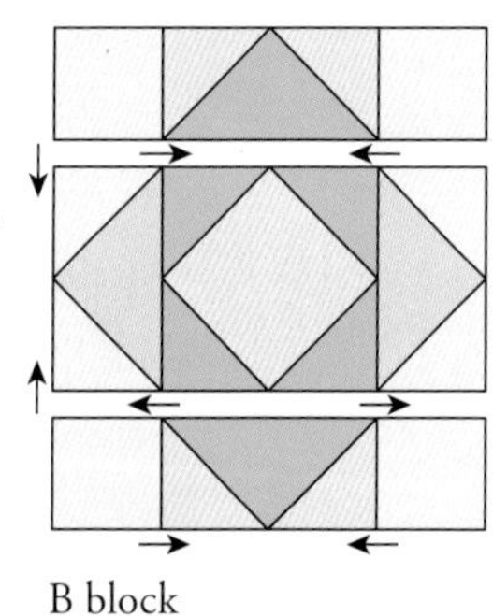

B block

9. Sew the A and B blocks into rows, as shown in the quilt assembly diagram. Press the odd rows to the left and the even rows to the right. Sew the rows together in order, matching the seam allowances and pressing all the seams toward the bottom of the quilt top.

Quilt assembly

FINISHING THE QUILT

For detailed instructions on finishing techniques, refer to Finishing Touches (page 29).

1. Cut and piece the backing fabric so it is 8″ wider and longer than the quilt top. Layer the quilt top with the batting and backing. Baste together the layers.

2. Hand or machine quilt as desired.

3. Square up the quilt sandwich.

4. Prepare and sew the binding to the quilt. Add your label and enjoy!

Pinwheel

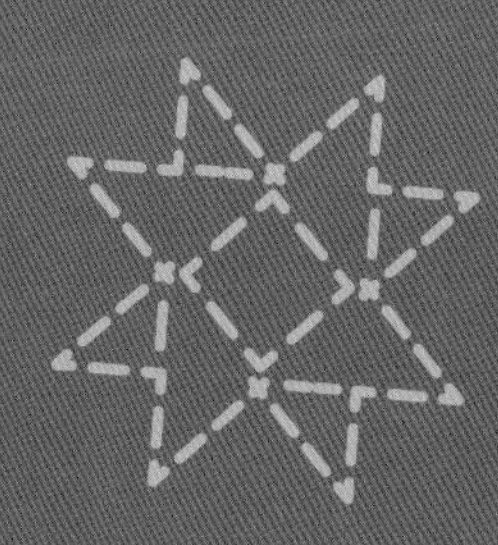

FINISHED QUILT: 45¼" × 58"

Pieced and quilted by Stacey Day

Summertime is a magical season when you are a child. The days are longer, the air is warmer, the sky seems bluer, and there is an explosion of bright, vibrant colors. My son loves summertime trappings like water parks, bubbles, and (above all) pinwheels. He has a small collection of pinwheels that grows every time we visit the dollar store. Watching him and my baby together, finding joy and pleasure in the movement and color—in the simplest of things—warms my heart like the summer sun.

MATERIALS

Yardage is based on 42″-wide fabric.

BACKGROUND: 2¾ yards of cream

FABRIC A: ⅜ yard of green

FABRIC B: ¼ yard of turquoise

FABRIC C: ⅜ yard of light pink

FABRIC D: ⅜ yard of deep pink

BINDING: ½ yard

BACKING: 3⅛ yards

BATTING: 54″ × 66″

TIP

Pinwheel is perfect for using up scrap squares. I pulled out all the stops with this quilt and used fabric pieces I'd been saving for years. My friend Sue Saylor even raided her stash for more background fabric when I ran short. Thanks, Sue!

CUTTING

BACKGROUND

- Cut 2 rectangles 4″ × 40½″.
- Cut 2 rectangles 4″ × 38¾″
- Cut 2 rectangles 4″ × 18½″.
- Cut 2 squares 14″ × 14″; subcut on both diagonals to make 8 quarter-square triangles.
- Cut 3 squares 8⅜″ × 8⅜″; subcut on the diagonal to make 6 half-square triangles.
- Cut 17 squares 4¼″ × 4¼″; subcut on both diagonals to make 68 quarter-square triangles.
- Cut 35 squares 3½″ × 3½″.
- Cut 6 rectangles 2″ × 8⅜″.
- Cut 50 rectangles 2″ × 3½″.
- Cut 50 squares 2″ × 2″.

FABRIC A

- Cut 17 squares 4¼″ × 4¼″; subcut on both diagonals to make 68 quarter-square triangles.

FABRIC B

- Cut 56 squares 2″ × 2″.

FABRIC C

- Cut 16 squares 3⅞″ × 3⅞″; subcut on the diagonal to make 32 half-square triangles.

FABRIC D

- Cut 18 squares 3⅞″ × 3⅞″; subcut on the diagonal to make 36 half-square triangles.

BINDING

- Cut 6 strips 2¼″ × 42″.

Making the Quilt

1. Sew together a 2″ fabric B square and a 2″ background square to make a two-patch. Press the seam toward fabric B. Add a 2″ × 3½″ background rectangle to the bottom, as shown, and press the seam toward the rectangle. Trim to 3½″ × 3½″ to make unit A. Make 56.

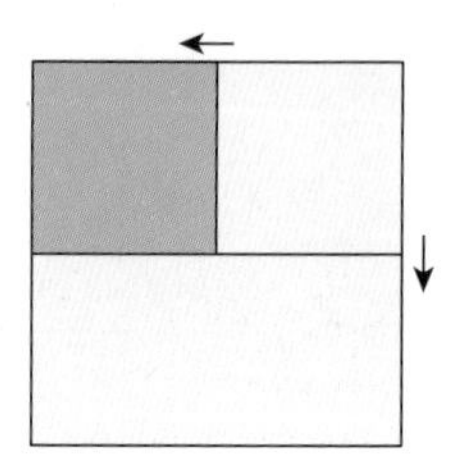

Unit A

2. Sew together a 4¼″ background quarter-square triangle and a 4¼″ fabric A quarter-square triangle, as shown. Press the seam toward fabric A. Add a 3⅞″ fabric D half-square triangle to the bottom. Trim to 3½″ × 3½″ to make unit B. Make 36.

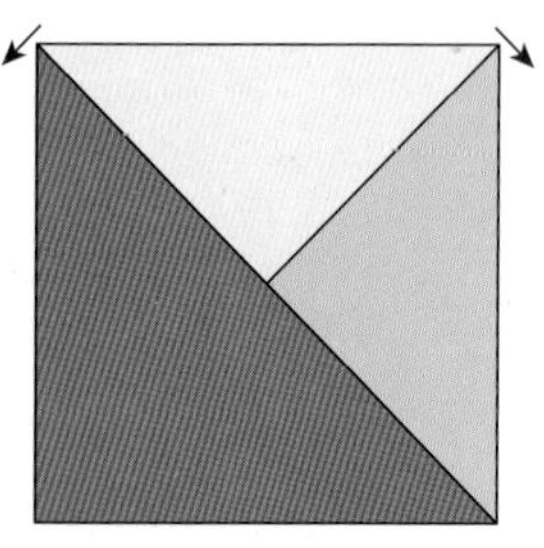

Unit B. Note the orientation of the quarter-square triangles, with fabric A on the right.

3. Sew together a 4¼″ background quarter-square triangle and a 4¼″ fabric A quarter-square triangle, as shown. Press the seam toward fabric A. Add a 3⅞″ fabric C half-square triangle to the bottom. Trim to 3½″ × 3½″ to make unit C. Make 32.

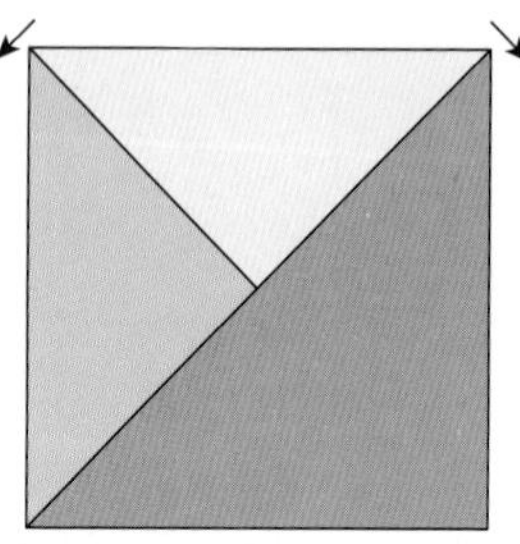

Unit C. Note the orientation of the quarter-square triangles, with fabric A on the left.

4. Sew together units A and B and a 3½″ background square, as shown, to make 1 A block. Trim to 9½″ × 9½″. Make 3.

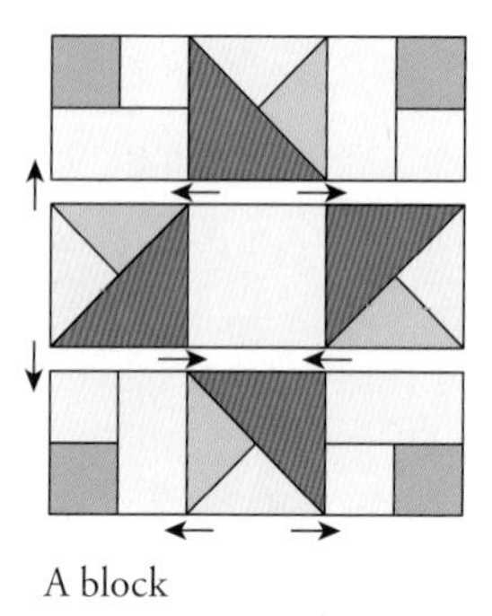

A block

5. Sew together units A and B and 3½″ background squares, as shown, to make 1 B block. Trim to 9½″ × 9½″. Make 4.

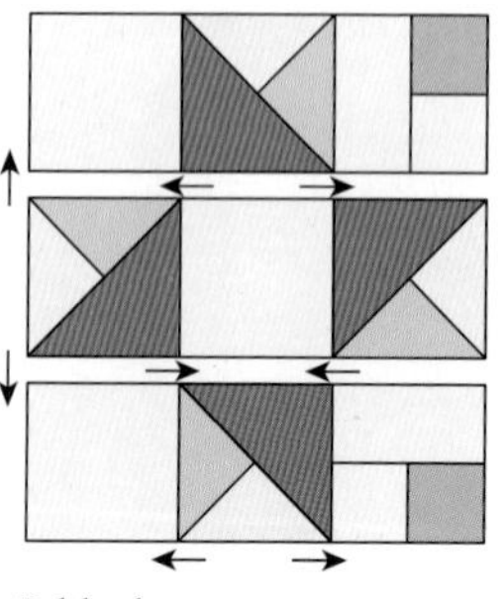

B block

6. Sew together units A and B and 3½″ background squares, as shown, to make 1 C block. Trim to 9½″ × 9½″. Make 2.

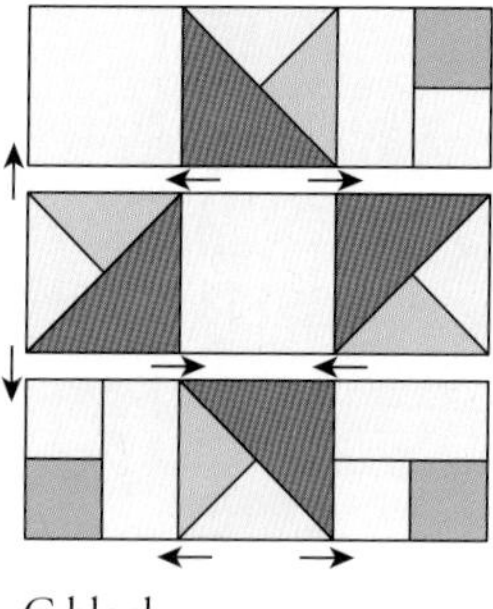

C block

7. Sew together units A and C and a 3½″ background square, as shown, to make 1 D block. Trim to 9½″ × 9½″. Make 4.

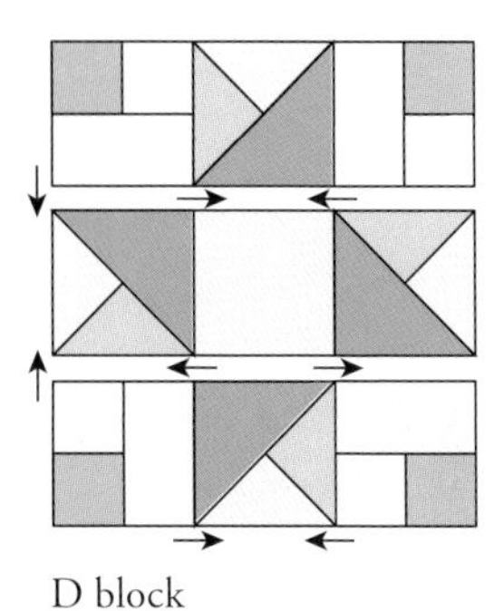
D block

8. Sew together units A and C and 3½″ background squares, as shown, to make 1 E block. Trim to 9½″ × 9½″. Make 4.

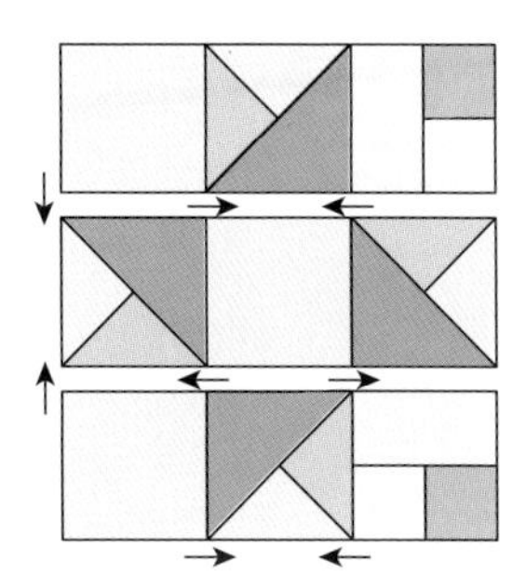
E block

9. Sew the 2″ × 8⅜″ background rectangles to the 2″ fabric B squares. Add a 8⅜″ background half-square triangle to the side, as shown. Trim the end of the rectangle in line with the half-square triangle to make 1 F block. Make 6.

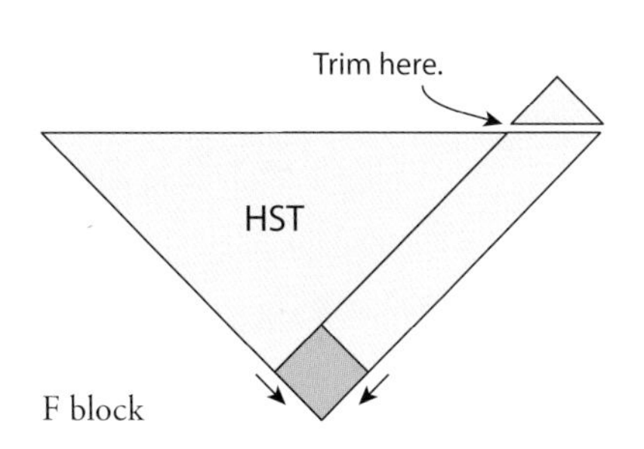

F block

10. Sew together the 14″ background quarter-square triangles (QST) and blocks A–F into diagonal rows, referring to the quilt assembly diagram. Press the even rows to the left and the odd rows to the right. Sew together the diagonal rows, matching the seam allowances and pressing the seams toward the bottom of the quilt.

11. Sew a 4″ × 38¾″ background strip to the top and bottom of the quilt top, matching the ends and centers. Press the seams toward the borders.

12. Sew together each 4″ × 40½″ strip with a 4″ × 18½″ strip to make 2 vertical 4″ × 58½″ borders. Sew them to both sides of the quilt top, matching the ends and centers and pressing the seams toward the border.

Quilt assembly

FINISHING THE QUILT

For detailed instructions on finishing techniques, refer to Finishing Touches (page 29).

1. Cut and piece the backing fabric so it is 8″ wider and longer than the quilt top. Layer the quilt top with the batting and backing. Baste together the layers.

2. Hand or machine quilt as desired.

3. Square up the quilt sandwich.

4. Prepare and sew the binding to the quilt. Add your label and enjoy!

Cool It Down!

The cool version of this quilt is a lot calmer. I used the same print for each pinwheel and chose prints of a very similar hue. The resulting pinwheels are like a soft breeze on a lazy day. Choose similar blues and a bright pop of yellow, and follow the rest of the project instructions as given.

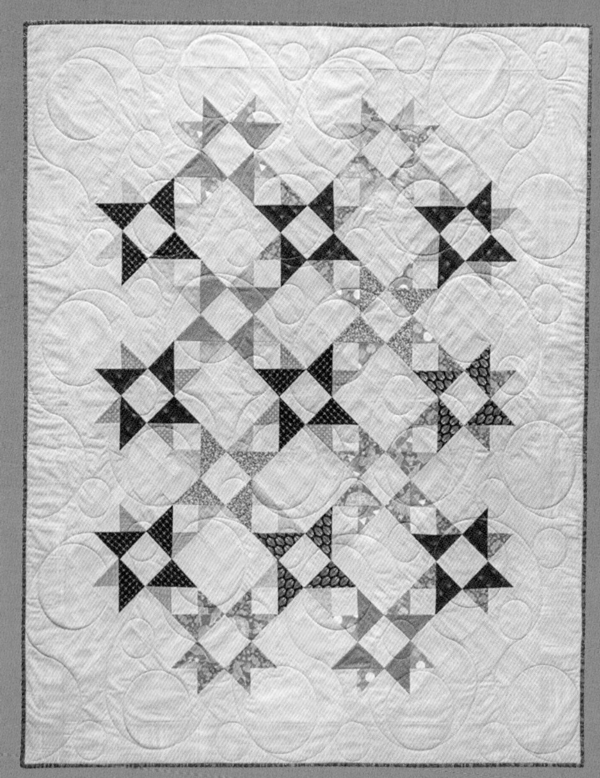

Pinwheel, 45¼″ × 58″, pieced and quilted by Stacey Day

Background: 2¾ yards of light gray

Fabric A: ⅜ yard of green

Fabric B: ¼ yard of light yellow

Fabric C: ⅜ yard of light blue

Fabric D: ⅜ yard of deep blue

Swish

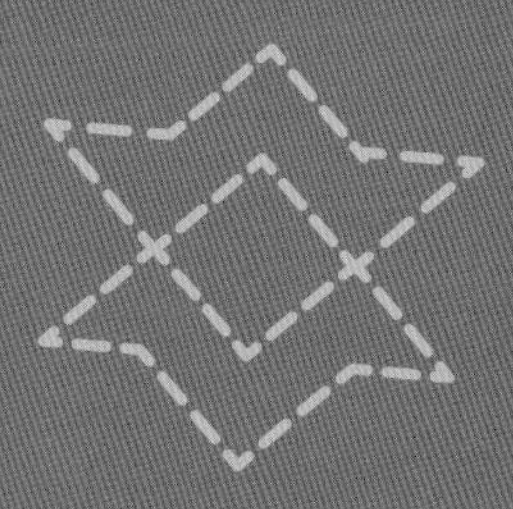

FINISHED QUILT: 52¼" × 61¾"

Pieced by Stacey Day and quilted by Miriam March

You don't truly appreciate just how fast a small child can be until you have to chase one down. It's usually because they have melted chocolate clenched in one little fist and spaghetti noodles in the other, running full tilt for the sewing room or grandma's couch. A toddler can be surprisingly hard to catch. But when you do, and they start that maniacal giggle, it makes the chase worthwhile. I wanted to capture that moment of fast fun and giggles in a quilt that will help your little one slow down at the end of a long day.

MATERIALS

Yardage is based on 42"-wide fabric.

BACKGROUND: 2½ yards of cream

FABRIC A: ⅝ yard of light pink

FABRIC B: 1 yard of medium pink

FABRIC C: 1 yard of medium purple

BINDING: ½ yard

BACKING: 3⅜ yards

BATTING: 60" × 70"

FUN TIPS

To accurately sew together triangles and squares, match up the centers first. Fold the pieces in half and finger-press. Line up the folds and pin. Voilà! Perfectly centered pieces make for accurate blocks that are easy to square up.

CUTTING

BACKGROUND

- Cut 15 squares 5⅞" × 5⅞"; subcut on both diagonals to make 60 quarter-square triangles for the D and E blocks and the border blocks.
- Cut 30 squares 3⅞" × 3⅞" for the B and C blocks.
- Cut 144 squares 3¼" × 3¼"; subcut on the diagonal to make 288 half-square triangles for the A, D, and E blocks and the border blocks.
- Cut 22 rectangles 2⅞" × 5¼" for the border blocks.

FABRIC A

- Cut 42 squares 3⅞" × 3⅞" for the A blocks.

FABRIC B

- Cut 8 squares 5⅞" × 5⅞"; subcut on both diagonals to make 32 quarter-square triangles for the D blocks and the border blocks. Put 2 in your scrap bin for another project.
- Cut 60 squares 3¼" × 3¼"; subcut on the diagonal to make 120 half-square triangles for the B and E blocks and the border blocks.

FABRIC C

- Cut 8 squares 5⅞" × 5⅞"; subcut on both diagonals to make 32 quarter-square triangles for the E blocks and the border blocks. Discard 2.
- Cut 60 squares 3¼" × 3¼"; subcut on the diagonal to make 120 half-square triangles for the C and D blocks and the border blocks.

BINDING

- Cut 6 strips 2¼" × 42".

MEMORY BOOK

Making the Quilt

1. Sew a pair of 3¼″ background half-square triangles to opposite sides of a 3⅞″ fabric A square. Press the seams toward the triangles. Sew a second pair of 3¼″ background half-square triangles to the remaining sides. Press the seams toward the triangles, and trim to 5¼″ × 5¼″ to make 1 A block. Make 42.

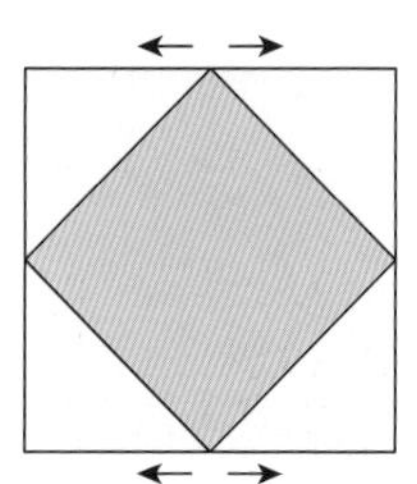

A block

2. Sew a pair of 3¼″ fabric B half-square triangles to opposite sides of a 3⅞″ background square. Press the seams toward the triangles. Sew another pair of 3¼″ fabric B half-square triangles to the remaining sides. Press the seams toward the triangles, and trim to 5¼″ × 5¼″ to make 1 B block. Make 15.

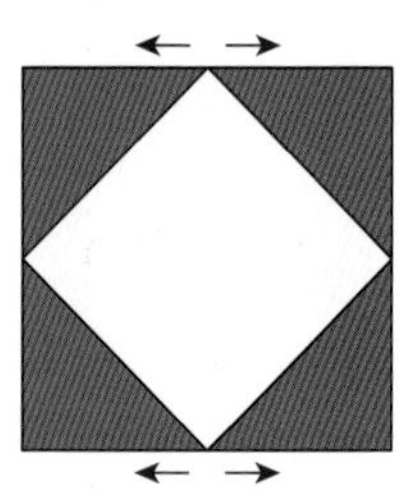

B block

3. Repeat Step 2 using the remaining 3⅞″ background squares and 3¼″ fabric C half-square triangles to make 1 C block. Make 15.

C block

4. Sew a pair of 3¼″ background half-square triangles to the short sides of a 5⅞″ fabric B quarter-square triangle. Press the seams toward fabric B. Trim to 2⅞″ × 5¼″ to make unit W. Repeat with the 5⅞″ fabric C quarter-square triangles to make unit X. Make 30 units W and 30 units X.

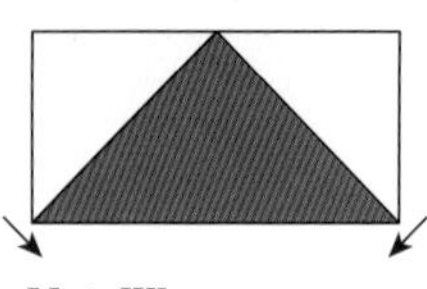

Unit W

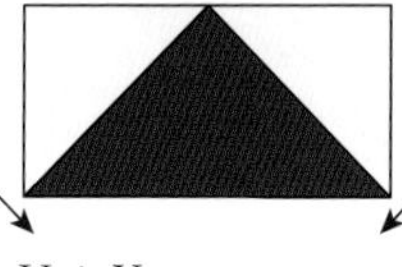

Unit X

5. Sew a pair of 3¼″ fabric B half-square triangles to the short sides of a 5⅞″ background quarter-square triangle. Press the seams toward fabric B. Trim to 2⅞″ × 5¼″ to make unit Y. Repeat with the remaining 5⅞″ background quarter-square triangles and the 3¼″ fabric C half-square triangles to make unit Z. Make 30 units Y and 30 units Z.

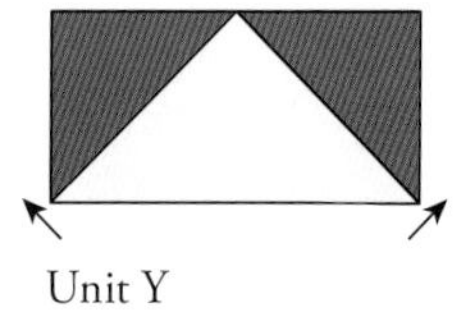

Unit Y

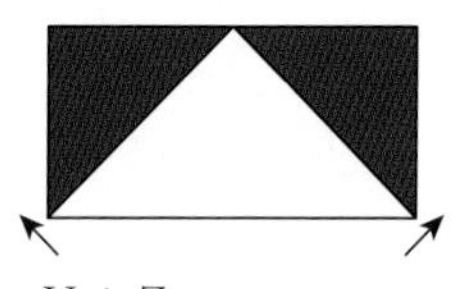

Unit Z

6. Sew together units W and Z, as shown. Press the seams toward unit Z, and trim to 5¼″ × 5¼″ to make 1 D block. Make 24.

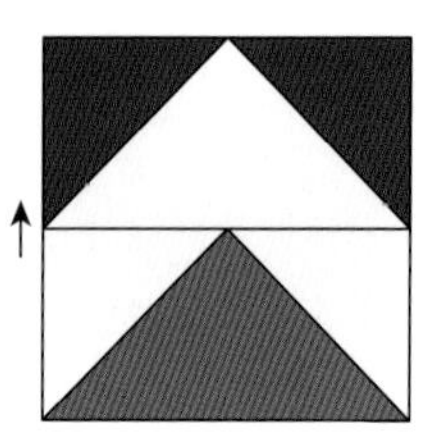

D block

7. Sew together units X and Y, as shown. Press the seams toward Y, and trim to 5¼″ × 5¼″ to make 1 E block. Make 25.

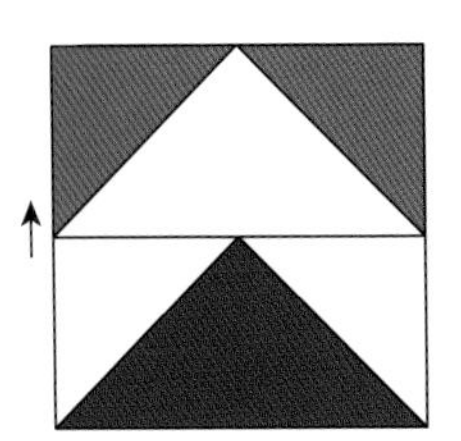

E block

8. Sew a 2⅞″ × 5¼″ background rectangle to the top of the remaining units W, X, Y, and Z to make the border blocks. Make 6 each using unit W and unit Z; make 5 each using unit X and unit Y. Press toward the background rectangle.

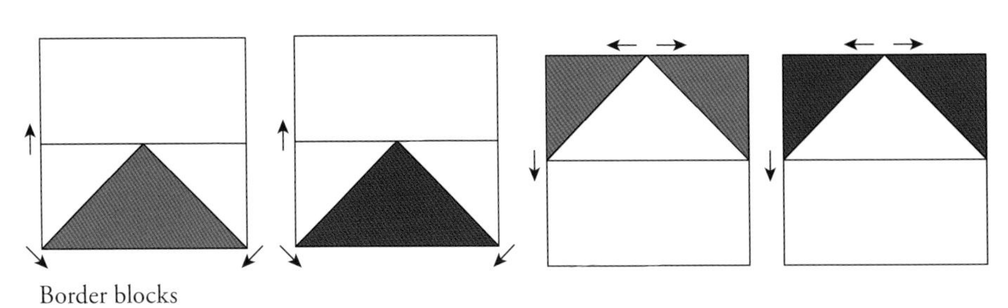

Border blocks

9. Sew together the blocks into rows, as shown in the quilt assembly diagram. Press the odd rows to the left and the even rows to the right. Sew the rows together in order, matching the seam allowances and pressing the seams toward the bottom of the quilt.

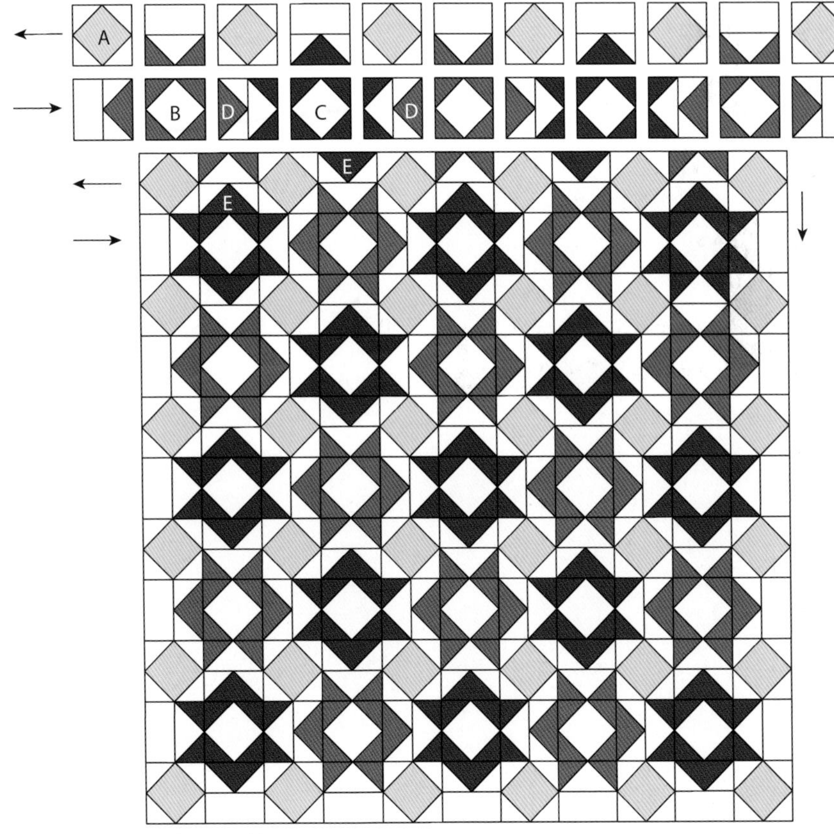

Quilt assembly

FINISHING THE QUILT

For detailed instructions on finishing techniques, refer to Finishing Touches (page 29).

1. Cut and piece the backing fabric so it is 8″ wider and longer than the quilt top. Layer the quilt top with the batting and backing. Baste together the layers.

2. Hand or machine quilt as desired.

3. Square up the quilt sandwich.

4. Prepare and sew the binding to the quilt. Add your label and enjoy!

Cool It Down!

I chose to use two similar-hue prints for this *Swish*, giving it a subtle scrappy look. I wanted the lime-green print to star; it is one of my all-time favorites, and I used it in the binding as well. To cool off, substitute with these blue and teal fabrics. Follow the rest of the project instructions as given.

Swish, 52¼″ × 61¾″, pieced by Stacey Day and quilted by Miriam March

Background: 2½ yards of light gray

Fabric A: ⅝ yard of lime green

Fabric B: 1 yard of medium teal

Fabric C: 1 yard of medium blue

Fox Hunt

FINISHED QUILT: 56″ × 72″

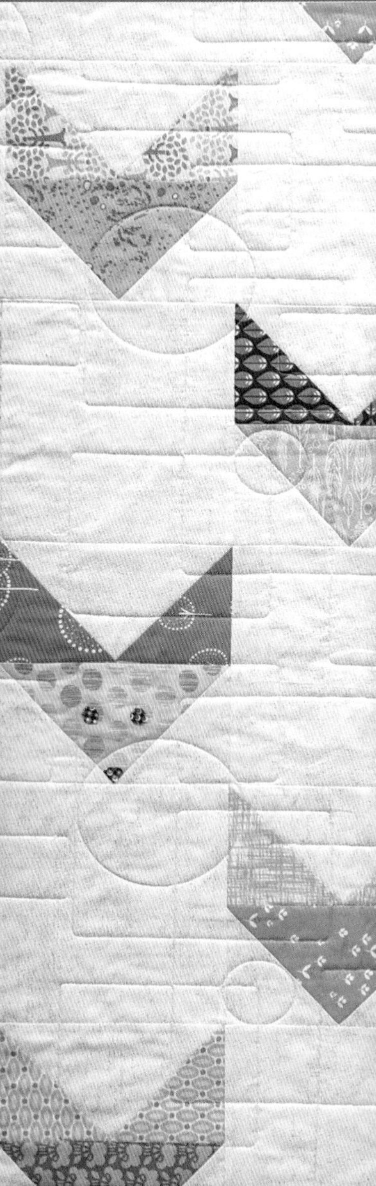

Pieced by Stacey Day and quilted by Miriam March

The year my eldest officially became a toddler, there was a highly popular song about foxes—he still randomly sings its chorus. Foxes are often featured in baby clothes these days, and my littlest one was even a fox for Halloween! It felt appropriate that the final pattern in the book reflect this current family theme.

MATERIALS

Yardage is based on 42″-wide fabric.

BACKGROUND: 3¼ yards of off-white

FABRIC A: ⅓ yard of medium green

FABRIC B: ⅓ yard of light orange

FABRIC C: ⅓ yard of light blue

FABRIC D: ⅓ yard of medium gold

FABRIC E: ⅓ yard of light green

FABRIC F: ⅓ yard of medium orange

FABRIC G: ⅓ yard of medium blue

FABRIC H: ⅓ yard of light gold

BINDING: ½ yard

BACKING: 3⅝ yards

BATTING: 64″ × 80″

TIP

Give your foxes some personality with a little dark gray or black appliqué. Cut out small circles for the eyes and a triangle for the nose. Add the features to a single colorway or to random foxes. Avoid buttons or beads because they are a choking hazard for children under three.

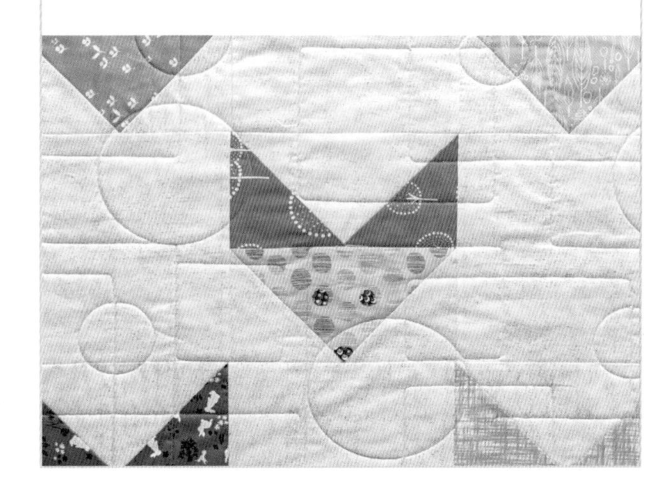

CUTTING

BACKGROUND

- Cut 8 squares 9¼″ × 9¼″; subcut on both diagonals to make 32 quarter-square triangles.
- Cut 31 squares 8½″ × 8½″.
- Cut 32 squares 4⅞″ × 4⅞″; subcut on the diagonal to make 64 half-square triangles.

FABRIC A

- Cut 3 squares 9¼″ × 9¼″; subcut on both diagonals to make 12 quarter-square triangles. Discard 2, or put them in your scrap bin for another project.

FABRIC B

- Cut 3 squares 9¼″ × 9¼″; subcut on both diagonals to make 12 quarter-square triangles. Discard 2.

FABRIC C

- Cut 2 squares 9¼″ × 9¼″; subcut on both diagonals to make 8 quarter-square triangles. Discard 2.

FABRIC D

- Cut 2 squares 9¼″ × 9¼″; subcut on both diagonals to make 8 quarter-square triangles. Discard 2.

FABRIC E

- Cut 10 squares 4⅞″ × 4⅞″; subcut on the diagonal to make 20 half-square triangles.

FABRIC F

- Cut 10 squares 4⅞″ × 4⅞″; subcut on the diagonal to make 20 half-square triangles.

FABRIC G

- Cut 6 squares 4⅞″ × 4⅞″; subcut on the diagonal to make 12 half-square triangles.

FABRIC H

- Cut 6 squares 4⅞″ × 4⅞″; subcut on the diagonal to make 12 half-square triangles.

BINDING

- Cut 7 strips 2¼″ × 42″.

Making the Quilt

1. Sew 2 background 4⅞″ half-square triangles to either side of a 9¼″ fabric A quarter-square triangle. Press the seams toward fabric A. Trim to 4½″ × 8½″ to make unit A. Repeat with the 9¼″ quarter-square triangles from fabrics B, C, and D. Make 10 each from fabrics A and B; make 6 each from fabrics C and D.

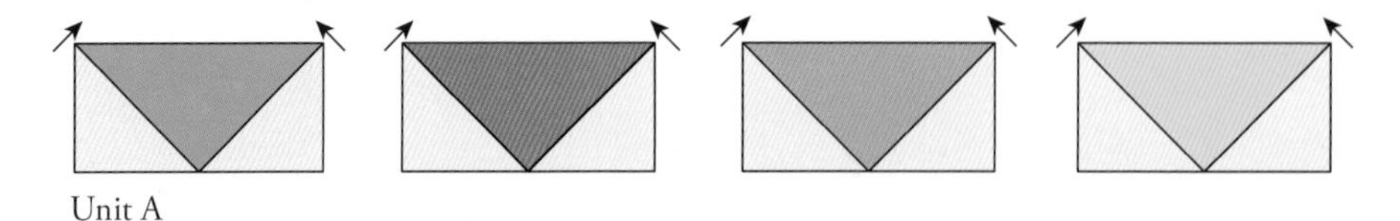

Unit A

2. Sew 2 fabric E 4⅞″ half-square triangles to either side of a 9¼″ background quarter-square triangle. Press the seams toward fabric E. Trim to 4½″ × 8½″ to make unit B. Repeat with the 4⅞″ half-square triangles from fabrics F, G, and H. Make 10 each with fabrics E and F; make 6 each with fabrics G and H.

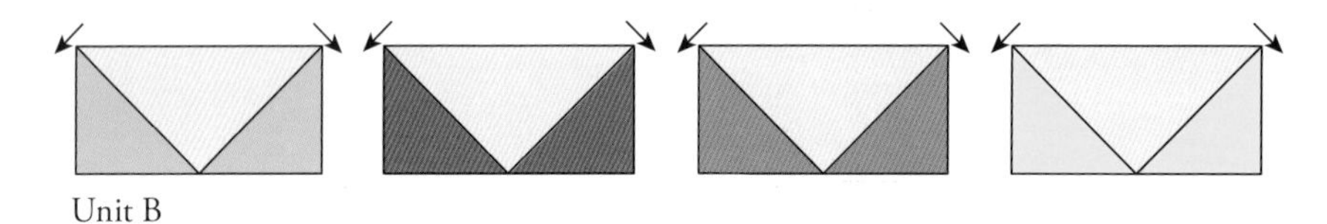

Unit B

3. Sew together pairs of units A and B, matching light and dark of the same color, to make Fox blocks. Press the seams toward unit A. Trim to 8½″ × 8½″. Make 32.

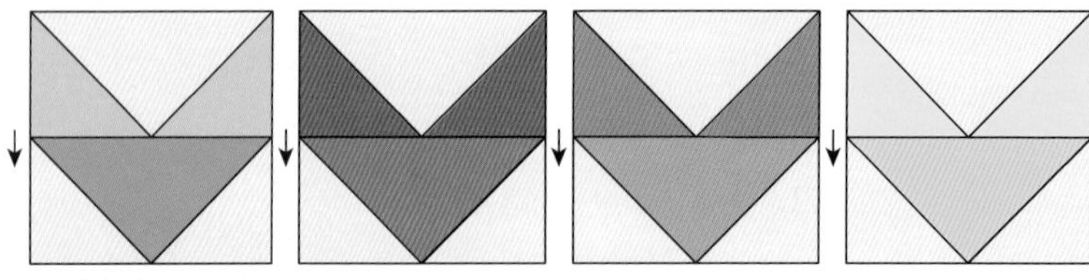

Fox blocks

4. Sew together the 8½″ background squares and the Fox blocks into rows, as shown in the quilt assembly diagram. Press the seams of the rows in opposite directions. Sew the rows together. Press the seams toward the bottom of the quilt.

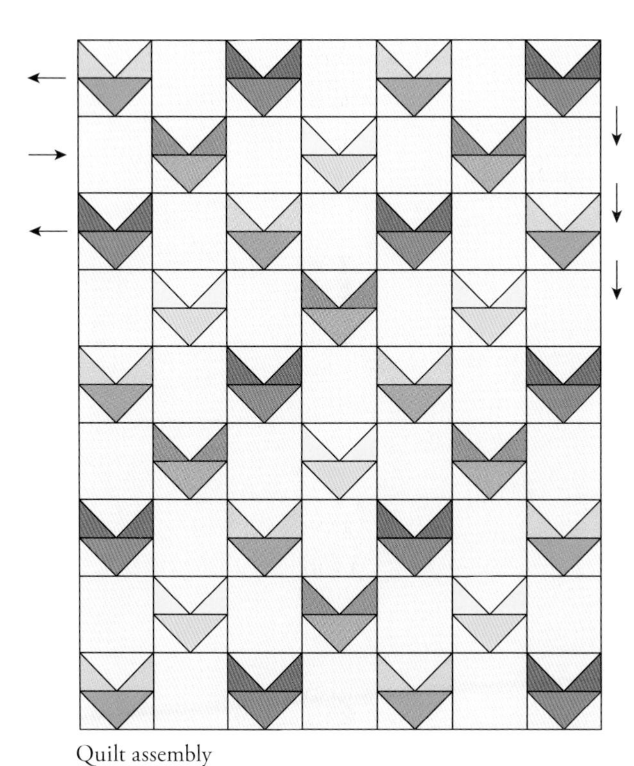
Quilt assembly

FINISHING THE QUILT

For detailed instructions on finishing techniques, refer to Finishing Touches (page 29).

1. Cut and piece the backing fabric so it is 8″ wider and longer than the quilt top. Layer the quilt top with the batting and backing. Baste together the layers.

2. Hand or machine quilt as desired.

3. Square up the quilt sandwich.

4. Prepare and sew the binding to the quilt. Add your label and enjoy!

Warm It Up!

This warm version combines desaturation and a hue shift on the color wheel. Each color is slightly off the pure on the color wheel, creating a soft alternate rainbow that's feminine without relying on traditionally "girly" colors. Substitute the tertiary colors listed below: coral, gold, aqua, and yellow-green. Follow the rest of the project instructions as given.

Fox Hunt, 56″ × 72″, pieced by Stacey Day and quilted by Miriam March

Background: 3¼ yards of light gray

Fabric A: ⅓ yard of medium lime green

Fabric B: ⅓ yard of light coral

Fabric C: ⅓ yard of light aqua

Fabric D: ⅓ yard of medium yellow

Fabric E: ⅓ yard of light lime green

Fabric F: ⅓ yard of medium coral

Fabric G: ⅓ yard of medium aqua

Fabric H: ⅓ yard of light yellow

Resources

Here you will find a comprehensive list of resources, books, and tools to help you expand your quilting experience. I have read, owned, or used each of these books, tools, or websites personally, and the techniques are the ones that I have tried and adapted into my own experience and style. These books explore in depth the theory and techniques used in *Child's Play Quilts*.

Books and Tools

The following books and tools can be found at C&T Publishing (ctpub.com).

COLOR THEORY

The Quilter's Practical Guide to Color, by Becky Goldsmith

Color Play, by Joen Wolfrom

Ultimate 3-in-1 Color Tool, by Joen Wolfrom

Studio Color Wheel, by Joen Wolfrom

APPLIQUÉ

Alex Anderson's Hand & Machine Appliqué, by Alex Anderson

The Modern Appliqué Workbook, by Jenifer Dick

QUILTMAKING

The Practical Guide to Patchwork, by Elizabeth Hartman

Piecing Makeover, by Patty Murphy

FREE-MOTION QUILTING

Beginner's Guide to Free-Motion Quilting, by Natalia Bonner

Free-Motion Quilting with Angela Walters, by Angela Walters

Free-Motion Quilting Idea Book, by Amanda Murphy

Step-by-Step Free-Motion Quilting, by Christina Cameli

Websites

FABRIC, THREAD, AND LONGARM QUILTING

Aurifil aurifil.com

Dashwood Studio dashwoodstudio.com

FreeSpirit Fabrics freespiritfabrics.com

Moda Fabrics unitednotions.com

Timeless Treasures ttfabrics.com

TinLizzie18 tinlizzie18.com

Windham Fabrics windhamfabrics.net

SAFE SLEEP

For more on safe sleep for your baby, visit the following websites:

The Public Health Agency of Canada
canada.ca/en > search "Safe Sleep" >
Safe Sleep - Canada.ca

Safe to Sleep campaign nichd.nih.gov/sts

About the Author

By day, Stacey is an unassuming x-ray technologist in hot-pink scrubs living in beautiful British Columbia. At night (and at nap time), she transforms into an award-winning quilter, pattern writer, author, and designer, whose superpowers are directly related to the amount of thread ends on the floor. A third-generation quilter, Stacey caught the sewing bug early, learning to quilt at the age of six and going on to earn a diploma in fashion production in 2005. Her work has appeared in numerous quilt and trunk shows across North America, and she has won ribbons for her quilts at AQS Quiltweek, the Canadian Quilters' Association's National Juried Show, and the Hoffman Challenge.

Follow Stacey on social media:

Website: staceyinstitches.com • **Instagram:** @staceyinstitches

Want even
more creative
content?
Go to ctpub.com/offer
& sign up to receive our gift to you!

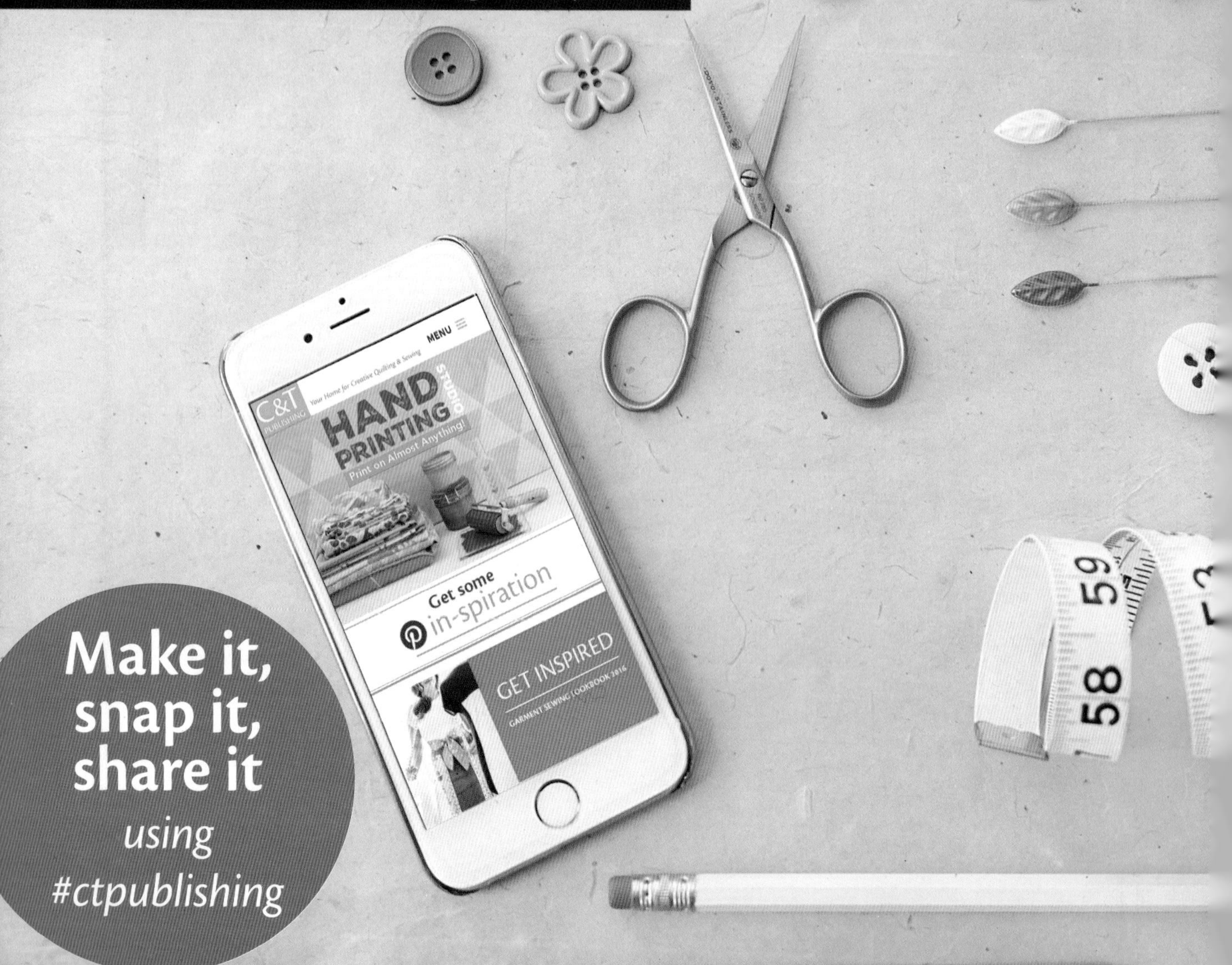
Make it,
snap it,
share it
using
#ctpublishing
MENU
C&T PUBLISHING
Your Home for Creative Quilting & Sewing
HAND PRINTING
STUDIO
Print on Almost Anything!
Get some
in-spiration
GET INSPIRED
GARMENT SEWING LOOKBOOK 2016